BOOMERANG

BOOMERANG

THE WORKS OF VALENTYN MOROZ

Introduction by Paul L. Gersper

Edited by Yaroslav Bihun

Smoloskyp Publishers

Baltimore - Paris - Toronto

BOOMERANG

Library of Congress Catalog Number: 74-77633

International Standard Book Number: 0-914834-00-2

Cover by Orest Polishchuk

Published in 1974 by Smoloskyp Publishers, a nonprofit organization, P.O. Box 6066, Patterson Station, Baltimore, Md. 21231.

Printed and bound in USA.

You wanted to hide people in the forests of Mordovia; instead, you placed them on a stage for all the world to see . . . You hurled a stone at every spark of life on the Ukrainian horizon, and every stone became a boomerang. . . .

V. Moroz

CONTENTS

EDITOR'S PREFACE

Boomerang is a story of Valentyn Moroz, a young history instructor at a teachers' college in Ivano-Frankivsk, a city in Western Ukraine with a population of under ninety thousand. At one point in this young man's life he began to realize that he and those around him were being spiritually robbed—of dignity and freedom as human beings, of culture and tradition as national beings, Ukrainians. He protested—revolted would be a better word, though not with force, but as would any young, educated man—in conversations with his colleagues, friends and in his writings. The exact date of this turning point in his life is not known, but it did happen before his thirtieth birthday, for by that time he was already experiencing the effects of his "dissent."

His stand on principle cost him dearly, for from 1965 until—ironically—1984, not counting nine months of unemployment between terms of imprisonment, he will have spent eighteen of the most productive years of a man's life behind bars, barbed wire, or in exile. If he survives, he will return to his wife and now young son as a man of almost fifty. Moroz's case is incomprehensible to the Western mind, which cannot envision such punishment for a person whose crimes were those of thought and expression, neither of which included violence. *Boomerang* will present all the facts about this man and his case, but the fundamental question will undoubtedly remain unanswered: How could this happen in the latter half of the twentieth century?

The story of Valentyn Moroz will unfold by itself through materials and documents that have reached the West. Part I of *Boomerang*, which includes his writings, begins with a short statement he delivered at his last trial—the trial that sealed his fate for the next fourteen years. Although chronologically out of place, this short statement serves as a good introduction to Moroz, for it gives an insight into his psychological make-up, his temperament, his uncompromising spirit, his stand on moral and ethical principles. In the essays that follow, Moroz gives his observations and thoughts on the state of human and national rights in Soviet Ukraine. Part I concludes with a few of his poems and a short narrative description of his first day in prison, which reveals a side of Moroz that is very much unlike the one who spoke of "boomerangs" in his court statement.

The chronological story of Moroz is told in Part II through a mosaic of documents: bits of information that reached the West about him, about his arrests and trials, letters, statements and appeals written by him and in his behalf.

Part III ends Moroz's story with poems dedicated to him and a foreboding, last eyewitness account of Moroz in prison written by a fellow inmate Anatoly Radygin, a Soviet Jew who has since emigrated to Israel.

The object of compiling and publishing *Boomerang* was to present Moroz's case and tell his story. Annotations were, therefore, added and limited with this purpose in mind. The reader will also find that the transliteration in *Boomerang* does not conform to tables currently used in the West. It is, however, a true and direct phonetic transliteration from Ukrainian into English, and not through Polish or Russian. Upon reading *Boomerang*, the reader will realize why it could not have been otherwise in a book about Moroz. This decision also covers Ukrainian place names, the only exception being that of the capital Kiev, which—fortunately or unfortunately—has long ago intrenched itself in Western languages by way of this Russian pronunciation (in Ukrainian —Kyiv). For this one compromise, we beg the author's forgiveness.

ACKNOWLEDGMENTS

The following primary sources are acknowledged with gratitude.

Part One: "Instead of a Last Word," *Ukrainsky Visnyk* (*Ukrainian Herald*), Issue VI, PIUF (Paris) and Smoloskyp (Baltimore), 1971; "A Report from the Beria Reservation," *Suchasnist* (Munich), Nos. 2-6, 1968; "Amid the Snows," *Suchasnist,* No. 3, 1971; "A Chronicle of Resistance," *Shyroke More Ukrainy* (*Wide Sea of Ukraine*), PIUF and Smoloskyp, 1972; "Moses and Dathan," *Ukrainsky Visnyk,* Issue I-II, PIUF and Smoloskyp, 1971; "From the 'Prelude' Collection" and "The First Day," *Ukrainsky Visnyk,* Issue IV, PIUF and Smoloskyp, 1971.

Part Two: Documents 1-3, *Lykho z Rozumu,* PIUF, 1967; Documents 4-7, 9, 32, 34-36, 42, 43, *Ukrainsky Visnyk,* Issue VI, PIUF and Smoloskyp, 1971; Documents 8, 10-14, *Ukrainsky Visnyk,* Issue I-II, PIUF and Smoloskyp, 1971; Documents 15-23, *Ukrainsky Visnyk,* Issue III, Smoloskyp and *The New Pathway* (Winnipeg), 1971; Documents 24-31, 33, 37-40, *Ukrainsky Visnyk,* Issue IV, PIUF and Smoloskyp, 1971.

Part Three: Poems by Kalynets and Chubay, *Ukrainsky Visnyk,* Issue IV, PIUF and Smoloskyp, 1971; "A Chance Meeting," by Anatoly Radygin, *Liberation Path* (London), Nos. 11-12, 1973.

The editor's special thanks are due to Andriy Fedynsky and Bohdan Yasen for their editorial assistance.

NOTES ON SOURCES

All articles, poems, and documents in *Boomerang* which have the *Ukrainian Herald* as their source were originally circulated in typescript or manuscript form in the underground *samvydav* (the self-publishing movement).

The underground journal *Ukrainian Herald* (*Ukrainsky Visnyk*) is the Ukrainian counterpart of the Russian journal, the *Chronicle of Current Events*. It appeared in six separate issues from January 1970 to March 1972, when its publication was stopped by the wave of arrests which rolled through Ukraine in the first few months of 1972 and the primary aim of which was the elimination of *samvydav*, in general, and the *Ukrainian Herald*, in particular. Five of the six issues of the *Herald* were smuggled to and published in the West.

The unsigned documents appeared in the various issues of the *Ukrainian Herald* in line with its policy, expressed in the credo of the journal, to give ". . . without generalization, information about violations of freedom of speech and other democratic freedoms guaranteed by the Constitution, about repressions through the courts and outside the courts taking place in Ukraine, about violations of national sovereignty (facts of chauvinism and Ukrainophobia), about attempts to disinform the public, about the situation of Ukrainian political prisoners in prisons and [labor] camps, about various protest actions and the like."

Signed documents appeared in the *Herald* in line with its declared intention of ". . . giving a review of, or printing in full, publicistic articles, documents, literary work and other materials which had circulated in the *samvydav*."

All other items, with the exception of Documents 41, 45 and A. Radygin's "A Chance Meeting" are *samvydav* materials which circulated widely but which were not included in the five issues of the *Ukrainian Herald* the contents of which are known in the West.

FROM THE CRIMINAL CODE
OF THE UKRAINIAN SSR

Article 62:
ANTI-SOVIET AGITATION AND PROPAGANDA

1. Agitation or propaganda conducted for the purpose of undermining or weakening Soviet rule or the commission of individual crimes which are of particular danger to the state; dissemination for the same purpose of slanderous fabrications which discredit the Soviet state and social systems; as well as the circulation, production, or keeping for the same purpose of literature of similar content—

> *are punishable by imprisonment for a term from six months to seven years, with exile for up to five years, or without same, or else by exile for a term of two to five years.*

2. These same acts, committed by an individual who has previously been sentenced for crimes which are of particular danger to the state, and also committed during times of war—

> *are punishable by imprisonment for a term from three to ten years, with exile for up to five years, or without same.*

Article 187-I:
DISSEMINATION OF DELIBERATELY FALSE FABRICATIONS WHICH DISCREDIT THE SOVIET STATE AND SOCIAL SYSTEM

Systematic verbal dissemination of deliberately false fabrications which discredit the Soviet state and social system, as well as the production or circulation in written, printed, or any other form of works of similar content—

> *are punishable by imprisonment for a term of up to three years or by corrective labor for a term of up to one year, or by a fine of up to one hundred rubles.*

ABBREVIATIONS

ASSR   Autonomous Soviet Socialist Republic

CC   Criminal Code

CC CPSU   Central Committee of the Communist Party of the Soviet Union

CC CPU   Central Committee of the Communist Party of Ukrainian SSR

CC UkrSSR   Criminal Code of Ukrainian SSR

CPSU   Communist Party of the Soviet Union

CPU   Communist Party of Ukrainian SSR

KGB   Committee for State Security (*Komitet Gosudarstvennoy Bezopasnosti*)

Komsomol   Communist Youth League

OUN   Organization of Ukrainian Nationalists

RSFSR   Russian Soviet Federative Socialist Republic

SSR   Soviet Socialist Republic

UCC   Criminal Code of Ukrainian SSR

UkrSSR   Ukrainian Soviet Socialist Republic

INTRODUCTION

VALENTYN MOROZ, a young Ukrainian historian, has been incarcerated within the penal system of the Soviet Union for all but nine months since August 1965. Moreover, he is not scheduled for release until 1984. For what "crimes" was Moroz twice sentenced to a total of eighteen years of incarceration? It seems that his advocacy of those individual, cultural, and national freedoms guaranteed by the Soviet Constitution was interpreted as "anti-Soviet propaganda and agitation," which, considering the severity of the punishment to Moroz, is apparently a very serious crime in the USSR.

Moroz's advocacy of a strict interpretation of the Soviet Constitution is clearly shown in his writings. Moreover, he has been unquestionably critical of the political institutions of the USSR in their disregard for those rights guaranteed by the Constitution and the resulting adverse effect on the behavior of Soviet citizens. However, it is difficult to see how Moroz's writings could be rationally interpreted as "anti-Soviet propaganda and agitation" and even more difficult to rationalize justification for the severity of punishment imposed. By any measure, Moroz's criticisms would be considered mild in the United States (similar criticism of US political institutions justifiably occur commonly), and punishment would be out of the question. For the Constitution of the United States guarantees, as does that of the USSR, freedoms of speech and of the press. These basic rights are essential to the well-being and stability of any society. This was recognized and well stated in the quotation attributed to Voltaire, "I disapprove of what you say, but I will defend to the death your *right* to say it."

According to the writings of Moroz, as well as other accounts, the Soviet Union excessively restricts individual freedom. Those who speak out against these excesses are systematically discouraged by direct government pressure or indirectly by the more subtle pressures of harassment, unemployment, or social ostracism. The ultimate sanction against those who do not bow to official edicts to curtail their criticisms is incarceration within the prisons, penal camps, or mental institutions of the vast, hidden empire of the Soviet penal system.

Moroz's eloquence and boldness as a defender of civil rights has branded him as an enemy of the Soviet regime, a particular enemy that, judging from the severity of the punishment, the government is fearful of. For his outspoken stand, Moroz has been singled out for special punishment, which may ultimately break his body and health, but which will surely leave his spirit uncompromised. Although he has been removed and hidden from society, his thoughts are not hidden. They, as well as his spirit, as champions of civil liberties live in his writings.

Valentyn Moroz was born on April 15, 1936, in Volyn region, Ukraine. He attended the University of Lviv where he studied history and graduated in 1958. For the next seven years he taught history while also working on his doctoral thesis. Then, in August of 1965, Moroz's life change abruptly. He was arrested and charged with "anti-Soviet propaganda and agitation." Specifically, according to accounts of his arrest, the charge was made because of Moroz's possession of several unpublished manuscripts and foreign publications that were unreleased in the Soviet Union.

Following his arrest, Moroz was tried and convicted in January 1966. He was sentenced to four years of hard labor and was sent to a special camp for political prisoners in the Mordovian ASSR. It was there that Moroz wrote his first significant essay, *A Report from the Beria Reservation*, in which he analyzed Soviet political methodology. Moroz addressed this work to the Supreme Soviet of the Ukrainian SSR. For his authorship of this essay, Moroz was tried by a camp court and sentenced to solitary confinement.

Although released from prison in 1969, Moroz continued to be punished. Because of his record as a political prisoner, he was unable to obtain employment. Moreover, his wife was dismissed from her job because of her loyalty to her husband. Thus the Moroz family, including their young son, was left with no means of support. In spite of this and other forms of nearly continuous harassment, during the nine months between his release from prison and his re-arrest in 1970, Moroz managed to write three more essays: *A Chronicle of Resistance, Amid the Snows, Moses and Dathan*, and several introspective, poetic accounts of his prison experience.

Moroz's works exhibit sharp criticism and ultimate rejection of Soviet policies of repression, denationalization, Russification, and debasement of individuality. At the same time, his writings affirm the highest human ideals and reach for the greatest possible fulfillment of the promise held in each human being. His style exhibits poetic qualities of sensitivity, a strong use of incisive logic, and a direct honesty that spares no one, that calls everyone to account for his ideas and actions. Throughout his writings his plea to his countrymen is similar to that of Abraham Lincoln, "Those who deny freedom to others deserve it not for themselves, and, under a just God, cannot long retain it." Above all, Moroz demands a consistency between ideas, words, and actions.

On June 1, 1970, Moroz was again arrested. In November of the same year, he was tried in a closed court. According to numerous accounts, Moroz and many of the prosecution witnesses, those who were friends of Moroz, who respected him and the human rights guaranteed by the constitution, refused to testify because of the illegal nature of the trial. The trial proceeded anyway. Armed guards kept crowds of friends and supporters away from the courtroom. On November 18, 1970, a prosecution-picked gallery heard Moroz receive a fourteen-year sentence for "anti-Soviet agitation."

Since his second conviction, Moroz has been reported to have been severely weakened by hunger and a hard-labor regime. These reports also indicate that he has been deliberately placed among vicious criminal elements and among genuinely insane individuals. As a consequence, he was reported to have been severely beaten and gravely wounded by criminal inmates in Vladimir Prison outside Moscow. Subsequently, he was transported to a prison hospital in Kiev, Ukraine. At present, fears have been expressed for his continued sanity because of incarceration among people suffering from severe mental illness.

In view of the reported brutal punishment, it is significant that none of the activities with which Moroz has been charged are illegal under Soviet law. In fact, Moroz himself is a victim of lawlessness, since the Soviet Constitution guarantees open trials and bans inhuman punishment. Since Moroz was convicted at a closed trial during which no significant testimony was given, his conviction and imprisonment are illegal.

When Moroz was arrested for the first time in 1965, his alleged crime was the possession of illegal articles and publications. At the trial, he freely admitted to the charges, but pointed out that Articles 125-126 of the Soviet Constitution guarantee Soviet citizens the freedoms of speech, of the press, the right to demonstrate, and to organize. Despite these constitutional rights, Moroz was convicted. Up to that time, he had written nothing really significant. His own mistreatment, as well as the mistreatment of other Soviet intellectuals, intensified his desire to systematically analyze Soviet society without compromising his own beliefs. These subsequent actions are also protected by the Soviet Constitution, but they brought Moroz further punishment.

In his essay *Amid the Snows,* Moroz observes that "devaluation of the word is the underlying moral problem left over from the Stalinist period." Because Moroz chose to take the Soviet Constitution at its word and then did not fear to express himself honestly and freely, he fell victim to the devalued word. As a political prisoner convicted for activities he had been taught were not a crime, Moroz had an opportunity to come to terms with himself. He was not naive, however, and had been under no delusions as to the realities of Soviet society. Moreover, he knew that he was risking severe punishment for his actions. He decided, however, to take a stand. As he expressed in *Amid the Snows,* "A person's moral stand today is more important than his word. Words are no longer believed—they have been terribly devalued. One's word must be backed by one's position." He decided, in a sense, to fight using the Soviet Union's own devalued currency, words, now made suddenly strong by his position, a position which can be described in the words of Collingwood, "Perfect freedom is reserved for the man who lives by his own work and in that work does what he wants to do."

In *A Report from the Beria Reservation,* Moroz analyzed real Soviet policies, which he claims are hidden behind devalued words. The basic reality of Soviet life, Moroz writes, is terror, violence coiled and ready to spring on anyone who deviates from the prescribed mode of conduct or thought. Yet most people of the USSR do not regard this violence as evil. Instead, it has become accepted as the everyday state of affairs. The people living in such an environment have ceased to be individuals and have become cogs in a huge Soviet machine which forcibly resists change. Terror is instituted, supposedly to maintain order. Moroz denounces this rationalization. Terror, he continues, "is instituted to maintain the *status quo*—to keep the powerful in power and

xix

suppress anyone who doubts their legitimacy or questions their policies." Moroz relates that order in Soviet society is bought at a fearful price: "And so order was built on the ruins of individuality." Moroz clearly believes that the death of individuality, in turn, leads to the death of creativity. According to him, a person who acts and thinks as he is told can create nothing, can arrive at no original work or ideas. The result, in this "Empire of Cogs," as Moroz calls it, is chaos in the Soviet economy and sterility in Soviet culture and art.

In this same report, Moroz historically compares the freedom of Western society with the repression of the Communist state and notes that the Soviet Union, and Tsarist Russia before, lagged and continues to lag behind the Western world in almost every aspect—in science, art, standard of living, economics, industry, and so on. Moroz cites evidence which shows that the potential for spectacular progress and innovations exists, but he predicts that the Soviet Union will continue to fall short of Western achievements so long as the individual continues to be destroyed and replaced by a programmed "cog."

Moroz writes that "We owe progress to those who have kept their ability to think and have preserved their individuality despite all attempts to erase it." And indeed, some of the finest achievements to come out of the Soviet Union are created by people like Solzhenitsyn, Sakharov, Pasternak, Rostropovich.

The importance that Moroz places on maximizing creativity through individual freedom of expression is well stated in the words of Romain Rolland: "The political life of a nation is only the most superficial aspect of its being. In order to know its inner life, the source of its action, one must penetrate to its soul by literature, philosophy and the arts, where are reflected the ideas, the passions, the dreams of a whole people." Moroz points out that despite the evidence that Soviet policies of repression, aimed at destroying individual expression, lead only to economic chaos, cultural sterility, and alienation of the best minds in the Soviet Union, Soviet authorities continue to pursue a policy whose goal is repression of the individual leading to a programmed uniformity of all people. He describes how the Soviet regime deals with the Ukrainian SSR; how Ukrainian culture, the Ukrainian language, the entire Ukrainian nation are being systematically altered and destroyed to achieve the desired uniformity within the Soviet Union. He states that the goal is to kill any possibility of individuality which could lead to people's demanding their constitutionally guaranteed rights, and then to ultimate questioning of Soviet policy and leadership.

As one example of this policy of "Russification," Moroz singles out the village of Kosmach in the Carpathian Mountains in his *A Chronicle of Resistance*. Kosmach is an old village steeped in tradition and mountain culture. It had been a showplace for Hutsul art (the Hutsul region is a segment of the Ukrainian Carpathians). Moroz writes that in 1963 a Soviet film company, filming the award-winning *Shadows of Forgotten Ancestors*, borrowed the renowned altar piece, the iconostasis (wall of icons), from Kosmach's historic church, as well as other Hutsul art objects. Seven years later, when Moroz wrote his essay, the objects were still not returned, despite extensive efforts by the Kosmach residents to have their property returned. According to Moroz, the art works were, in effect, stolen. A piece of Ukrainian culture ceased to exist. Moroz points further to the burning of libraries in Kiev, Tartu, Samarkhand, and in other cities of the Soviet Union, all outside of the Russian Republic proper. Moroz refused to accept the official explanations that the loss of art objects from Kosmach resulted from "administrative mix-ups" or that the burning of libraries was accidental. According to him, too many "accidents" involving items of Ukrainian and other non-Russian culture had occurred. Moroz points out that official policy appears to be

xxi

the systematic destruction of all vestiges of national individuality and replacement with a Russified uniformity. He objects most strongly to this policy of cultural genocide and asserts his right to be an individual, to be a Ukrainian.

Because Moroz has been bold enough to honestly express himself, he has become the target of terrible repression. His punishment is unusually long and brutal, even by Soviet standards, although he is by no means unique in his ordeal. There is increasing evidence, however, that Moroz's brand of truth and resulting punishments have become particularly embarrassing for the Soviet leaders as world opinion becomes louder.

To Moroz, a man who kills innocent people is a murderer, and he is not afraid to use the word when it applies. He denounces those Soviet officials who continue to encourage the kinds of murder he describes in *A Report from the Beria Reservation*. Moroz further denounces those officials whose actions violate the Soviet Constitution, who suppress the rights and individuality of Soviet citizens, and who destroy the cultural identity of an entire nation. Moroz rejects the leadership of the Soviet Union and demands retribution for their crimes and freedom for their victims.

For his assertions, Moroz is punished and his pen is silenced; however, he believes that even his silence can be powerful. In his final statement following his second trial, he declared that his silence, in the face of severe pressure to recant, will sound louder than roars. The tactic to pressure him to recant indicates that Soviet officials want a submissive Moroz, but he vowed that this is something they will never see.

Moroz's literary output has been rather small. A man of his talent might have been expected to have created more. However, when viewed against the great obstacles that have been put in the way of his creativity, his output is almost incredible. In a short period of time amidst an atmosphere of constant hardships and harassment, Moroz has created lengthy, inductive essays, beautifully sensitive poems, and other short pieces of writing.

Perhaps Moroz's greatest work is his life. He appears to have understood perfectly what he was accepting when he defied Soviet authorities that are infinitely more powerful than he is. He was apparently willing to risk enduring half a lifetime of miserable incarceration and exile, a particularly difficult risk to accept since a man in prison becomes, as Moroz puts it, "a man without his skin; every memory a scalding drop, every thought a hot coal." But Moroz endures because, as he says in his final statement, losing your self-respect is worse than imprisonment. Even behind bars, Moroz more than most people ever do, retains and exercises his freedom. For, as Bertold Brecht said, "A man can be free even within prison walls. Freedom is something spiritual. Whoever has once had it, can never lose it. There are some people who are never free outside a prison." Moroz, above all, is an individual.

May, 1974

Paul L. Gersper

University of California at Berkeley

PART ONE

The Works of Valentyn Moroz

INSTEAD OF A LAST WORD

I SHALL not attempt to prove my innocence by citing articles of the Criminal Code. As you well know, I am not being tried for any crime. I am being tried for my role in a movement of which you disapprove. You would be on sounder legal grounds to arrest in my place certain other individuals; however, you find it more convenient that they remain free, for they—unwittingly, of course—impede and undermine the spirit of Ukrainian reawakening. You would never intentionally trouble them; if, by chance, they ever fell into your hands, you would see to their immediate release. You have concluded, that since V. Moroz accelerates certain undesirable processes in Ukraine, it would be best to isolate him by placing him behind bars—a logical solution, were it not for one "but" . . . .

Since 1965, you have jailed several dozen men. *What have you achieved?* I shall not consider the movement itself, for no one has been able to stop it. But have you at least succeeded in destroying its concrete, external manifestations? Have you, for instance, stemmed the flow of unofficial, uncensored literature, which has already acquired a name: *Samvydav?*[1] No! It seems to be beyond your power. *Samvy-*

[1]*Samvydav*, literally "self-published," clandestinely circulated literature in Ukraine. Periodically compiled into a journal called *Ukrainian Herald*. Russian equivalents are *Samizdat* and *Chronicle of Current Events*.

dav is expanding, improving its form and content, and attracting an ever-widening circle of authors and readers. But most importantly, it has become so deeply rooted that no increase in your staff of informers or electronic surveillance will help. At best, your efforts can be compared to those of *Martushka*.[2] Perhaps even this analogy may be misleading, for it implies effort without result. Your efforts, however, have had results, but opposite to what you had expected. You wanted to intimidate people, but aroused their interest; you wanted to extinguish the fire, but added fuel. Nothing could have revitalized Ukrainian community life as effectively as your repressions; nothing could have drawn as much public attention to the process of Ukrainian reawakening as your trials. You wanted to hide people in the forests of Mordovia;[3] instead, you placed them on a stage for all the world to see. Your persecutions gave birth to most of the revival's activists. You should have realized by now that your repressions are first and foremost detrimental to your cause, and yet you continue these trials. Why? In order to fulfill some quota? To appease your bureaucratic conscience? To vent your anger? More than likely, the reason is inertia. You have given the Ukrainian reawakening movement of the post-Stalinist period the element without which the movement would never fully mature—the element of *sacrifice*. Faith is born where there are martyrs, and you have given them to us.

You hurled a stone at every spark of life on the Ukrainian horizon, and every stone became a boomerang; it returned and struck . . . you! What went wrong? Why do repressions no longer produce the usual results? Why has a tried-and-proven weapon backfired? The times have changed—there is your answer. Stalin had enough water to put out any fire. But you live in a different age; the reserves are depleted. As any child knows: do not tease fire with water, unless you

[2]Allusion to Russian fable by Ivan A. Krylov (1769-1844).
[3]Mordovian ASSR (Central Soviet Union), where the Dubrovlag complex of correctional labor colonies are located. See map on p. 61.

2

have enough to put it out. You took a poker to scatter the coals, but succeeded in stoking the flames. You have lost control, for our society has reached a stage of development when repressions no longer produce the intended, but the opposite, effect. From now on every act of repression will *boomerang*.

By throwing me behind bars on June 1, 1970, you launched another boomerang. You know from experience what will happen. Five years ago you placed me in the prisoner's dock . . . and released an arrow. Then you put me behind barbed wire in Mordovia . . . and launched a bomb. Having learned nothing, apparently, you again embark upon the same course. Only this time the boomerang will return with greater force. Moroz was an unknown history instructor in 1965; today he is widely known.

So Moroz will once again taste prison cabbage. What will you gain? Moroz would be *extremely useful* to you as a penitent author of a repudiating confession that would undermine the movement. But you will *never* see that day. Were you seriously hoping to create a vacuum in the movement by jailing me? When will you understand? *There will never be a vacuum.* The spiritual potential of Ukraine has grown enough to fill any vacuum, to replace any activist who leaves the movement on his own or by way of prison. The 1960's gave us the beginning of the great reawakening of Ukrainian life; the 1970's will not bring its demise. That "Golden Age," when every aspect of life was set into a tight official frame, is gone forever. We now have a culture without the Ministry of Culture; a philosophy without *Problems of Philosophy*.[4] These phenomena, born without official sanction, are here to stay, and they will grow.

I am to be tried behind closed doors. But your trial will boomerang even if no one hears me, or if I sit in silent isola-

---

[4] *Voprosy Filosofii*, monthly journal published in Moscow by the Philosophy Institute of the Soviet Academy of Sciences.

tion in my cell in Vladimir Prison.[5] *Silence can sometimes be more deafening than shouting.* You could not muffle it even by killing me, which is, of course, the easiest thing to do. But have you considered the fact that the dead are often more important than the living? *They become symbols*—the building blocks of spiritual fortresses in the hearts of men.

No doubt you will say that Moroz thinks too highly of himself. Actually, Moroz is of little consequence here. We are concerned here with any honest man in a similar position. After all, there is little room for ambition in Vladimir Prison, where one awaits slow death by chemical additives.

The awakening of national consciousness is the deepest of all spiritual processes. This phenomenon can take on a thousand unpredictable forms that are impossible to contain. Your dams are strong, but they now stand on dry land, bypassed by the spring streams that found other channels. Your draw gates are closed, but they stop no one. The process of national reawakening has unlimited resources, for every man—even one thought to be spiritually dead—has within his soul a spark of national identity. We saw an example of this during the recent debates on the expulsion of Ivan Dzyuba from the Writers' Union, when votes against his expulsion were cast by those of whom this was not expected.[6]

You stubbornly insist that all whom you place behind bars are dangerous criminals. You close your eyes, pretending

[5]Vladimir Prison, located in city with that name, northeast of Moscow.

[6]Ivan M. Dzyuba, literary critic (b. 1931), author of *Internationalism or Russification?* Originally written in the form of a memorandum, and forwarded in 1965 to the First Secretary of the Ukrainian Communist Party, P. Shelest, and Prime Minister V. Scherbytsky. It cites the Soviet nationalities policy for not being a policy of internationalism but, in fact, a policy of Russification. Copies of this memorandum were circulated by *Samvydav*; subsequently it was published in the West (The work was published in English by Weidenfeld and Nicolson, London, 1968). Although from 1965 Dzyuba's works ceased to be published in Soviet Ukrainian periodicals, an intensive campaign against him did

4

there is no problem. You can pursue this absurd policy for, let us say, ten more years . . . but then what? These movements in Ukraine and in the whole Union *are only beginning*. The Ukrainian renaissance has yet to become a mass movement; however, do not deceive yourselves that it will remain that way forever. With universal literacy in Ukraine, 800,000 students and a radio in every home, every socially significant movement becomes a *mass* movement. Is it possible you do not comprehend that soon you will be dealing with *mass social movements?* New processes are only beginning, and your repressive measures have long ceased to be effective. What of the future . . . ?

There is only one alternative: abandon obsolete repressive policies and seek a form of coexistance with these movements, which are permanently entrenched in our society. Such is reality. It evolved without asking for permission, but its results *demand a new approach*. Those called upon to serve the state have much to rethink . . . and you amuse yourselves by throwing boomerangs.

There will be a trial. Very well, we shall fight. We need an example of strength especially now, when one man has published a retraction,[7] another acquiesced to a change in profession and others ceased to be active in the movement. Someone must erase the shame; apparently, I shall have to be the one. It is not an easy mission. Life behind bars is not easy, but life without self-respect is worse. So we will fight!

not begin until late 1969. An attempt was made to expel him from the Writers' Union of Ukraine. The attempt was unsuccessful, but Dzyuba was pressured into writing a statement, deploring the fact that his work was being used by "bourgeois nationalists" in the West, but he did not retract his original thesis. In 1972 Dzyuba was arrested, released, and finally expelled from the Writers' Union. Subsequently, he was arrested again and released upon the publication in 1973 of a full retracting confession, in which he promised to refute in print every point made in *Internationalism or Russification?*

[7]An apparent reference to Dzyuba's first "retraction" mentioned in fn. 6 above.

There will be a trial, and all will begin anew: protests, petitions, world-wide press and radio coverage. Interest in Moroz's writings will increase tenfold. In short, more fuel will be added to the very same fire you are trying to extinguish.

No doubt, this is subversion. But do not point the accusing finger at me . . . I did not jail Moroz; I did not throw the boomerang.

A REPORT FROM THE BERIA RESERVATION

*To the Deputies of the Supreme Soviet of the Ukrainian
    SSR*
*From Valentyn Moroz, a political prisoner illegally convicted
    in Lutsk on January 20, 1966.*

THE CHASE ended. The fugitive came out of the bushes. "I
surrender, don't shoot! I'm unarmed." The pursuer drew
closer, almost touching the fugitive, cocked his submachine
gun in a businesslike manner and sent three rounds, one
after another, through the live target. Two more bursts:
two more fugitives, who had also surrendered, were shot.
The bodies were carried out onto the road. The police dogs
licked the blood. As usual, the victims were brought to the
camp and thrown down near the gate—as a warning to
others. Suddenly the corpses moved; two of them were alive.
One could not shoot them now; there were people around.
This is not the beginning of a detective novel. This is not a
story about fugitives from Buchenwald or Kolyma. This
happened in September 1956, after the 20th Congress had
censured the personality cult, when the criticism of Stalin's
crimes was going full speed ahead. Everything written here
can be confirmed by Algidas Petrusiavicus, who is in Camp
No. 11 in Mordovia. He remained alive. Two others—

Lorentas and Jursa—died. Such incidents were everyday occurrences.

The green land of Mordovia stretches in a narrow strip from west to east. It is green on the map and green in reality. In the middle of the Slav sea there is an island of sonorous Mordovian names: Vindrey, Yavas, Potma, Lyambir. In the northwest corner is the Mordovian State Reservation. The law reigns here; hunting is strictly forbidden. But there is another reservation, not marked on any map, where hunting is allowed all the year round. Man hunting. If one were to prepare an exact map of Mordovia, one would have to divide its southwest corner into squares, fenced off by barbed wire and dotted with watchtowers. These are the Mordovian political camps—a land of barbed wire, police dogs and manhunting. Here, amidst the barbed wire, children grow up. Their parents mow the hay and dig potatoes after work. "Daddy, has there been a search? What have you found?" Then they will grow up and learn the first rule of popular wisdom in these parts: "Camp is bread." For each fugitive captured a pood[1] of flour is issued. Things were simpler in the Aldan camps: a Yakut brought a head and received gunpowder, salt and vodka—just as among the Dyaks of Borneo. The head, however, was brought not to the tribal chief decked out in necklaces of human teeth, but to a major or captain who took correspondence courses from some university and lectured about legality. That tradition had to be abandoned in Mordovia: Moscow is too near. If, by some chance, such a trophy fell into the hands of a foreign correspondent, just try and prove that it was a fake invented by the "yellow press."

The three Lithuanians were shot although they had not been sentenced to death. Article 183 CC permits escape to be punished by three years' imprisonment, while Article 22 UCC forbids the "causing of physical suffering or the lower-

[1] 36 pounds.

ing of human dignity" of prisoners. The Court of the Lithuanian SSR (a sovereign state, according to its Constitution) gave the KGB permission to hold the prisoners in isolation —nothing more. Ukraine, according to its Constitution, is also a sovereign state and even maintains a mission to the United Nations Organization. Her courts sentence thousands of Ukrainian citizens and send them abroad—a procedure unheard of in history. Perhaps Ukraine, like the principality of Monaco, lacks space for camps? Room was, however, found for seven million Russian settlers[2]—yet there is not enough room for Ukrainian political prisoners in their native land. Thousands of Ukrainians have been transported to the East and swallowed up by the gray unknown. They have been swallowed up by the dungeons of the Solovki Islands, the sands of Mangyshlak, then by Stalin's "construction projects"—twentieth-century pyramids—that devoured millions of slaves. People have been transported not only in prison trucks; "volunteers" for resettlement are also devoured by the mincing-machine of Russification in the boundless expanses of Siberia and Kazakhstan, and are forever lost to the Ukrainian nation. Primitive peoples located their Land of the Dead where the sun sets. In future Ukrainian legends such a land will be in the East.

The level of civilization of a society is determined by the concern it shows for the fate of its citizens. A disaster in a Belgian coal mine buried several dozen Italian migrant workers. Italy erupted in protests; there was a shower of official notes and questions in Parliament. Ukraine also has a parliament—the Supreme Soviet of the Ukrainian SSR. I do not know whether any members remember their right to question the Government. I do not know whether these people remember any of the rights of a deputy except the one which allows him to raise his hand during a vote. But I do

[2]According to the 1959 census, Russians in Ukraine numbered 7,091,-000 (16.9 percent of the Ukrainian SSR population), as compared with 2,677,000 (9.2 percent) in 1926.

know that according to the Constitution, the Supreme Soviet of the Ukrainian SSR is the highest authority in Ukraine. It has given one of its subordinate bodies—the KGB—the power to arrest, put on trial, and decide the fate of people accused of "anti-Soviet activities." Honorable Deputies of the Ukrainian Parliament, let us for once rouse ourselves, put aside talk about sows, concrete mixers and the effects of the use of superphosphate on the national economy. Let the experts decide these questions. Let us for once leave the Land of Nod and visit Mordovia to find out: (a) who are these people that are taken from their normal lives and given over into the undivided power of the KGB, and (b) who are the men to whom these people's fate has been entrusted.

The Message of Thought

In 1958 a lecturer in philosophy at the Frunze Medical Institute, Makhmed Kulmagambetov (now in Camp No. 11), brought an application to the rector's office: "Please terminate my appointment." The reason?—Disagreement with the teaching program. This caused a sensation. The herd of careerists, vying for a place at the trough, trampling on their own consciences, dignity and convictions in order to climb higher and grab their neighbor's booty, could never understand—how could a man renounce 1200 roubles only because his views had changed! Kulmagambetov became a laborer. In 1962 he was arrested. The court in Kustanay sentenced him to seven years' imprisonment and three years' exile for "anti-Soviet *activity*." How did this manifest itself? The chief witness for the prosecution was the personnel manager at the "Sokolovrudstroy" Trust, Makhmudov. The only thing he could tell the court was Kulmagambetov's own words: "I do not want to teach what I do not believe in." That was his reply to the question: "Why don't you work in your profession?" Other accusations were similar. Even the investigator admitted: "Generally speaking, there is nothing even to try you for, but you have *a dangerous way of think-*

ing." A typical case for the KGB, but unique in the frankness of its disregard for the law. As a rule, the KGB tries to fabricate at least a semblance of "anti-Soviet" *activity*. But in this remote province it did not even consider this necessary and admitted that Kulmagambetov had been *convicted for his views*. Thousands upon thousands of people are sentenced in this way, although the matter is "played out" more subtly. Article 125 of the USSR Constitution proclaims freedom of speech, press, assembly and organization. Article 19 of the United Nations Declaration of Human Rights proclaims the "freedom . . . to seek, receive and impart information and ideas through any media and regardless of frontiers." Therefore, Article 62 UCC is in violation of the above-mentioned documents—a Stalinist leftover. The formula "agitation or propaganda carried on for the purpose of subverting or weakening Soviet authority," if the KGB men themselves determine the degree of the "subversiveness" of the material, serves the purposes of an unlimited disregard of the law.

In Moscow dozens of books by foreign authors are published every year which are stuffed with sharp criticism of the Soviet order and communist ideology. If Article 62 of the Criminal Code is truly the law, then the publication of such books is a punishable matter. A law is a law only if it binds everybody. What logic is there if I may freely propagate Hitler's views, published in the journal *Problems of History*,[3] but if I myself retype Hitler's memoirs, I will be tried! Thus Article 62 is simply a weapon of arbitrary power in the hands of the KGB, enabling it to put behind bars any *persona non grata* for possessing any book which has been published outside the Soviet Union.

My comrades and I were convicted "for propaganda di-
to secede is laid down in the Covenant on Civil and Political
rected at separating Ukraine from the USSR." But Article

[3] *Voprosy istorii*, monthly journal published in Moscow by the Historical Institute of the Soviet Academy of Sciences.

17 of the USSR Constitution clearly states the right of each republic to secede from the Union. The right of every people Rights adopted by the 21st Session of the United Nations General Assembly.

The KGB dearly loves the phrase *nationalist literature*. What does this phrase mean, and what are the criteria for determining *nationalist character?* Until recently, the works of Oles,[4] Hrinchenko,[5] and Zerov[6] were considered "nationalist"; now they are no longer nationalist. Mice have yet to nibble away the pamphlets in which "theoreticians" of Malanchuk's[7] ilk called Hrushevsky[8] "a fierce enemy of the Ukrainian people," while the *Ukrainian Historical Journal*[9] (No. 11, 1966) considers him a scholar of world renown, and quotes a government decree that speaks of Hrushevsky's services to Ukraine. The works of Hrushevsky and Vynny-

[4]Oleksander Oles (1878-1944): outstanding Ukrainian poet. Emigrated after the Revolution; not published in the USSR between 1931 and 1957.

[5]Borys Hrinchenko (1863-1910): Ukrainian lexicographer and prose writer. His prose was not published in the USSR between 1932 and 1957.

[6]Mykola Zerov (1890-1941): Ukrainian literary historian, poet and translator; arrested in 1935, died in Siberian camp. Partially rehabilitated in 1963.

[7]Valentyn Malanchuk (b. 1928): secretary of the CPU Lviv Regional Committee in charge of agitation and propaganda.

[8]Mykhaylo Hrushevsky (1866-1934): historian, head of Ukrainian national government after Revolution; emigrated after Red Army's victory. Returned to Ukraine in 1924, became member of Ukrainian and Soviet Academies of Science. Ten-volume *History of Ukraine-Rus* and five-volue *History of Ukrainian Literature* officially considered bourgeois for lack of class struggle interpretation of history and for "attempting to prove the lack of any relationship between the Ukrainian and Russian peoples, their united struggle against tsarism and capitalism" (*Ukrainian Encyclopedic Dictionary*, Kiev, 1966).

[9]*Ukrainsky istorychny zhurnal*, monthly journal published in Kiev by the Institutes of History of the Ukrainian Academy of Science and of the CC CPU.

chenko[10] are being prepared for publication. What are the criteria? But this is the point—the KGB never had any logical criteria. In its attitude to Ukrainian culture it follows the old Stalinist line: "Strangle whatever you can, and what you cannot—falsify." Shevchenko[11] wrote: "Why did we fight the Poles, why did we fight the hordes, why did we rake *Muscovite* ribs with our lances?" He was too great to be thrown into oblivion, and the Kiev "academicians" were therefore ordered to scratch these words out of *Kobzar* with their dirty hooves. "Muscovite ribs" became "Tartar ribs." Russian chauvinists dislike exposing their own ribs to the blows of the forces of national liberation; they have the habit of hiding behind Tartar, Polish or English ribs. They have to tolerate Shevchenko. But if a contemporary poet wrote something similar, those "Muscovite ribs" would cost him dearly.

During the 1930's most names were purged from Ukrainian culture. The purpose is not difficult to guess: to bleed Ukrainian culture white and prevent it from acting as a dam against the flood of Russification. The great *Ukrainian* historian, Hrushevsky, was hidden from the Ukrainian people. Instead, the pitiful two-volume *History of the Ukrainian SSR*,[12] in which Peter I, the executioner of Ukrainian freedom, figured as the chief Ukrainian national hero. At the same time Solovyov and Klyuchevsky, just as "bourgeois," just as "un-Soviet," filled up the bookshelves—they were *Russian* historians. Everything was done so that a young Ukrainian could find satisfactory spiritual nourishment only in Russian culture, and would thus become Russified.

If the KGB were consistent in its Stalinist interpretation of nationalism, it would proclaim all prominent Ukrainians,

[10]Volodymyr Vynnychenko (1880-1951): Ukrainian writer and member of 1917-20 Ukrainian national governments; emigrated after Red Army's victory.
[11]Taras Shevchenko (1814-61): Ukraine's greatest poet; born a peasant, persecuted by tsarist regime for his writings.
[12]*Istoria Ukrainskoyi RSR* (Kiev, 1953-58).

13

with Shevchenko in the lead, as nationalists; nor would they leave out Prince Volodymyr,[13] who carried on nationalist agitation as early as the tenth century "by preparing"[14] tridents[15] on his coins. Indeed, if anyone in the KGB should wish to earn an additional star for his shoulder boards and demonstrate his "vigilance" in combatting Ukrainian nationalism, an interesting "case" could be suggested to him. It turns out that Ukrainian nationalism existed as early as the seventh century, as witnessed by the tridents found during excavations on the Starokievsky Hill. True, there is a snag: no one knows the name of the "Bandera"[16] who prepared these tridents, but for Beria's pupils—who once managed to find Stalin's pipe in ten different places at the same time—this is a trifle.

The trident business dates back even further: it was known as a symbol of the tree of life among southern peoples even before our era,[17] as well as the symbol of Neptune's power. But this is a subject for Malanchuk: to discover the still unexplored connection between Ukrainian nationalism and international imperialism before our era aimed at undermining the sea power of a one-and-indivisible Russia. True, the name "Ukraine" did not exist before our era, but this is no problem for Malanchuk. For he succeeded in making the leader of the USDRP[18] Lev Rybalka (Yurkevych) an active member of the SVU,[19] although Yurkevych and his paper

13Volodymyr the Great, Grand Prince of Kiev (c. 978-1015).

14An allusion to the use of this word in the Criminal Code.

15Selected as state emblem by Ukrainian national government.

16Allusion to any Ukrainian nationalist, often referred to in the Soviet Union by using the name of Stepan Bandera (1909-59), leader of a faction of the Organization of Ukrainian Nationalists (OUN). Bandera was killed in 1959 in Munich by a Soviet agent.

17B.C.

18Ukrainian Social-Democratic Workers' Party (active 1905-20).

19Union for the Liberation of Ukraine (active in Western Ukraine during World War I).

14

The Struggle[20] were opposed to the SVU. An old member of the Communist Party of Western Ukraine, Adrian Hoshovsky (living in Warsaw),[21] wrote of Malanchuk's book *The Triumph of Leninist Nationalities Policy*:[22] "One can only greatly wonder how any responsible person could have made Yurkevych a member of the SVU when Yurkevych was a fierce enemy of the SVU" (*Ukrainian Calendar*,[23] Warsaw, 1966, p. 220). Actually, there is no cause for wonder. For "historians" like Malanchuk, brought up on good Stalinist traditions, a petty detail such as an historical fact is unimportant when the protection of Russian chauvinism's positions in Ukraine is at stake.

Malanchuk is not alone. If Hoshovsky lived in Ukraine, he would see even stranger things. After the war zealous fighters against Ukrainian nationalism even cut the trident off Neptune's statue in the Market Place in Lviv. And so the disarmed nationalist Neptune stood until 1957 as a monument to the immortal cretinism of the Black Hundreds[24] in a new guise.

All thick and thin pamphlets state that King Danylo of Galicia refused the royal crown from the Pope's nuncio, even though the Galician-Volynian Chronicle asserts the opposite, and Danylo was called king after his coronation, and Galicia a kingdom. (And so it is marked on a map in the *History of the Middle Ages*.) Such efforts hardly hurt the "bourgeois nationalism" against which the Malanchuks claim to be fight-

[20]*Borotba*, a Ukrainian Social-Democratic newspaper published in Geneva from February 1915 to September 1916.
[21]Until his death in August 1967, he was deputy editor of the Ukrainian paper *Nashe Slovo* in Warsaw.
[22]V. Malanchuk (see fn. 7 above), *Torzhestvo leninskoyi natsionalnoyi polityky* (Lviv, 1963). Subtitled: "The Communist Party—the organizer of the solution of the nationalities problem in the western regions of the Ukrainian SSR."
[23]*Ukrainsky kalendar*, an almanac.
[24]The popular name of the Union of the Russian People, a pre-Revolutionary right-wing extremist organization.

15

ing. Who could be hurt by such puny and pitiful scribbling? But in the struggle against Truth these scholars have achieved tangible results.

Enough facts, maybe a conclusion can be drawn: people convicted for "anti-Soviet agitation and propaganda" *think differently* or, simply, think, and their spiritual world does not fit the Procrustean bed of Stalinist standards which the KGB carefully defends. They have dared to claim the rights proclaimed in the Constitution and raised their voices against the shameful stranglehold of the KGB and the violations of the Constitution. They do not want to accept the slavish wisdom with a false bottom which says that the phrase in the Constitution* "the Ukraine's right to secede from the USSR," should be read as: "Keep quiet while you're alive."

Let us now see who has been granted the monopoly to "re-educate" those who do not conform with the standard.

---

*The right of secession is guaranteed both in the Constitution of the USSR and the Constitution of the UkrSSR.

Article 17 of the USSR Constitution states:

> **To every Union Republic of the Union of Soviet Socialist Republics is reserved the right to secede freely from the USSR.**

Article 14 of the UkrSSR Constitution states:

> **The Ukrainian Soviet Socialist Republic reserves its right to secede from the Union of Soviet Socialist Republics.**

Under Article 15 of its Constitution, the UkrSSR also "has the right to enter into direct relations with foreign states, conclude agreements with them and exchange diplomatic and consular representatives."

16

The Descendants of Yezhov and Beria

The characterization of a human being or of an environment is always liable to err towards subjectivity. It is therefore best to rely on self-characterization. It is also fortunate that the author of these lines has received a rich bouquet of self-characterizations from the KGB men about themselves and their system. The KGB men did not stint words or stand on ceremony when talking to the prisoners; they were certain that their words would not get beyond the heavy doors of their offices, and that the icy terror of silence on which they had built their Golgotha would never melt. But ice melts sooner or later, and the words barked into our faces during interrogation and in the camp have echoed in a thousand voices throughout the world as if they had been proclaimed through a giant megaphone.

Where are the roots of the KGB? If we retrace the paths along which the KGB entered our reality, we will find ourselves in the nightmarish thicket of the Stalinist jungle. In the Khartsyzsk constituency of the Donetsk region, General Shulzhenko, Deputy Chairman of the KGB attached to the Council of Ministers of the Ukrainian SSR, was elected as a deputy to the Ukrainian Parliament. Where did this parliamentarian make his career? In order to become a KGB general in 1967, one must have been one of Beria's lieutenants or captains in 1937. What did KGB[25] captains do in 1937? They killed people for not fulfilling their quotas (or simply for fun) in Kolyma. This is no longer a secret; Moscow journals write about it. In Ukraine they shot innocent people *three days* after arrest. Just to listen to them—Beria was responsible for everything, while they simply followed orders. Lawyers at the Nuremberg Trials used exactly the same

[25]Known as NKVD in 1937.

17

arguments. It seemed that only Hitler was guilty. But this was not good enough. A new concept even appeared in German—"a murderer at the desk." I do not doubt that this concept will some day also find expression in Ukrainian.

Maybe the KGB men have changed? No, they proudly regard themselves as descendants of Stalin. The Ukrainian KGB representative in the Mordovian camps, Captain Krut, said to me: "What have you got against Stalin? True, there were isolated shortcomings, but, on the whole, he deserves high praise." In a conversation with Mykhaylo Horyn,[26] Krut said openly, with regret: "Pity we're in Mordovia, and not up north." Nadiradze, the chief of the investigative department of the Georgian KGB, said to the poet Zauri Kobaliya (he is in Camp No. 11) during interrogation in 1963: "Do you know that I was here in 1937? Keep that in mind!"

Now they no longer wear "stalinkas"[27] and they "study" by correspondence in institutes of higher education. This is study by correspondence in the full sense of the word. The student's credits book is taken to the institute, and the "professors," hypnotized from the cradle by the term "KGB," enter his marks without ever having laid eyes on the student. The representative of the Ivano-Frankivsk KGB, Kazakov, admitted to me: "You spoke here of totalitarianism. *But I am not a totalizator.*"[28] Harashchenko, a representative of the Ukrainian KGB at Camp No. 11, made short work of all Masyutko's[29] evidence concerning the unresolved nationalities problem in the Ukraine: "You say—the nationalities problem . . . But when a widow asks the chairman of the collective farm for some straw, surely he won't refuse?" These are the

[26]Arrested in 1965, sentenced in 1966 to six years of imprisonment. Laboratory technician, born 1930.

[27]Peak-caps or tunics of the pattern worn by Stalin.

[28]The semi-literate KGB captain confused "totalitarian" with "totalizator."

[29]Mykhaylo Masyutko (b. 1918): retired teacher; arrested in 1965, tried and sentenced in 1966 to six years of imprisonment.

18

intellectuals who have been entrusted with making final peremptory decisions on questions which are subjects for discussion even in specialized journals. Kazakov, Krut, and the KGB man from Kiev, Lytvyn, were all "re-educating" me. "Well, what did you need? You had a good job, an apartment. . . . " They spent several hours proving that a man had nothing more than a stomach and so many meters of intestines. An idea? Protection of Ukraine from the threat of Russification? Here, as far as my interlocutors were concerned, the discussion definitely left reality and moved into the realm of children's fairy tales. They did not pretend to take this conversation seriously.

An idea. . . . Of course, much is written about this in books, and, in general, it is unacceptable to admit that one is without any ideas. But that an idea should actually be a motive of human activity—this is unheard of in the KGB environment. Mykhaylo Horyn heard in the Lviv KGB offices: "Today is Chekists' day." "What kind of Chekists' day?" "It's pay day." Well, even if an idea is to be given serious consideration, then only as a myth which befuddles and distracts people from normal existence, that stands on three whales:[30] lust for money, power, and women. An idea is a psychological disorder, which is, admittedly, not completely understandable, but it has to be taken into consideration as a factor with the other three, which are normal and understandable. Captain Kozlov (Ivano-Frankivsk) explained it to me like this: "One man is bought with money, another through women, and some are caught by an idea." The possibility that a man's brain could *independently* give birth to an idea is never admitted. Such are the men who have been entrusted with "regulating" the spiritual life of society.

It would be naive to consider this state of affairs a chance "violation of socialist legality," a deviation from the norm.

---

[30]According to ancient cosmological mythology, carried over to Old Slavonic literature and folklore, the earth stands on three whales.

On the contrary, this is the standard at certain stages of the development of society. An order of society, in which a poet receives a catalogue of permissible imagery and a painter a list of permissible and forbidden paints, has strong roots in the past and is an outcome of certain forces and relationships. These forces are gradually fading before our eyes, and these relationships are ceasing to be the standard of relationships among people. The KGB men feel this and put the entire blame on Khrushchev, who supposedly toppled the idols before whom one had previously bowed without stopping to think. One can, with equal success, regard the rooster as the creator of dawn, but this is too great a truth to fit into the skulls of generals and majors with blue collar tabs.[31]

"When There Was Stalin—Then There Was Order"

These words spoken by Captain Volodin (Lviv) at Masyutko's interrogation provide for a better understanding of the origins of the KGB and its present role than whole volumes.

There are various kinds of order. When the ice breaks up in the spring and is carried chaotically downstream—this is order, a precise conformity to the laws of life. There is also order in the calm of a cemetery, achieved by killing all that is alive. So it is in society: there is stability achieved through a harmonious balance of all social forces and factors, and there is "order" built on their destruction. Such an "order" is not difficult to achieve; the degree of maturity of a nation, however, is measured not by it, but by the ability to achieve social stability while allowing maximum scope for the individual's creative activity, the only force of progress.

Intellect is an individual matter. The history of progress is therefore the history of the development of individuality. The so-called masses *create nothing;* they are the building material of history. "Everything gained through the activity

[31]The insignia of the KGB.

20

of the intellect must be created in the minds of individuals. . . . Only the excitations of a lower, undeveloped level, which may generally be classified as moods, arise as epidemics in many people simultaneously and conform to the intellectual make-up of a nation. Intellectual achievements come from individuals." (Ratzel)[32]

The emergence of something new (progress) is possible only by stepping beyond the existing standard, by the emergence of something which previously did not exist. The very nature of creativity is rooted in the unprecedented and in the *unrepeatable,* and the carrier of the latter is the individual. Each individual consciousness embraces *one* facet of the all-embracing, boundless existence, an *unrepeatable* facet which can be reflected *only* by this particular individual and by no other. The more of these facets of consciousness there are, the more complete is our picture of the world. Therein lies the value of the individual; with the disappearance of each individual point of view, we *irrevocably* lose one of the possibilities, and at the same time one facet of the million-faceted mosaic of the human spirit stops sparkling.

In society there always have been and will be forces for whom progress is undesirable, for whom the maintenance of the *status quo* is a guarantee of the maintenance of their privileges. (A typical example is Stalin in the past, and the Stalinists who have survived him.) Time, however, does not stand still; within twenty-four hours, today becomes yesterday, and it is yesterday that the forces which oppose change are always defending. But who will admit that he is swimming against the current of the mighty river called History? Therefore, all standardizers, from the stupid Sergeant Major Prishibeyev[33] to Plato, the genius, have repeated the same thesis on various levels: "Changes destroy order; they destroy society." Since the seed of all changes is hidden in the

[32]Friedrich Ratzel (1844-1904) : German geographer and traveller.
[33]From Chekhov's story *Unter Prishibeyev* (1885).

uniqueness of the individual, they at first try to standardize him, to kill the originality within him. This cannot be achieved completely, but the degree of standardization of the individual has always been the measure of the power of the brake at the disposal of the forces of stagnation. Plato exiled Homer from his ideal state and gave high praise to the tyrant who ordered the lyre strings above the "prescribed" seven to be broken. Why? With primitive candor Plato argues that poetry and music are the Trojan horse which imperceptibly introduces changes into the spirit of the nation. Poetry and music are therefore best driven out, and, since this cannot be done, they should be rigidly standardized to insure against obscurities and innovations. Later reactionaries were no longer so candid; they assumed the mask of "the workers' interests." In the 1930's, innovation became a negative concept, when poetic experiment was "if not always a catastrophe, then always at least both a creative and ideological setback" (*Soviet Literature*[34] [1938] No. 78, p. 224). This leads to a situation in which "creativity begins to serve as a mask for enemy ideology" (*Literary Gazette*[35] June 24, 1934). "The poetry of socialist realism must not tolerate obscurity, even if beautiful" (*The Fatherland*[36] [1949] p. 147).

The fact is, however, that changes do not destroy society at all; they destroy only those social standards which have become obsolete and a hindrance. Evolution must not be set against tradition. Evolution is not the denial of tradition; it is its natural continuation, the life sap which prevents it from ossifying. An explosion by no means always destroys; it is also used to remove obstacles when building new roads.

[34]*Radyanska literatura*, magazine published by the Ukrainian Writers' Union between 1933-41. During World War II, called *Ukrainska literatura* (Ukrainian literature); from 1946 *Vitchyzna* (Fatherland).

[35]*Literaturnaya gazeta*, newspaper published in Moscow by the Soviet Writers' Union.

[36]See fn. 34 above.

And when a man begins to hold different opinions this does not mean that he puts himself outside the standards of his society. The general is an abstraction; *in reality* it exists and manifests itself only in the *particular,* the individual. "The raven is perched in the forest" is an abstraction; in reality, it has to perch on one of the trees. When a man begins to hold different opinions he does not destroy the standards of society; on the contrary, he makes them more full-blooded. "They be two things, Unity and Uniformity" (Francis Bacon). *Uniformity* is not essential for achieving *unity.* At this point it is quite easy to catch any despot red-handed at cheating when he tries to equate unity and uniformity. Every point of view a despot wishes to impose on all under the guise of "truth" is just as individual as all others, and has by no means greater rights than any of the others. Therefore, the maintenance of an order in which all points of view must fit the Procrustean bed of a "truth" proclaimed by the great "Dalai Lama" is necessary not to society, but to the "Dalai Lama" himself, for whom development means death.

An explorer of Africa (Segeli) wrote of the Africans:

When the chief loved hunting, all his people got dogs and hunted with him. If he loved music and dancing, all showed an inclination for this entertainment. If he loved beer, everyone got drunk on it. . . . The chiefs paid their sycophants. So among all the tribes of the Bechuanas there are individuals who have mastered the art of pleasing their chief's ear with songs of praise in his honor. In this they develop considerable eloquence and always have a great number of images at their disposal; they are skilled at dances with battle-axes and gourds. The chief rewards their sweet words with a bull or a sheep. These songs, which endlessly repeat one and the same theme, unfortunately hold first place in the poetry of the Negroes.[37]

If it were not for the word "Negroes" everyone would have

[37]Not located. ("Segeli" may be copyist's misreading.)

been certain that this was a description of our own not-too-distant past. It is not only in Negro poetry that songs with battle-axes endlessly repeated before the chief's throne hold first place. When we recall the speed with which every word not only of Stalin but also of Khrushchev was seized upon, and how half the collection of aphorisms entitled *In the World of Wise Thoughts*[38] was filled with the drunken babblings of Khrushchev, one must admit that the Africans lagged far behind. "Such are our people; it is enough to wink and they understand immediately" (Khrushchev). Twin societies, one might think. But this is far from being the case. Such an order was not forced by anyone on the Africans; it was their natural state, dictated by the level of their development. For them the chief was simultaneously an idol, an object of adulation, a magician, a doctor, a sage, and a warrior leader —a demigod. The slavish adoration was therefore sincere and did not infringe the inner harmony of individuality. The African court singer's songs were praises of the chief, and yet artistic creations in their own right, because the creative personality of the singer was not split. Ratzel wrote of the Africans of the nineteenth century that they "submitted only to absolute and irresistable rule, the origins of which are hidden in the darkness of the past, or, if it originates in the present, which they are able to connect with a belief in the supernatural"; therefore, "even the best rulers of the Africans, in our sense of the word, must be called despots. *Even if they themselves do not want to be despots, their subjects will force them to be such.*"

Thus, primitive despotism was natural, based less on power than on voluntary worship. (This is the answer to the mystery that has always puzzled Europeans—how an African or American Indian despot could maintain his dominion over great territories with almost no military-bureaucratic appa-

---

[38]*V mire mudrykh mysley* (Moscow, 1962). Out of a total of thirty pages of source references, nearly a whole page is taken up by references to Khrushchev—more than the space occupied by any other author.

ratus.) How can despotism be maintained in the twentieth century among people for whom he who holds power has long ceased to be a god and is simply the first among equals, an individual chosen to perform certain functions? How can stone-age despotism be set up in the soul of a Ukrainian, who (in his tradition) as early as the Middle Ages elected and deposed a "koshovy"[39] and could himself become a "koshovy," who gave birth to Skovoroda's[40] philosophy—a hymn to human individuality, even though in traditional scholastic garb, with the motto "Know thyself" on the first page?—a philosophy in which the Ego is the basis of everything, even of the kingdom of God, and in which even God Himself is nothing other than a fully developed Ego: "He who knows himself has found the desired treasure of God. He has found its source and fulfillment in himself. . . . *The true man and God are one and the same.*" How can the contemporary artist, for whom the corporal-despot is simply an inferior being, be forced to perform a battle-axe dance before the despot's throne?

No one worshipped Khrushchev; on the contrary, he was a public laughing-stock. And yet, dozens of toadies leaped at a flick of his finger, and a system of "levers" was set in motion. How was this managed? Very simply. When worship passes away, brute force takes over. Only this can force contemporary man to endure a despot. As individuality develops, the more man resists attempts to enslave him, the greater the efforts that despotism must make in order to maintain the standards that earlier existed "by force of inertia." In the end, it sheds its patriarchal features and changes into an octopus that fetters all movement in the social organism. The twentieth century has seen the emergence of unprecedented controls over all aspects of community life, even family life. The entire course of a man's life—from

[39]Head of Zaporozhian Cossacks (sixteenth to eighteenth centuries).
[40]Hryhoriy Skovoroda (1722-94): Ukrainian humanist, philosopher, poet.

the cradle to the grave—is controlled. Even leisure is standardized; evading the roundup for a "cultural excursion" to the museum is proclaimed a sin. Despotic forms become more and more disgusting, and degenerate into Auschwitzes. In this some see regression, "the end of the world." Actually, it proves the opposite: despotism ceases to be the accepted norm of human relationships and must continually assert itself in order to survive.

But even with maximum standardization and subjugation of life, the despot meets a problem that cannot be solved by purely bureaucratic means. One can dress people in identical gray, build gray barracks, burn all books except the official Talmud, and still a tiny crack remains through which a ray of light, lethal to the mustiness of despotism, penetrates. Man's spiritual world remains. KGB Captain Kazakov, sent from Ivano-Frankivsk to Mordovia to check how far I had been "re-educated" (*i.e.,* how far my individuality had been eroded), frankly admitted to me that: *"Unfortunately we can't see what is in your head. If we could do this, and throw out (!!!) everything that prevents you from being a normal Soviet man, there would be no need for so much talk."*

This would indeed be very convenient—to remove and insert thoughts into a person's head, like an element into an electronic device. Firstly, it would then be easy to destroy all memory of the past. For example, a campaign to condemn the cult of Stalin must be started, so a certain program is inserted; tomorrow it is removed, and there is no further mention of Stalin. Or it has been decided to liquidate nations and national languages; the same procedure, and there is no bother with such unsuitable things for programming as national dignity, honor, or the desire to preserve spiritual and cultural values. Secondly, there would be a guarantee that nothing unknown or uncontrolled existed anywhere.

But this is only a dream. You cannot catch thought and put it behind bars. You cannot even see it. How horrible! Even a thought forced into a man's head does not lie there like an element in an electronic device; it grows and develops (sometimes in the direction opposite from that programmed), and no apparatus can control this process. Many a tyrant has awoken in a cold sweat, paralyzed by the realization that he is powerless to stop this invisible but constant activity within human skulls. The fear of this force, which is subject to nobody, made Stalin spend the last years of his life in a voluntary prison and turned him into a maniac. Hence the desire to remove the Homers from society, to break "superfluous" strings in the lyre, and the age-old hatred of corporals for the intellectual who remains unstandardized and potentially explosive, be he in a soldier's uniform or in prisoner rags.[41]

"Comrades, fear those who have concealed their thoughts behind obscurity of expression. They conceal an anti-class nature." (Pokrovsky).[42] Hence the wholesale struggle not only—needless to say—against those who think *differently,* but also against those who think *for themselves.* During my arrest, a poem by Ivan Drach, "Tale about Wings," was confiscated. "Why?" I asked; the poem had been published, and the author himself had long since stopped being berated for his "washed trousers"[43] and had suddenly begun to be praised. They gave me this explanation: there was nothing against either the poem or the author, but the poem had been typed *on someone's own initiative.* And that unknown someone had distributed it, also on his own initiative. In this lies the greatest sin: a man generates thoughts *on his own* and does not accept them ready-made. One can do anything, but only when ordered. One may drink only from that spring of dis-

[41]An allusion to Shevchenko (fn. 11 above), who was punished in 1847 for his revolutionary poetry by military service of indefinite period as a private in remote regions. He was amnestied in 1857.

[42]M. N. Pokrovsky (1868-1932): leading Soviet Russian Marxist historian.

[43]Ivan Drach (b. 1936), poet, translator, critic. The "Ballad about Washed Trousers" was included in Drach's first book of poetry, *Sonyashnyk* (Kiev, 1962); some critics took exception to it.

tilled water which is common to all and strictly controlled; all other springs must be filled in, even though the water in them is in no way different. In 1964 the representative of the Volyn KGB, whose task it was to note the appearance of every thinking being in the local pedagogical institute and immediately switch on the alarm, persistently put the question to me: "What is this association of thinking people?" The idea of forming an association of thinking people was born over a drink, as a joke, but it was more than a joke to the KGB. The Constitution gives the right to form associations; the KGB knows this—but provided the order to form an association comes *from above.* Then everything is all right—even if this association intended to bring about an earthquake. But if some people wished to form even an association for the protection of cattle *independently,* the KGB would doubtless look into the matter.

How then can this endless, spontaneous movement of thought be stopped when it remains alive after undergoing all stages of standardization and sterilization? One last resort remains—to *freeze* it; freeze it by means of icy *terror.* To build a giant refrigerator for human minds. Shooting, three days after arrest, mysterious disappearance in the middle of the night, shooting for failing to fulfill the quota, Kolyma, from which one does not return—these are the bricks with which Stalin constructed his "Empire of Terror." Terror filled both days and nights. Terror was in the air, and a single mention of it paralyzed thought. The goal was reached: people were *afraid to think;* the human brain stopped producing criteria and standards *on its own* and instead considered it normal to accept them ready-made. Despotism begins when people stop regarding violence aimed at them as evil and begin to think of it as normal. ("The authorities make things awkward. And what of it? That is what authorities are for—to make things awkward.") There grew up a whole generation of *people in fear,* and on the ruins of individuality arose. . . .

An Empire Of Cogs

STALIN did not recognize cybernetics, and yet he made a great contribution to this discipline; he invented the programmed man. Stalin is the creator of the Cog. After reading Solzhenitsyn's novel, some people said: "One wants to hide in a corner and not show oneself." It is easy to imagine how much stronger this feeling was twenty years ago, when people were eyewitnesses of mass executions and other horrors, and one did not know in the evening where one would be by the morning. The desire not to be conspicuous, to lose oneself in the masses, to look like the next person in order not to draw attention to oneself, became universal. This meant a complete levelling of individuality. At one time the separation of the individual from the mass of matter meant the birth of life, the origin of the organic world. Now the opposite process had begun: the blending of individuals into a gray mass, a return to a solid non-organic, non-individual existence. Society was overcome by the spirit of gray facelessness. It was considered a crime to be an individual. "What do you think you are—someone special?" One heard this dozens of times both before and after arrest. The team method reached even poetry and produced such a marvel as a collective poem "Ivan Holota" appeared in 1937, signed in alphabetical order, as in a telephone directory: Bazhan, Holovanivsky, Yohansen, Kulyk, Pervomaysky, Rylsky, Sosyura, Tereshchenko, Tychyna, Feffer, Usenko, Ushakov. But even this seemed inadequate; a year later there was an order to compose the "Duma about Ostap Nechay," which had twenty signatures under it. This was probably a record.

Here are some impressions of a former member of the Communist Party of Western Ukraine who was arrested five times by the Polish Defenzywa[44] and after 1939 finally got to Eastern Ukraine, about which he had dreamed in prison for years:

[44]Security police, pre-1938.

The train crossed the line of the no longer existing border. The first stop was in the Zhytomyr region. A crowd on the platform. The first thing that caught my eye was the unaccustomed monotonous grayness of the people, who were dressed in sweaters. A woman in a red coat looked like an exotic flower, strange and even out of place here.

But clothes may be colorful, even gaudy, yet the grayness does not vanish. It does not spring from the clothes. And no matter how Cogs may publicize themselves and bedeck themselves with tapestries rented from a shop for the visit of a delegation, a bystander will always notice the grayness—it floats in the air, people breathe it, they cannot imagine themselves without it; it has become their daily bread.

Lastly, the ruling power claims to be the only fount of "the mind, honor and conscience" of the whole society—and then solemnly proclaims the "politico-moral unity of society." In so far as the Cog is concerned, the eternal question "Where to go?" is made into a formula which requires no exertion of the intellect: "Wherever they lead me." A human deprived of the ability to distinguish between good and evil for himself becomes like a police dog that is moved to rage only on orders and perceives only the evil that is pointed out to it. A Cog reads in the paper that Blacks are forbidden to live in Capetown or Johannesburg, that Africans are forbidden to live in South African cities without permits, and he regards this as a manifestation of arbitrary power. But his frozen brain is unable to discriminate between facts and to draw the conclusion that registration in towns—familiar to him since birth—is just as much of a violation of Art. 13 of the Declaration of Human Rights ("Everyone has the right to freedom of movement and residence within the borders of each state") and that in our reality *the pale* is legalized, and not as formerly just for Jews, but *for everybody*. For those not born in a large city a ghetto has been designated whose boundaries end in the suburbs of Kiev, Lviv, or Odessa. The Cog writes angry poems about Buchenwald; this is allowed. "Your hearts have turned into ashes, but your voice has not been consumed." But the ashes of victims mouldering in the Siberian tundra do not perturb the Cog. And it would be a mistake to see only fear in this; it is already a feature of his character.

Everyone condemns the crimes of fascism against the Jewish population. Yet one walks serenely over the gravestones from Jewish cemeteries with which the pavements of many cities are laid. True, the pavements were laid by the Germans. The Germans, however, have long since departed, but one goes on walking over the desecrated names of the dead in the courtyards of the Lviv and Ivano-Frankivsk prisons. Lecturers and candidates of sciences of the Ivano-Frankivsk Pedagogical Institute walk over them. And if by now any of them have succeeded in defending their doctoral theses, professors also walk over people's names. A spare pile of gravestones lay in the courtyard of the Institute before my arrest. They were broken and used for domestic needs. They were broken to the accompaniment of lectures on aesthetics and philosophy. This will go on until an order from above is issued that one is to show indignation at German barbarity and to erect a monument of these gravestones. Until then they may be slighted.

The Cog is the dream of every "totalizator." An obedient herd of Cogs may be called a parliament or an academic council, and it will give rise to no worries or surprises. A Cog called a professor or an academician will never say anything new, and if he does surprise one it will not be by saying something new but by the lightning speed of the change in his beliefs. A herd of Cogs can be called the Red Cross, and it will count calories in Africa, but say nothing of the hunger in its own land. The Cog will be released from prison and immediately write that he was never there, and he will also call whoever demanded his release a liar (as Ostap Vyshnya did).[45] The Cog will shoot whomever he is told to and then, at an order, fight for peace. Last and most important, it is safe to introduce any constitution and grant every right after turning people into Cogs. The whole trick of it is that it will not even occur to the Cog to take advantage of these rights.

It is not surprising that the Cog was highly publicized and held up as an ideal. That is not history; it is reality. In some school corridor pupils enthusiastically read Symonenko: "We are not an infinity of standard egos, but an infinity of different universes." Nearby a standard wall newspaper, placed there by the Pioneer leader, tells the story of the Pioneer girls who saved some calves during a fire. Everything was enveloped by flames, and the roof was about to cave in, but she herded out the calves. And if the girl had perished, the Cogs would not have seen anything strange in this; on the contrary, they would have made this case an example for others.

In the society of Cogs there are laws which protect tigers and boa constrictors from poachers. "Humanitarianism" has a level where men are imprisoned in Moscow for killing Borka, a swan. We hope that humanitarianism will some day extend to humans as well. But as long as the life of a Pioneer girl is valued below that of a calf, one cannot take the slogan "All for man, all for the good of man" seriously. The value of individuality is realized only where it is regarded as unique and separate. Where it has been turned into a Cog, a component which can be replaced by another, an individual's value is measured by his muscular strength. In such a society, humanitarianism is seen as a false slogan that has

[45]Popular Soviet Ukrainian humorist writer (1889-1956); in 1933 arrested and sentenced to death on a trumped-up charge of planning the assassination of Postyshev and others; the sentence was commuted to ten years of labor camp. One of the very few survivors of these camps, he wrote to official requirements after his release in 1943. In *My Life Story* (Moscow, 1958) he derided those in the West who had been indignant about his presumed liquidation.

nothing in common with reality. A calf is the material-technical basis, the prime principle, for which a spiritual principle (found in the Pioneer) is a pitiful superstructure. The calf is a finished product; the Pioneer is a kind of raw material which is known as manpower reserves. In cannibal days this Pioneer would undoubtedly have been valued higher; she would at least have been regarded as having material value, along with the calf.

An "edifying" article about a fireman appeared in *Izvestia*. The engine that had brought a train to Finland developed trouble at one of the Finnish stations. The furnace had to be put out for the engine to be repaired. But the fireman decided to show the Finns "how to do it": repairing without putting out the furnace. That is, the fireman decided what his protectors, who had solicitously accompanied him across the frontier so that he should not get lost, "advised" him to decide. True, the paper forgot to mention this. But be that as it may, the furnace was not put out and the fireman risked his life and carried out the repair. The paper says that the Finns were impressed by the fireman's courage. Yes, the Finns were impressed, but not by his courage. It was simply the first time that they had seen a man value his life less than a hundred kilos of coal. This, however, is regarded as heroism among the Cogs.

> Behind the drums
> The calves do trot.
> They themselves
> Supply the drum skins.

> (Brecht)

An Orgy On The Ruins Of Individuality

AN INTELLIGENT engineer, when asked why he had become an engineer rather than, say, an art historian, replied: "There are fewer x's here." That is the essential difference between the so-called exact sciences and the humanities which stand, together with art, with one foot on the plane of logic and with the other on the plane of the irrational. The so-called technical intellectual who is firmly convinced that philosophy is "concerned with nonsense" and "is mere empty talk" has not learned the simple truth: that philosophy draws the objects of investigation out of the fog of irrational depths, puts them in his hands and enables him to measure them with a tape measure. It gives him things that have stopped being x's and can be measured with a tape measure. But the point is that spiritual concepts, which make human beings human, cannot be measured with a tape measure or a stopwatch. This is a higher sphere, not accessible to the applied sciences. "Mathematics, medicine, physics, mechanics . . . the more plentifully we partake of them, the more is our heart consumed by thirst and hunger; our crude stupidity cannot grasp that they are all *the servants of the lady of the house* and the tail of a head without which the whole body is not real" (Skovoroda). A chemist taking out and adding substances into a test tube can demonstrate exactly which is the cause of the reaction. A historian, even if he has no doubts about his vision of the truth, can never show the causes of a historical phenomenon so convincingly and graphically; he cannot carry out an experiment; he has to deal with an abstraction. After losing the war against Japan in 1894, the Chinese concluded that the cause of the failure was—the replacement of bows by flintlocks. Attempts were made to prove to them that the cause lay in the complete stifling of individuality, which led to a standstill in material production, but no one could demonstrate this to them *perfectly*, with mathematical precision. No wonder Shaw wrote: "We learn from history that men never learn anything from history."

Yes, it is much more difficult to understand a history than a chemistry lesson. This has always been convenient for despots; they proclaimed themselves to be the authors of all the achievements of society, and their enemies the cause of all evil. Not everyone will understand that the "order" introduced by Stalin decades ago is the direct cause of the present bedlam in agriculture, or that "lofty ideas" forcibly fed to people for decades, and not "bourgeois propaganda," are the cause of the notorious absence of idealism among present-day youth. When a man is taught to accept unhesitatingly all spiritual values ready-made from a single source, and when the mechanism for producing them independently is destroyed within him, society, so it would seem, must become an indestructible monolith. All the conditions for this appear to be present: first, the identical nature of human needs and values; second, the unconditional, though naive, worship of one idol; all leading to unanimity. It would seem that such a society must also be militarily strong. Let us take China as an example, where medical standards have not changed for four thousand years. The Chinese really believed their empire to be an indestructible monolith, the most powerful in the world. And then? At the beginning of the twentieth century one European power after another tore hunks off this vast centralized China, virtually without opposition.

In Paris or London, a Russian nobleman would look down on the demonstrations and revolutions that had become a common occurrence there, and see in them a symptom of weakness in comparison to the serene peace in his Mother Russia. A myth was even created about the "rotten West" which has survived to our own times. The philistine who acquires it daily from the newspapers and novels does not even suspect that this wisdom stems from the Slavophiles[46] and

[46]The opponents of the Westernizers (the other main school of thought in Russian intellectual life in the 1840's).

Dostoyevsky. As early as the middle of the nineteenth century one could read in the pages of *Moskvityanin*[47] the admonitions to "Europe, old and blind, sick as an old dog." Mother Russia flowered and was fragrant in uniformity and indivisibility; the rotten West lived on, barely managing to give birth to the theory of relativity and the quantum theory. Russia adopted them, fifty years later, with the reservation that Lomonosov had foreseen these discoveries two hundred years ago, and went on speaking of the "rotten West." A typical example of complete atrophy of thought! "In Petersburg they sing songs which have gone out of fashion in Paris," wrote Chernyshevsky a hundred years ago. He could write the same today. So Russia is mighty; the West is rotten. And then? The Crimean War came, and it became evident that an equal battle between these forces was impossible. The Russian fleet had to be sunk at the entrance to Sevastopol Bay. Not only could it not win, but it could not even engage the Anglo-French fleet. This was an encounter between two worlds: one that regarded individuality as the prime source of all power, and another that saw in it the principal evil. The latter was occasionally victorious, but the ultimate victory had always been carried off by the former. This was already demonstrated in ancient times by the Greek phalanxes and the Roman legions, which looked like David against Goliath facing the gigantic armies of the Eastern despots. But they routed them, because *individuals* opposed *Cogs*.

Such encounters opened the eyes of many—but not all, by a long shot. The majority managed to see only the results: "With our order we would do wonders if only we had their weapons." But that is precisely the point: this very "order" is the cause of our lagging in production and arms. Nothing will replace the free, unregimented thought of an individual, whose creative ability is the only motive force of progress.

[47]The Slavophiles' journal.

We owe progress to those who have kept their ability to think and preserved their individuality despite all attempts to erase it. A person without an individuality becomes a machine that will execute everything, but will not *create* anything. He is spiritually impotent—the manure of progress, but not its motor. All totalitarian concepts, regardless of the garb in which they appear, regard man precisely in this way —as manure. "We will, as you did, become the fertilizer for future generations." But can it be that man has travelled the long road of evolution to *Homo sapiens* solely in order to become manure, and the world—a garden in which utopian despots conduct mad experiments to satisfy their ambition?

No program can foresee everything needed for complete social development; only the unfettered creative force of individuality can cope with this. Before cybernetics could become a factor of social development and be supported by the state, it had to be born and exist as an idea in an individual brain. By driving thousands of slaves to the Ural Mountains, Peter I made Russia England's rival as the largest producer of iron. But a century later, England's output was *tens of times* greater than that of Russia! One can still use his method; it does not require a great deal of intelligence. But one cannot expect lasting results from it. The mechanism of cause and effect, beginning with creative individuality and culminating in a practical result, is complex and difficult to grasp. A savage cannot grasp the connection between a shot on one bank of a river and the death of a living being on the other, but the mechanism of interaction between the gunpowder, the bullet and the gun could be explained to him in half an hour. If only it were as simple to explain the workings of social causes and effects!

The Cog spreads a similar deadening atmosphere in the realm of morals and ethics. If anyone considers the present "Tower of Babel" in China the outcome of fanaticism, and a Red Guard a fanatic, he is greatly mistaken. Herds of thousands pushed their way to the last remains of the earthly

37

god during Stalin's funeral, crushing dozens of weaker men to death, and the world also thought that they were fanatics. Three years went by. The embalmed "Dalai Lama" was first reviled and later thrown out of the mausoleum altogether. And what happened? Perhaps a revolt? Perhaps thousands of fanatics shielded the shrine with their bodies? Not a word! The herd trampled over the body of the herd leader and then ate his remains. Those who were taken for fanatics filled with blind devotion turned out to be quite empty. They turned out to be mere robots. There was an order to love and mourn Stalin, and everyone wore crape armbands. Their wrath, grief, joy, enthusiasm—all were programmed. Today's "wrath" against "the traitor Tito" which the "citizenry" has shown at "meetings" will tomorrow automatically turn into "enthusiasm" of the same "citizenry" neatly drawn up along the road from the airport to the city, obediently holding placards and waving.

In vain does the "older generation," ensconced in its comfortable chairs, wonder where this "younger generation" which "holds nothing sacred" has come from. The business with Stalin showed that they also held nothing sacred. They merely did not notice this because of their blindness and the atrophy of their reasoning ability. The "young" finally noticed that the emperor had no clothes. This is a good thing. Only those who have lost their illusions and can see the broken trough[48] will begin to seek new values.

An *empty man*—this is probably the main charge against despotism and its essential product. For when a despot proclaims his monopoly over reason, honor and conscience, and forbids the independent development of these qualities, it is the beginning of the spiritual emptying of man. Each living being needs self-expression. When this need cannot be fulfilled in the spiritual sphere, an individual's spiritual faculties become useless and atrophy. Even the idea that a man can

[48]Allusion to Pushkin's "The Tale of the Fisherman and the Fish."

develop something *independently* is not permitted.

Before and after our trial we were repeatedly told that we were "the brood of Antonenko-Davydovych[49] and company." From the KGB's point of view an idea can be put into a man's head only *from without*. And when a movement against intellectual and moral stagnation and against the chauvinist stranglehold developed among the young Ukrainian intelligentsia, the KGB rushed to find out who *introduced* it, and who influenced them?

The instinct of self-determination, banished from the realm of the spirit, rushes with redoubled energy into the material sphere. So we see a man "set free" from spiritual inwardness developing an unnatural material shell. Base passions become the sole motivating force of behavior. But no one dares to say so openly. It is officially agreed that the Cog is guided by dedication, self-denial, honor, etc. The Cog, however, does not perceive them within himself and concludes that all these moral principles are simply ridiculous superstitions, which everyone talks about but which in this world lead to perdition. A double moral standard thus comes into existence, and falsehood becomes a social standard. By force of inertia, the dictator receives divine honors, and his portraits hang on every pillar, but the soccer center forward becomes the real god. Only in the stadium and in the tearoom does the Cog wake up briefly from his lethargic slumber.

The Cog develops a certain virtuosity in spreading subsidence. When ordered to join a new conservation organization, he will not refuse, and in a month's time the organization will have as many members as there are Cogs. But Nature will not benefit from it. This organization, like all the rest, will be stillborn. The finest net cannot draw the Cog— a shapeless, resilient mass of an amoeba—into creative, useful

[49]Borys Antonenko-Davydovych (b. 1899) : Soviet Ukrainian writer; sent to labor camp in 1934, rehabilitated in 1956. Recent works on maintaining the integrity of the Ukrainian language have been objects of controversy.

work. The Cog will silently accept and carry out the most extravagant experiments; he will build factories where no electric power is planned for at least twenty years, or where raw materials are not accessible, his work destined to collapse through years of disuse.

And so order was built on the ruins of individuality, sowing the earth with languor. "It is worse than a plague. The plague kills indiscriminately, but despotism selects its victims from the flower of the nation," wrote Stepnyak-Kravchinsky.[50]

The Dragon

ICY TERROR, without which an empire of Cogs cannot be built, must be constantly maintained. Ice cannot exist forever in its natural state, and so a special refrigerator is essential. Each dictator must create one—this a matter of life or death for him. During Stalin's rule the KGB became such a refrigerator in which the spiritual development of society was frozen for decades. The total destruction of individual thought and the mass standardization of thinking and life placed a great burden on the KGB, but also gave it unlimited power. So it has always been: the agent assigned to drain the blood from the living organism hypertrophies from the blood it has sucked from it. Its functional role comes to an end; it no longer fulfills any useful function in the organism and becomes a parasite. It transforms the body which has given it birth into a nourishing medium for itself, into food. A satellite has been launched from the planet; it suddenly turns out that not only has it entered its own orbit, but has captured the gravity of the planet, concentrated it in itself, and forced the planet to orbit around it. In the end, the

[50]S. Stepnyak, *Russia under the Tzars* (1885). The original English edition has the term "the present regime." Moroz is quoting from a recent translation into Russian (Stepnyak-Kravchinsky, *Rossiya pod vlastyu tsarey*, Moscow, 1964, p. 238) in which this term is translated as "despotism."

40

parasite loses all semblance of connection with the organism. It grows to the proportions of a dragon and demands regular sacrifices. As a rule it swallows even the despot who has reared it. So it was with the praetorian guard in Rome when it developed from the emperor's bodyguard into the power which raised them to the throne and deposed them from it. The same was true of the janissaries. Stalin realized this well and feared the same fate. Therefore, just in case, he dispatched Yezhov and Yagoda into the hereafter. But even so, the principle almost prevailed. After Stalin's death, Beria nearly became the new dictator.

The dragon becomes the quintessence and the symbol of the terror required for the manufacture of Cogs. The position of the KGB above society is perhaps evidenced less by their exclusive material privileges (including private hunting grounds) than by the magic terror which "KGB" spells everywhere. In order to justify their position of a state within the state, the "agencies" must constantly create the impression that they are protecting society from terrible danger. They, first of all, put up a sign: protectors of "state security." The dragon must regularly devour people in order to remain alive. All energy is directed at fabricating "anti-Soviet" plots and organizations. All cultural forces were destroyed, 95 percent of the General Staff was executed—and then the KGB agents began shooting each other. They reached a mad, nightmarish state when the question: "Where is Comrade Ivanov? I have come to arrest him," was answered by: "He left not long ago to arrest you." The deadly serpent began to devour its own tail, while the actual function of the "agencies"—the protection of state security—receded into last place. Real spies never had it so good. In the madness of wholesale suspicion and spy-mania, when all feeling of reality vanished, their work was very easy. This became obvious during the first years of the war.

In Camp No. 11, a mentally ill Estonian, Heino Nurmsaar, claimed to be the pantheistic god in human form. In his mind, all evil on earth was due to the fact that he is badly treated. Because of this the glaciers moved south, and the polar regions are still ice-bound. But after he is released and well fed, everything will change, and it will be possible to plant potatoes on the North Pole, while he lives in the forest, planting trees and keeping bees. Nikolay Tregubov, a Siberian, has proclaimed himself president of "United Russia" and thus signs his appeals. And so the KGB and camp authorities, some ten men all told, in all seriousness tried to persuade him to abandon this anti-Soviet intention of becoming president. The Siberian proved adamant: "I will die as president!" Both men were sent to Vladimir prison as "incorrigible anti-Soviets." Both are regarded as malingerers, although everyone knows that they are mentally ill. A third, Yura Kazinsky, is the "ruler of the world." He thinks he is a shaman. He formulates his anti-Soviet intentions thus: "One must stick feathers in one's hair, put on an old jacket, take off one's trousers, bind one's legs with colored ribbons and perform the dance of the Rattlesnake. Then the prisons, the camps and . . . the collective farms (an interesting classification of things!) will fly across to America." He is in the camp prison for "anti-Sovietism" and will probably also go to Vladimir soon.

This is how the KGB men take the sting out of the numerous dangers that threaten the state. It is a lunatic asylum in which the demarcation between doctors and patients vanished long ago. Not only children, but even some adults should never be allowed to play with matches. But strange as it may seem, they have been given the monopoly to control the spiritual life of society!

No one, however, has yet succeeded in creating everlasting terror or everlasting ice. Every story of a dragon, whether it is the one which ruled the Kievites, or Smok, which lived in the Wawell Hill above Krakow, ends in the same way: along comes a Kyrylo Kozhumyaka, a hero, and makes an end of it. Refrigeration works only while there is something to be frozen. But when people have become Cogs, the mechanism is automatically cut off. The Cog is interested neither in social nor in political questions ("this is not a matter for our minds . . . never get mixed up in politics"); this realm is beyond his interests. But in all other things, in judging football games, for example, the Cog feels completely at ease and makes up his own criteria. So, the next generation of Cogs is freed from a feeling of inferiority; it is the product no longer of terror, but of tradition. And no matter how primitive his world may be, it is nevertheless a world founded on common sense. A score of 4-0 is better than 2-0; there is no room for sophistry here. All the dogmas which are pumped under pressure into the young Cog contradict his primitively obvious world, founded on common sense. It is a very important moment when the heavyweight champion replaces the dictator as god. No one openly opposes dogmas, but they are felt to be something alien. And since the young Cog is no longer familiar with his parents' terror, he begins to view dogmas with silent scepticism and imperceptibly moves on to the road of silent opposition—destructive opposition, because he still has not been programmed for constructive opposition.

But thought does not stand still; first it shyly peers in, and then ventures further into the forbidden area of history, philosophy, literature. It now begins to regard everything it sees from the point of view of common sense. And imperceptibly a miracle takes place—the Cog becomes human!

The dragon suspects nothing as yet, but he has already been morally slain. His rule could be maintained only because he had stolen people's awareness of their own power, because he was able to convince people that they were nothing. But, sooner or later, a Prometheus gets into his kingdom and restores to men the power stolen from them. Everything appears to be the same; those who incur displeasure are put behind bars or fired from their jobs, but the curse no longer holds. Before, they were afraid even to raise their eyes at the dragon, let alone rummage inside him. Now, he is morally dead, and one can start the autopsy without hesitation. It turns out that there is more of the swine in him than of the devil.

A new generation has thus entered Ukrainian life, creating a new problem for the defenders of the Stalinist order. "Order" was maintained on the basis that the people *themselves* had renounced all rights and reconciled themselves to this. As a result, everything could be promised, it being known in advance that nothing need be given. Now, a new generation has arrived and says, "The Constitution mentions freedom of speech, and we want to take advantage of it." This variation had not been foreseen. It has suddenly turned out that the dummy gun made for display can shoot. The gods have always hated Prometheuses, who light up the darkness and show men that nothing is there except what their own fear has created, and that the power of evil comes only from their own weaknesses.

It is very important to gag the first man to cry out: "The king has no clothes!" before others pick up the cry. But the king really is naked. That is the truth. To whose disadvantage is it? To those who will lose their privileges when Stalinist lawlessness has been completely wiped out. First of all, it will be the KGB men. Next, the collective farm chairman who is afraid that if all legal norms are actually complied with he will not even be given the job of a swineherd. The academician who walked to his chair over the bodies of his betrayed comrades in 1937. The chauvinist who will have to give up his Russification program. *These are the powers that defend the past and, with their dead weight, block the path of progress in society. They* are *the only ones* who require men to be Cogs. Yet they claim with all their might to be protectors of society and defenders of "socialist legality." Behind their closed office doors, however, the KGB men express an entirely different view of "socialist legality."

When Levko Lukyanenko asked Captain Denisov, the investigator of the Lviv KGB, "For what purposes does Article

44

17, which gives each republic the right to secede freely from the USSR, exist?" the latter answered, "For foreign use." (!) That's how it is! It appears that the KGB men are perfectly aware that they are not defending "socialist legality," but the right to violate it with impunity. They have no illusions about their organization and see it simply as a place where the pay is highest and there is no queue for housing.

The KGB officer Kazakov brought me a letter from the principal of the Ivano-Frankivsk Pedagogical Institute, where I had worked. I told him, "If anyone wants to write to me, let him send it through the mail." Kazakov answered, *"That would be too great an honor."* So he considers that the KGB can never command even the respect that the Post Office deserves. Why then does the KGB dislike it when people have no respect for it?

Lytvyn, the representative of the Kiev KGB, said to me, "We arrested you because the public demanded it. People would have torn you to bits." Strange! Why, then, are political prisoners tried in camera, and not a word is said about them in the papers? The KGB, well aware of the illegality of its actions, conceals political trials from the people, while trials of German police assassins are widely publicized.

In general, all the means used by the KGB to deal with those who incur its displeasure form a continuous sequence of illegal acts. Immediately after the conviction of Dmytro Ivashchenko in Lutsk, his wife, Vira Ivashchenko, was dismissed from her position as a teacher of Ukrainian literature in School No. 3. On what grounds? She had for many years been considered an exemplary teacher; the journal *Soviet Woman*[51] had written about her achievements, and as a result of her efforts, a Lesya Ukrainka[52] museum was opened in the city. But she refused to sign incriminating testimony against her husband, as demanded by the KGB, and was thrown out

[51]*Radyanska zhinka*, monthly magazine published in Kiev.
[52]Emminent Ukrainian poetess (1871-1913).

of her job on their orders. What law gives the KGB the right to fire people from their jobs?

A student of the Lutsk Pedagogical Institute, Anatoliya Panas, who appeared as a witness at the trial, dared to speak about the chauvinist stranglehold in the Crimea, where she did her practical training as a teacher of Ukrainian literature. They called her a "Bandera-ite" to her face, and her colleagues openly declared: "If Lenin were still alive, he would have gagged this *national riff-raff*," and advised her not to speak Ukrainian "if you want to be on good terms with us." Article 66 UCC states: "Propaganda or agitation for the purpose of arousing hostility or dissension between races or nationalities, or the direct or indirect restriction of rights, or the establishment of direct or indirect privileges for citizens depending on the race or nationality to which they belong" shall be punished by 6 months' to 3 years' imprisonment or 2 to 5 years' exile. No one mentioned any punishment for the chauvinists in the Crimea, but the student who dared to uphold the law and her national dignity was failed in her state examinations.

The KGB men always talk as if they were faced with a "small group of renegades" whom "the people" oppose. But they themselves are well aware that this is a lie. Otherwise, they would not hide political prisoners from the people behind the doors of secret trials, which are a mockery of justice. Nor do the KGB men have the right to include among their supporters those who remain silent. Silence is not always a sign of consent. This was convincingly shown by the Fifth Writers' Congress of Ukraine. Not only the speakers but also the audience of the Congress were carefully screened. There were, so it would seem, no "wrong-minded" people present. Yet the Congress became a platform from which voices for the defense of national culture and against the Russian chauvinist stranglehold rang out. The defenders of Stalinism turned out to be in the minority. At the Byelorussian Writers' Congress, Bykav[53] criticized great-power assimilationists; at the Georgian Congress, Abashidze[54] did so.

The KGB register of "renegades" is increasing catastrophically. To Osadchy's question, "Why didn't you bring Novychenko[55] to Mordovia? For he said things as we did," Marusenko (Lviv KGB) replied, *"Honchar[56] deserves it too."* A revealing admission! This is the kind of society served by the KGB! This society is not beyond putting Honchar behind bars, or the Vice-Chairman of the Soviet of Nationalities Stelmakh,[57] or Malyshko,[58] or many other well-known intellectuals in Ukraine who protested against the arbitrary arrests in 1965 in Ukraine. The KGB is an isolated clique which makes every effort to hang on to society's neck, where it has been since Stalin's days. The ring of isolation around it is irreversibly shrinking as people cast off their shameful, slavish fear. Marusenko himself admitted this. In reply to Osadchy's question, "What is the mood of the Lviv intelligentsia?" he said, "Some have accepted the Writers' Congress line, others vaccilate. They do not want to live in the old way; they dare not live in the new way."

They do not want the old ways; they cannot have the new way. . . . The situation is not new; it has always characterized epochal turning points. The present events in Ukraine

[53]V. Bykav (b. 1924) : notable Byelorussian writer.

[54]I. Abashidze (b. 1909) : Georgian poet; Chairman of the Board of the Writers' Union of Georgia.

[55]Leonid Novychenko (b. 1914) : Ukrainian literary critic and scholar; usually follows the Party line.

[56]Oles Honchar (b. 1918) : prominent Soviet Ukrainian novelist, holder of several state literary prizes; Chairman of the Writers' Union of Ukraine; decorated for war service; CPSU member.

[57]Mykhaylo Stelmakh (b. 1912) : Soviet Ukrainian writer; holder of numerous state prizes in literature; deputy chairman of the Council of the Union.

[58]Andriy Malyshko (1912-1970) : Soviet Ukrainian poet; awarded several state and literary prizes; was Party member.

also mark a turning point: the glacier of terror which for many years has immovably fettered the spiritual life of the nation is breaking up. People are, as before, thrown behind bars and, as before, transported to the East. But this time they have not sunk into the unknown. To the great surprise of the KGB, *public opinion* has risen up for the first time in recent decades. For the first time a protest campaign has emerged; for the first time, the journalist Chornovil[59] has refused to testify at a closed, illegal, trumped-up trial; and for the first time the KGB has felt powerless to suppress all this. With all the more satisfaction, they find their revenge on those who fall into their hands, those who are . . .

In The Reservation

THIS IS the only place where the KGB may dispense completely with all laws and standards. Here, they continue to forge terror. Their effort is directed at destroying the humanity in man; only then does he become putty which can be given any shape. A prisoner may not break the rules of the regime in any way, but as soon as the KGB men feel that he has not submitted, that he has not yet accepted evil and violence as the normal state of affairs and that he has preserved his dignity, they will resort to every pressure. They will not rest until they are convinced that the man has sunk

[59]Vyacheslav Chornovil (b. 1938): Soviet Ukrainian journalist; documented secret trials of Ukrainian intellectuals in mid-1960's. These materials were published in the West (*The Chornovil Papers*, McGraw-Hill, 1968). Arrested, tried and sentenced in 1967 to three years of imprisonment; sentence later commuted under general amnesty to 18 months. Rearrested in January 1972; tried and sentenced in February 1973 to 7 years of severe regime labor camp and 5 years of exile.

48

to the level of a mere consumer of food.

The Ossete Fedor Byazrov was a thief. Then he became a Jehovah's Witness and stopped stealing. One would think that the "re-educators" would be satisfied. Byazrov thought so too. "What do you want from me? I no longer steal and I am doing no wrong. Nobody is forbidden to believe in God." *"It would be better if you stole."* This is no exception. Many political prisoners were shown criminal offenders and told: "They are thieves, but they are *our people*. You are enemies." These are the people whom the KGB protects. They take to morally corrupt individuals, as a fish takes to water. A bandit is a bird of the same feather to them. The KGB knows how to talk to him. He is a willing informer in return for a dose of drugs. He has no dignity, no incomprehensible, powerful force that requires destroying.

Agents are not used only as eavesdroppers. Prisoner Lashchuk was a known KGB agent. Everyone was aware of this. In Tayshet Camp No. 11, in 1958, the prisoners took from him a denunciation he had written. In April 1964 in Mordovian Camp No. 7 he wounded Stepan Virun (one of the jurists' group sentenced in Lviv in 1961) with a knife. After his release from the hospital, Virun spoke to Captain Krut about this; the latter said, without fussing: *"You'll lose your head too if you don't wise up."* (Virun, refusing to acknowledge the legality of his sentence, wrote appeals.)

Art. 22 UCC states: "Punishment does not have the purpose of causing physical suffering or the lowering of human dignity." *Therefore, all the methods which the KGB applies to put pressure on the prisoners are in violation of the law.* But where are those who have been appointed to supervise adherence to the law, *i.e.*, the prosecutors? There is a prosecutor's office in Mordovia. It would be untrue to say that it shuts its eyes to arbitrary action, or washes its hands of it. On the contrary, rolling up their sleeves, the local prosecutors join in and spare no effort to help the KGB men perpetrate their dirty deeds. During a conversation with the deputy

49

prosecutor of the Dubrovlag camp administration, I informed him that people seriously ill with stomach ulcers were kept on a starvation diet, which was contrary to the law. He calmly answered, *"That's precisely what punishment should do—hit the stomach."* What right do these sadists have to call themselves defenders of legality?

Compulsory labor for political prisoners is a violation of the United Nations Convention Concerning the Abolition of Forced Labor. But then the KGB men themselves admit that they regard labor as a means of pressure. They have told many a prisoner: "We don't need your work; we want you to correct yourself." Those prisoners who have to be put in the camp prison ("kartser") are transferred to heavy work. There they are punished for not fulfilling their quota, which is impossible to fulfill. All prisoners' rights are looked upon as privileges that can be withdrawn. For example, Lukyanenko and Mykhaylo Horyn were deprived of a personal visit from their families in 1967, although this is a right (and not a privilege) which cannot be withdrawn by anybody, any more than the right to food. Only one single visit a year from one's family, and even this may be taken away! For comparison it is enough to mention that in England a prisoner has the right to see his family *every week!*

The system of education by hunger is also unprecedented. Political prisoners everywhere have always received food parcels in unlimited quantities, while we have the right to receive two parcels a year after completing half our sentence, "subject to good conduct." Is there any need to comment on this? The essential food minimum specified by the FAO (a UNESCO agency) is 2,700 calories; the famine line is drawn at 2,400. Below this, a man's physical and mental capacities begin to deteriorate. In the camp prison where I am held, the "higher" quota is 2,020 calories. But there is also the lower one, a mere 1,324 calories. *A continuous crime has thus been perpetrated for decades. Nobody should forget that the Nuremberg Trials were not only for murder by steel, but also for murder by hunger. One wonders whether the Ukrainian Red Cross will take at least as much interest in the Mordovian crimes as in those committeed in Africa.* The camp diet has made half the people ill. At this point, a new means of pressure—medicine—takes over. Indeed, it is not necessary to have anything to do with medicine in order to be a doctor or a doctor's assistant in a camp. In Camp No. 7, Malykhin, an ex-policeman in the service of the Germans and the murderer of many people, was the doctor's assistant (he is now in Camp No. 11). He has no medical training, or, indeed, any education whatsoever. Instead, he has been of service to the KGB. True, this is not always so. At present we are looked after by an Estonian, Braun, who once worked as an ambulance driver. Say what you like, one cannot call him a stranger to medicine.

The rules state that prisoners thrown into the camp prison are not to be deprived of medical aid. But what do rules matter when the camp doctors openly say: "We are Chekists first, and doctors only second." Mykhaylo Masyutko is in serious condition, ill with a stomach ulcer. But all attempts to obtain his release, or at least a special diet, have been useless. The KGB men in white coats said, *"Of course we should send you back, but we would pay for it . . ."* "You are not allowed any injections," and some simply say, "You shouldn't have got caught. . . . " This, of course, does not exhaust the tales of camp medicine. Is the high rate of mental illness in camps accidental? *The function of camp medicine awaits its researcher. . . .*

The tentacles of the octopus also hold the prisoner tight after he goes out through the camp gates. Captain Krut told Yarema Tkachuk, sentenced in 1958 in Stanyslaviv: "You won't have any life unless you get wiser. We'll see to it that you have neither family nor a roof over your head." Kazakov promised me that I "would live to regret it."

And this is not simply intimidation. In 1957, Danylo Shumuk (now in Camp No. 11) was arrested in Dnipropetrovsk for "anti-Soviet agitation." Major Sverdlov of the KGB admitted without much ado that the charge was trumped up. Something else was at stake. Shumuk, a man who had recently been released from imprisonment, was given a choice: return behind bars or become an informer; as a man of spotless reputation among ex-prisoners he would not be suspected. Shumuk was illegally detained for two days at the KGB administration office without being shown an order for arrest while they tried to persuade him. Major Sverdlov declared: "If you agree to cooperate with us, I will, here in front of you, tear up this order for arrest and these records of interrogation." Art. 174 UCC states that "The institution of criminal proceedings against a person known to be innocent . . . combined with an accusation of an especially dangerous crime against the state . . . shall be punished by deprivation of freedom for a term not exceeding eight years." Nobody sentenced Sverdlov to either eight years or even eight months; he had the right to violate all laws with impunity. He is not a KGB man for nothing. Shumuk returned to Siberia to do ten more years of penal servitude for remaining an honest man. And now, before his release, the sick man who began his prison career back in the days of the Polish Defenzywa and has spent 27 years behind bars is again summoned by Captain Krut and promised, "You'll have no life." Shumuk has been put in the camp prison for "preparing anti-Soviet manuscripts." This is how the KGB described his experiences: five arrests under Polish rule; a German prisoner-of-war camp; escape from it, crossing the whole Ukraine from the Poltava region to Volyn on foot, avoiding roads and the German police.

When someone has to be put in the camp prison, he will be put there not only for "anti-Soviet remarks," but also for "anti-Soviet silence." The prisoner Vovchansky is in detention because he is "bitter against Soviet rule"—that is how it appears in the order! To end up in a camp, one still has to have at least a "dangerous way of *thinking*." The way from camp to camp prison is much simpler: as we can see, people are put there not merely for their thoughts but even for their *moods*. Masyutko, Lukyanenko, Shumuk and I were put here for appeals which were treated as "anti-Soviet manuscripts." Mykhaylo Horyn did not write any "manuscripts," but he was put here with us all the same. Why? Captain Krut asserts that he found Ivan Dzyuba's memorandum[60] addressed to the CC CPU among Horyn's belongings. Bohdan Horyn, in a conversation with Lytvyn and Marusenko, asked, "Is Dzyuba's memorandum an anti-Soviet document?"—"*No, it is not.*"—"Then why has my brother been jailed?" Marusenko replied, "There has been a misunderstanding." There was no misunderstanding. Horyn, like the others, is kept in the camp prison because they brought the truth about events in Ukraine into the camp and would not keep silent about it.

Certain aspects of the camp regime have been brought down direct from the times of Nicholas Palkin.[61] A portrait of the Latvian poet Knut Skujenieks was taken from the painter Zalyvakha, and the painter himself (!) was forced to cut up his work! Does such a society have the right to criticize the Chinese Red Guards? The uniformed robots destroyed all Zalyvakha's paintings they could find and took away his paints. When the painter demanded to be shown the law which allowed them to do all this, the answer he received was this: "*I am your law!*" The corporal told the truth. He is the embodiment of the law introduced back in the time of Shevchenko, who was also forbidden to write and paint.

Such are the methods of "re-education" used by the KGB. And what is the result? What do the individuals who "have mended their ways" and are held up to us as examples and receive parcels and drugs from the KGB look like? One can

[60]See fn. 6, p. 4.

[61]Nicholas I, Emperor of Russia 1825-55. It was his rider to Shevchenko's sentence that forbade him to write and paint. (See fn. 11 and 41 above.)

see them gathered at celebration concerts before May Day or November 7.[62] On stage—a rare collection of faces ravaged by all possible vices, a bouquet of criminals of all hues who seem to have emerged specially for the occasion from the pages of a criminology textbook. Here are all the war criminals who killed thousands upon thousands of Jewish children, specimens of all sexual perversions, and drug addicts who inject cat's blood into their veins when nothing else is handy. This is the choir. "The Party is Our Helmsman," "Lenin is Ever Alive" ring out solemnly. *If even a single KGB man really believed in the ideals which he claims to defend, would he allow this?* The "re-educated" walk around camp with little diamond-shaped insignia on their sleeves bearing the letters SVP ("Sektsiya Vnutrennego Poryadka"—Section for Internal Order, *i.e.*, auxiliary police). The prisoners interpret these initials as "Soyuz Voyennykh Prestupnikov" (Union of War Criminals).

Can one seriously say after all this that the KGB *defends* the Soviet order? On the contrary: all its activity *undermines* and *compromises* it, and drives people to resistance.

A Finn, Vilho Forsel (now in Vladimir Prison), graduated from Petrozavodsk University with distinction and worked in the Karelian National Economic Council. He accompanied a Canadian communist delegation touring Karelia as an interpreter. After the tour, the KGB demanded that Forsel report the contents of conversations carried on by the Canadians with individuals who had met them. Forsel refused, saying that the law did not give anyone the right to treat him in this way. So he was told, "All right, a time will come when you will be begging to cooperate with us." A few days later Forsel was dismissed from his work and could not get another job. If this is a crime, only the KGB should be tried for it.

Churchill said: "No anti-communist wrought as much

---

[62]Anniversary of the October 1917 Revolution.

damage to communism as Khrushchev." Who, if not the KGB, picked up Khrushchev's shoe, like a baton in a relay-race, and now bang away with it on every rostrum, at the United Nations and elsewhere, degrading the state whose defenders they claim to be? When searching us, they regularly confiscate the UN Declaration of Human Rights. To my demand to have it returned, Krut replied: "The Declaration is not allowed." The assistant prosecutor to whom I spoke admitted that he had not read it. At the "political training" sessions conducted by semi-literate corporals for artists and writers, the prisoners once began a discussion with Senior Lieutenant Lyubayev (Camp No. 11) using the Declaration as an argument. He retorted indulgently: *"Listen, but that is for Negroes."*

Indeed, there is no need to show which particular actions compromise communism. Poltoratsky, who lately has been specializing in the Chinese Red Guards, clearly indicates what should be regarded as "a malicious caricature, an attempt to discredit the just socialist society which has been the dream of centuries." This is, first and foremost. Mao's command "to send actors, poets and scholars . . . to be re-educated in the villages, that is, in the people's communes. It is not hard to imagine what will happen to an aged scholar or writer if he spends several days tilling the soil, harnessed to a wooden plow" (*Literary Ukraine*,[63] Feb. 24, 1967). Indeed it is not hard to imagine. Let Poltoratsky come to Mordovia and see how the painter Zalyvakha, sent here to be re-educated, shovels coal into a furnace. He was given a stoker's job on purpose, so that this work would kill all his desires except one—to sleep.

If Poltoratsky's new "hobby" has not yet dimmed his interest in linguistics, I can inform him that here, just as in China, the word "to plow" is a popular one. We were all

[63]*Literaturna Ukraina*: newspaper published in Kiev; official organ of the Writers' Union of Ukraine.

sent here "to plow" in order to be turned into mindless beasts of burden. But it is not only here that one "plows," and the village is regarded as a place of exile not only in China. Harashchenko, a camp representative of the Ukrainian KGB, when demanding "repentance" from Osadchy, threatened to take away his Lviv apartment and "chase him out into the countryside." Harashchenko may be congratulated. Osadchy is the only one among us whom they managed to "re-educate." On the evening of April 11 he wrote a petition for pardon, and expressed a hope that he might benefit the people (?) by working as a lecturer at the university. (Osadchy did not mention whether he counted on any benefit for himself.) A few hours before this, in the morning of April 11, he wrote, and read to his friends a document in which he denied his guilt, called the 1965 arrests a blood-letting of the Ukrainian intelligentsia, and accused the investigator, Galsky, of rough physical treatment. On the next day, after his comrades had unanimously expressed their contempt for Osadchy, he wrote a new document, *the third in two days,* in which he withdrew his repentance. It is not known how many more repentances and withdrawals Osadchy will write. He can write—after all, he is a journalist. . . . One thing is clear—if Osadchy follows his present road any further, he will not be thrown out of his Lviv flat. And he will be allowed to lecture at the university "for the benefit of the people." Curiously, Galsky did not dare to beat anyone other than Osadchy—this is not 1937. But he did beat Osadchy—his ears and neck—as he himself later related. But then Galsky is an experienced Chekist; he well knew with whom he was dealing.

Forcing dunces caps on people's heads is also a degradation of communism. "The fact that the female workers in the factory wore kerchiefs of various colors or no kerchiefs at all was immediately apparent. Apprentices and women who were not fulfilling their quota wore no kerchiefs. Those who fulfilled their quota wore yellow kerchiefs. And only those who exceeded their quota could put on red kerchiefs."

56

(*Science and Religion*,[64] No. 3, 1967, p. 7.) If this had happened in Tientsin or Wuhan, Poltoratsky would immediately have talked about holding human beings up to ridicule. But I must disillusion you: this routine has been adopted in the sewing factory in Osh in Kirghizia. If so, then it simply cannot be ridicule; it is merely a way of emancipating women in Central Asia.

Poltoratsky derides Chinese poetry, ("The general Party line, like a spring breeze sweeping over the land, gives life to the crops."). Is it really only in Chinese periodicals that such poetry can be found? His eyesight seems to be failing. . . . Here is an article reviewing the illustrations in a periodical: "The saturation of black makes them difficult to understand. The editors *are directed* to note the necessity . . ." etc. Where was this printed? In China? No, this is the paper *Youth of Ukraine*[65] re-educating the periodical *Dnieper*.[66] To attack Mao, whose vision of the China of the future is "a communist barracks with hungry but obedient slave Cogs" (*Literary Ukraine*, Feb. 24, 1967) and at the same time to *direct* an artist what colors he is to use—what an Everest of hypocrisy! Poltoratsky is struck most of all by the "absolute lack of a sense of humor" in China. He quotes these lines as an example:

> If you must sing, sing revolutionary songs,
> If you must read, read books by Chairman Mao . . .
> . . . .
> If you are one of us. But if you are detached
> and love the dreamt-of times,
> *rear your culture in a swamp,*
> *like a stork.* . . . Not for us!
> We need songs—storm, thunder,
> We need—words like bombs! . . .
> We need each one a soldier
> For our everyday and our fronts!

[64]*Nauka i religiya* (Moscow).

[65]*Molod Ukrainy*: newspaper published in Kiev; official organ of the Ukrainian Komsomol youth organization.

[66]*Dnipro*: monthly magazine published in Kiev by Komsomol.

Who would notice that the first part is a poem by Liao Chu-tsan, a Chinese, and the second part a poem by Oleksa Vlyzko,[67] published in 1927 in *Literary Gazette*? Poltoratsky began his career as a critic by publicizing such poems. For some reason he did not mention a sense of humor then. . . . Poets such as Liao Chu-tsan learned from such models. Honestly, it isn't nice to censure one's own children like this. . . .

The newspaper *Izvestia* (No. 78, 1967) wrote that "the Maoists, openly challenging Marxism-Leninism . . . have declared as their goal the assimilation of the non-Han (non-Chinese—V.M.) peoples." If this is a "challenge" to Marxism-Leninism, then one must include among the Maoists such learned men as Agayev and Kravtsev. Their "works" are regularly published in Moscow and Kiev. The former maintains that all the languages of USSR, except for Lithuanian, Latvian, Estonian, Georgian and Armenian, have no future— in other words, they must be Russified. The latter tries to persuade Ukrainians that being "up to date" means substituting Russian for their native tongue.

As we see, Mao is not the only author of "malicious caricatures and attempts to discredit the socialist society which has been the dream of centuries."

When men are sentenced for "a dangerous way of thinking";
When those who think differently are re-educated by means of hunger in camp prisons;
When an artist is ordered what colors to use;
When the UN Declaration of Human Rights is considered to be a seditious document even though it has been ratified by the Government;
When officials in Ukraine call the Ukrainian language the "Bandera-ite tongue" with impunity;

[67]Soviet Ukrainian poet (1908-34). A deaf mute, he was shot, together with several other writers, on faked charges of belonging to a "fascist Ukrainian nationalist organization" and of "organizing sabotage." Now rehabilitated.

58

When men who fight against the Russian chauvinist stranglehold in Ukraine are thrown behind bars while the world passes through an era of the rebirth of nations: *all this degrades the state which allows such phenomena.*

The height of this degradation is the rule of Beria's brood over the spiritual life of society. Wretched is the society in which philosophical problems are solved behind barbed wire by the penal agencies. It is doomed to an everlasting lurching from kok-saghyz[68] to maize[69] to "great leaps forward" and to "cultural revolutions." It will always accept Einstein and cybernetics after a delay of fifty years—so long as the KGB regulates social life. And in that society, men who wish to drag it out of the mire will always sit behind bars. One prisoner began his complaints with the words: "Demented horses . . . into what other jungles of horror, shame and idiocy are they thinking of leading us?"

In 1946 Europe put the last full stop to the verdict of the Nuremberg Trials. The nightmares of Auschwitz had passed into history. The knell of Buchenwald rang out, and petals fluttered over the world from a small flower that had faded in the dawn of life—a young Jewish girl, Anne Frank, who left only a diary. Meanwhile permafrost still held sway in the distant Siberian tundra. There they crushed innocent, worn-out human beings with tanks for demanding humane treatment. One hand was signing the sentence at Nuremberg, the other a sentence of death by starvation for hundreds of thousands of people in Norilsk and Verkhoyansk.

Tomorrow I shall go out to work and meet, as always, the truck with sawdust leaving "for freedom" beyond the camp gates. And, as always, a figure in a great-coat will jump onto the truck and start prodding the sawdust with a long pike,

[68]*Taraxacum kok-saghyz*, a dandelion of the class *Scoriosa*. Its discovery in 1932 as a rubber-bearing plant roused great hopes that it would fill all Soviet needs for rubber. It turned out to be a failure.

[69]Khrushchev's belief that this crop would solve difficulties in agriculture has been abandoned by his successors.

every centimeter of it, quietly and efficiently, lest a prisoner should hide under the sawdust. True, the law allows him to be punished with three years' imprisonment for escaping. Nobody is allowed to kill him. It is a criminal offense. Yet the robot in uniform prods with his pike again and again. Quietly and efficiently. In the hope that he will hit something. . . . That is an advertisement by the KGB: "Look at what all the rights and laws to which you appeal are worth. Our most insignificant wage-slave can spike them through and through with a single movement, and you as well!"

But does anyone really naively imagine that there will be no need to answer for all this? No—on these great plains everything comes about fifty years late. . . . But it inevitably comes about!

> And when they had driven us to the cursed site,
> We saw human leg bones. . . .

This song will someday ring through the world's concert halls along with "The Knell of Buchenwald."

A crime is a crime and it is inevitably followed by retribution. In accordance with the Constitution which, after all, will some day become the law, there will be no evading responsibility for those who were shot and those who were put to death by hunger. Someone will also have to be held responsible for the robot capable of calmly running a man through with a pike—someone who robbed him of his soul and of his humanity.

A lie has short legs—that has long been known. But it is only half the truth. Let no one forget:

TRUTH HAS LONG ARMS!

April 15, 1967

60

DUBROVLAG COMPLEX

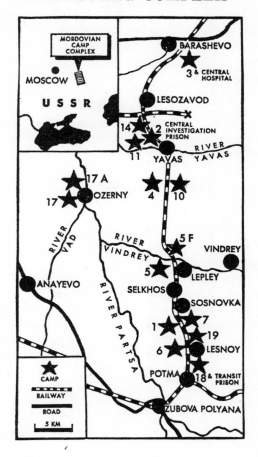

Labor camps in the Dubrovlag Complex in the Mordovian ASSR are marked with a star; special prisons with a circle. (This map was presented by Avraham Shifrin, a Soviet Jew who has emigrated from the USSR, during testimony before the Subcommittee to Investigate the Administration of the Internal Security Act and Other Internal Security Laws of the Committee on the Judiciary, United States Senate, on February 1, 1973.)

AMID THE SNOWS

MARCH 1953. Moscow.

Crowds of sobbing people, pressing on to get to the bier of the dead Leader. Scores suffocate, trampled underfoot. . . .

Many a foreigner, casual witness of this "national mourning," must have thought: Surely, it will take a hundred years for this fanaticism to dissipate. But one did not have to wait so long. Three years later, the Leader (dead!) was put in the pillory and proclaimed a criminal. And . . . not a word in his defense. Of course, some indignation was expressed, but privately. . . . No one immolated himself; no one cut off even his little finger. What happened to all those fanatics who surged toward the sacred bier not too long before? There were none, apparently. There were only sleepy jades that did not even notice being turned around and driven in a different direction. Nowadays, it is easy to distinguish between genuine and artificial diamonds; with emotions, however, it is more difficult. By tickling one can provoke artificial laughter; much in the same way one can elicit artificial emotions of tragedy and fanaticism. The greatest secret of the Stalinist period was that, despite the "tremendous pledges" of "loyalty," "faithfulness" and "readiness," this was the period of the nihilist, the man who does not believe in anything. The jades truly thought they were "loyal," "faithful," "ready." They had convinced themselves of it (it is easiest to convince *oneself*). But all these feelings were elicited artificially.

One cannot endlessly issue banknotes, for they will become valueless. One cannot endlessly stuff the human brain with words for the same reason. Devaluation of the word is the underlying moral problem left over from the Stalinist period. Epithets of the comparative and superlative degrees, exclamation points, appeals and expletives—all criteria was lost through their oversaturation. Inflated to its limit, a huge hot-air balloon, bearing boisterous slogans, rose from the ground and drifted away. And the leader himself no longer had control over where he would land and which winds would carry him.

No one believed in the existence of reality, nor in the obligations accepted by the collective farm manager, nor in the critic's review of a new poem. Two worlds evolved, one diametrically opposed to the other. One world was mundane, lacking not only in heroism but even in basic decency. The other world existed in cinema and books, where Young Guardists[1] sang arias before the mine shaft into which they would be thrown five minutes later. The Young Guardists— as everything else in this exaggerated world—were also bound to become unreal.

No one dared say it out loud, but the doubts kept surfacing: Did the Young Guardists really exist, and is it true about all their achievements? Or is it all the same "eyewash" like the collective farm yield figures, percentages of passing grades in school and the number of lectures in the "Knowledge" society? "Sharks do not exist"—this logic of an excessively sober youth in Chukovsky's book became a tacit creed. The narrow-minded love of the sensational, like (did you hear that?) Oleh Koshovy[2] was not killed after all, but lives in West Germany, and that everything about him is a pack of lies.

[1]*Moloda hvardiya* (Young Guard), an underground Komsomol organization that existed during the German occupation in the Krasnodon area of Donbas.

[2]Young Guard member executed by the Germans.

Devaluation of the word brought with it the devaluation of all concepts. Aim, ideal, heroism, achievement—all fell victim. Cut off from anything spiritual by his nihilism, the "working man" threw everything overboard. He knew of Tychyna[3] as a poet who "writes in verse, each time worse." But what could he say about Tychyna's genius when no one accepted this concept seriously, when the mark of genius was associated with Demyan Byedny,[4] when it was pinned on the trousers of every commissar?

This was especially tragic for Ukraine, as it was for all the "nationalities" of the Soviet Union, for such concepts as nation, patriotism, native language, Fatherland, also found themselves on the list of "fictitious," "bookish" notions. A person who did not believe in anything was bound to become indifferent also to Ukraine.

Into these cold ruins, wind-swept of ashes long ago, came the poets of the sixties—"Symonenko's[5] generation." Not all of their first works were invaluable and profound; yet, their arrival was an *epoch*. They restored *meaning* to words and concepts, and they renewed the faith of the people in the *reality* of the spiritual world. Theirs was a genuine feat: to have faith in an atmosphere of complete nihilism, and rekindle that faith in others.

"The people await nothing so earnestly as a living example of heroic civic action. They need this example not because they cannot envision true civic action, but because they need proof that it is possible and fruitful even today."

Characterizing the significance of Symonenko, Dzyuba[6] was, in fact, evaluating the role of the "poets of the sixties" as a whole. Every epoch has its sages who revive devalued words and concepts and give them living meaning. Moral

[3]Pavlo Tychyna (1891-1969): emminent Ukrainian poet whose earlier lyricism turned "proletarian" in the 1930's.
[4]Russian "proletarian" poet (1883-1945).
[5]Vasyl Symonenko (1935-63): leading Ukrainian "poet of the sixties."
[6]See fn. 6, p. 4.

decay is caused not only by "cults"—as that of Stalin, for example. It often comes when spirituality grows old, exhausts itself, and retreats into its shell. So it was with late Rome, when all its traditional moral precepts based on the worship of Venus and Jupiter ceased to be obligatory and became formal; there was no longer a Marcus Scevola to calmly put his hand into the fire.

Rome was renewed by the Christians. But what was it that gave strength to the illiterate Christian with his naive preachings of overcoming the Roman philosopher, the bearer of all Greek and pre-Greek wisdom? Could it be that the Christian preacher knew something the Roman philosopher did not know? No, but that is beside the point. The Roman philosopher knew more. The basic difference, however, lies not in the degree of knowledge nor lack thereof, but in the degree of *emotionality* with which a person accepts this or that truth. One man simply knows the truth; another lives by it. For one man, truth is merely information, knowledge; for another, it is *revelation*, without which life has no meaning. A truth, warmed in the soul to a certain "degree," attains *value*. Knowledge becomes faith. And only then does a man begin to live. Lesya Ukrainka[7] called this state *obsession*.

Obsession is neither a fine art, a science, nor a journalistic trait. Obsession is a singular characteristic, one of the necessary components of a truly meaningful spiritual life. One can have the best ore, but it will never become an alloy without being heated in the oven. One can have the greatest spiritual values, and they will remain unnoticed until an *obsessed* person melts them in the hearth of his obsession. Until Lonnrott compiled the epic *Kalevala,* the Finns were unaware of the power it possessed. We had Tychyna and his brilliant poems; but even with this treasure in his hands he could not make Ukrainians of those nearest to him, he could

[7]See fn. 52, p. 45.

not raise them so they would speak Ukrainian. What was lacking? He had not a spark of obsession left in his cold freedom; the sparks were extinguished by Siberian snows— those sparks that once flew as if from golden waterfalls, and set aflame the Ukrainian renaissance of the 1920's. But Symonenko and Vinhranovsky[8] awakened with one touch the slumbering Ukrainian soul and gave it life.

And that was the mission of the "poets of the sixties"— to bring the spark of obsession into the frozen reality of Ukraine. Without it even Shevchenko[9] was powerless. His works were read, but unnoticed . . .

A tiny group of people in Kiev scattered sparks all over Ukraine, and wherever they fell, the permafrost of indifference and nihilism melted away. Their every word burned with obsession, with a fanatical hatred of the cold and *slimy*, and with a fanatical desire to accelerate the end of the *ice age* in Ukraine.

> You—loudmouths, haughty and rotund,
> Bribe-takers, stuffed with tallow,
> Who bow before a lowly crayfish,
> And march to meetings in formation.
>
> Potbellied monks without the faith,
> And slimy-tailed speculators,
> You—thick-skinned kettle drums,
> Stretched out on ideological bones.

Most importantly, their avalanche could not be stopped. Everything placed in their path was made of ice, which melted from their sparks. The greatest surprise of the past decade was that the arrests of 1965 did not slow down, but accelerated the current Ukrainian renaissance. The era of the *Great Terror* had passed. Arrests did not frighten, but

[8]Mykola Vinhranovsky (b. 1936): film actor, producer and "poet of the sixties."
[9]See fn. 11, p. 13.

aroused intense interest—not only in Ukraine, but in the whole world. To persecute someone today is to place a halo on his head, to make a martyr of him, regardless of whether he actually suffers or not.

This was a miscalculation, and they immediately began to correct their mistake. They freed Ivan Svitlychny[10] from prison, although he was regarded as one of the "principals." Their tactics responded to the daily change of events. Since intimidation did not work, it was necessary to *discredit* and *disillusion*. The first achievement in this direction was Ivan Drach's article in *Literary Ukraine*.[11] It was necessary that Drach publicly shine Poltoratsky's[12] boots. Though there were enough candidates for this, just anyone would not do; it had to be Drach or at least someone from his circle. *It was necessary to kill the legend about the poets of the sixties* —a new breed of man—to show that there was nothing new about them, to show that Drach could write the same diatribes about "nationalists" as could Taras Myhal.[13] It was necessary to kill the faith, the fervor, to extinguish the spark of obsession and turn the people back into a state of jaundiced nihilism. It was necessary to remove from the people the example of courage, to convince them that their god was no god at all but a stage prop. Ivan Dzyuba announced a boycott of Drach after this article. The *one obsessed* could not do otherwise.

I recall this now, reading Dzyuba's statement in the same *Literary Ukraine*, which in many ways resembles that of Drach: the same abusive language from the Poltoratsky

[10]Ivan Svitlychny (b. 1929): literary critic; arrested in January 1972; sentenced in March 1973 to 7 years severe regime labor camp and 5 years exile.

[11]See fn. 43, p. 27.

[12]Oleksiy Poltoratsky (b. 1905): Ukrainian writer and critic noted for attacks against "bourgeois nationalism."

[13]Taras Myhal (b. 1920): journalist and writer of short stories; noted for his pamphlets and lampoons on "Ukrainian bourgeois nationalism."

vocabulary ("provocative hallucinations," "political double talk"), the same anathema on "nationalists." . . . Without a doubt, the slimy-tailed can congratulate themselves on this new success.

I read Dzyuba's arguments and listened to his defenders. I listened and wondered: How petty and immaterial. . . . Those who defend Dzyuba's statement give, among others, this excuse: Had Dzyuba not written the statement, a translation he had ready for printing would not have been published. His expulsion from the Writers' Union would have automatically cost him his job. Well, if these are serious reasons, then we must forego all plans. Each step, each new work that deviates in any way from the canons of poor Demyan automatically results in a certain degree of unpleasantness. And whoever wants to avoid it, should then fold his hands and do absolutely nothing.

The defenders of Dzyuba's statement accuse us, its opponents, of the grave sin of Don Quixote—lack of realism. We need not even formulate our own arguments in our defense; we can take them from a speech that Dzyuba made in 1965, when he viewed "Don Quixotes" and "realists" in a different light:

"At that time, when they were big-hearted realists, they knew well what was permitted and what was not, which undertaking was a winner and which a loser, at that time, Vasyl Symonenko seemed to their commercial sobriety a hopeless Don Quixote, who—as Lesya Ukrainka put it—refused to recognize the so-called 'historical gap" as a real gap, and demanded the impossible: 'Let the Americas and Russias keep silent when I talk with you'—and with whom he was talking was well-known [Ukraine—Ed.]. And that was that; but, oh, how impossible and hopeless this was from the point of view of the learned and all-knowing piglet."

"From the point of view of the learned and all-knowing piglet," the speech by Dzyuba at the cinema on September 4,

1965, was stark madness.[14] This was the height of "Don-Quixotism"—coming out with protests in the midst of a wave of arrests. "Commercial sobriety" dictated otherwise: sit still, keep silent and be happy that not everyone was apprehended. But "hopeless Don Quixote" Dzyuba still was not satisfied; he chose this time to give the world his book. And, as it happened, this "Don-Quixotism" produced greater results than the "realism" of all the all-wise piglets. For some reason, flowers grow best when sown in the frost. Whoever disregards the weather creates his own weather, and catches colds infrequently. The paradox here is strictly external. The "realist" and the one obsessed by themselves represent neither the logical nor the illogical; they represent two forms of logic. The "realist" follows the shallow, mundane logic of *today;* but the future is built on a different logic—the logic of *tomorrow*—which only the obsessed can discover. Every discovery, every invention, everything new—has been the work of a Don Quixote. The obsessed do not always find the road to the future; they often stray from the path. But with the caution of the all-knowing piglet it is impossible even to budge. Sown in the frost, not every flower grows. Most of them die, but there is no other way. A nation that has spent centuries in the *ice age,* in conditions of the *endless winter,* has no other recourse: "I shall sow the flowers in the frost." Ukraine is a flower that grew amid the snows. And Ukraine is a flower, a breakstone. Ukrainian life is illogical, irrational, paradoxical, if perceived through the logic of the "realists"—as is the blooming *edelweiss* atop the icy peaks. Ukraine lives in the framework of a different logic—the *logic of obsession.* Only the obsessed could consider himself Ukrainian in Kiev and Kharkiv in the 19th century, when Ukraine was considered nonexistent, buried. Only the obsessed can be a Ukrainian in that same Kharkiv today, when the "all-wise piglets" are convinced that all nations will soon

[14]Made in the "Ukraina" theater in Kiev.

merge into one, and that Ukraine will not exist in the next Seven-Year Plan. The "realists" in Ukraine were never Ukrainians; they always became Little Russians. Fear the "realist," as you fear fire, if you want to remain Ukrainians! From the "realists' " point of view, the Ukrainian cause has always been hopeless. Consequently, it was always espoused by those who "hoped without hope," by those who were not frightened by "hopeless" reality and stubbornly followed their dream "as Israel followed the pillar of fire."

It has become a tradition for us to complain about our weakness. But, really, Ukraine has been a unique example of strength. Other nations in our circumstances have long ceased to exist and became a Provence.[15] And we have survived! What other forbidden language has such a rich literature? The strength of the Ukrainian character must truly be considerable if both the Russians and the Poles came up with the same: *Upryam kak khakhol* and *Uparty jak rusin*.[16] This is the basis of a strange Ukrainian firmness—to find strength and hope within *oneself*, to be independent of outside sources of strength and hope. Hryhoriy Skovoroda's[17] commandment "search for everything within yourself" repeatedly comes alive in a Ukrainian. A Jehovah's Witness once asked Levko Lukyanenko[18] in a Mordovian camp: "Are you sure that your Ukraine is everlasting?" He answered: "No, I am not sure, for no one can be certain of that." The other laughed and

[15]It is interesting that Lunacharsky [see fn. 27 below] called Provence "French Ukraine," wishing to stress the similarity of conditions that decided the destinies of the two people. Ukraine survived these conditions; Provence did not, and fell to the level of a French province. [This is an original note by Moroz.]

[16]Both derogatory, meaning "stubborn like a Ukrainian."

[17]See fn. 40, p. 25.

[18]Ukrainian lawyer (b. 1927), founder of Ukrainian Workers' and Peasants' Union, an underground organization formed in 1960; sentenced in May 1961 to death—later commuted to 15 years of imprisonment at hard labor—for propagating the separation of Ukraine from the USSR.

said, "So, you do not even know what you are fighting for. And I know that we, Jehovah's Witnesses, will gain eternal life. And what do you know?" Then Lukyanenko answered, *"If I were the last Ukrainian on earth, I would still continue to fight for Ukraine."* On this logic Ukrainian life has lasted for several centuries. Few Ukrainians do not love Ukraine, and even fewer would like to see her disappear from the face of the earth. People become Russified not because they do not love or want Ukraine; they become Russified because they lack the strength to believe in Ukraine, to keep the faith in the filthy atmosphere of Kharkiv and Odessa, where the selection of a language—as one would a suit—is considered neither shameful nor horrible, but normal. They need an *example.* "The people are waiting for nothing so much as a living example."

Not everyone found something new in Dzyuba's *Internationalism or Russification?* And yet the book opened everyone's eyes. Everyone knew the necessity of fighting Russification. But this was not enough; they had to see a real person who really fought against this process. A spark was needed to ignite the long-awaiting bonfire. Therein lies the meaning of Dzyuba and the other poets of the sixties—in that spark of obsession which they introduced into the frozen Ukrainian reality. It is here that one should search for answers to the question: Why seemingly insignificant facts and events of the 1960's evoked great interest and loud reaction. People did not search for arguments in Dzyuba's book; they searched for *faith—the explosive charge of obsession.* Externally it appears that a person is first persuaded, and then he begins to believe. In fact, the opposite is true; the person is first *inflamed* by faith, and only then seeks arguments for his *already formed* conviction. If one believes, he will find arguments. They will often be naive, but that is of no consequence.

Look about, are there many conscious Ukrainians left in our bankrupt, Russified Kiev? To increase their number is to fight Russification. Without this, our work is meaningless. We see a ruined, Russified Ukrainian, a person without his "I." What will awaken his sleeping Ukrainian soul? Arguments? An apostle never converted anyone to his faith by using arguments. Rhetoric and eloquence are powerless; Christian apostles had neither.

"Limited, narrow-minded, uneducated and without any experience in propaganda, the disciples of Jesus were, in the full sense of the word, small men." "The language of the authors of the New Testament was limited by their minuscule vocabulary," writes Renan (E. Renan, *The Apostles*).

And yet these uneducated, inexperienced people within a short period of time made the Roman Empire Christian. Apostles! That is what Ukraine needs today, and not the contented timeserving "realists" with their arguments. There has yet to be a spiritual revolution without apostles, and without them the rebirth of Ukraine is impossible.

The importance of Dzyuba and his kind lies in their burning apostolic zeal. Without it they fade, become nothing. For them to languish is to die. Let us not lose the sacred flame of obsession! For then we will be left with arguments; thick monographs will multiply, but they will awaken no one. A cold sceptic and his rhetoric never inflamed and never will inflame. Dzyuba himself characterized it best in 1965: "There are epochs when decisive battles are fought on the field of social morality and civic conduct, when even basic human dignity, resisting brutal pressure, can become an important, rebellious, revolutionary force. Ours, I think, is one of those epochs. ... And that is why nothing is more important today than maintaining a high standard of civic conduct."

A person's moral stand today is more important than his word. Words are no longer believed, they have been terribly devalued. One's word must be backed by one's position. We live at a time when both Sverstyuk[19] and Shamota[20] speak the same words about Shevchenko: both call him a genuis. They differ not in word but in position.

A lecturer once attended a conference addressed by Dzyuba. "Well, how was it," they asked him. "Well . . . the man wanted to show off," the lecturer replied. This small realist will never understand the meaning of position. He will sincerely think of it as a theatrical pose or, at best, as naivete. And now the defenders of Dzyuba's statement tell us, "We have had enough theatrical poses. It's time to work." And they argue how important it is for Dzyuba to remain in the Writers' Union, and that there should be more like him in the Union, and that people should strive to attain higher "positions." They waste their words. No one is planning to refute their arguments. Of course, we should very much like to see such people as Dzyuba take control, and not only of the Writers' Union. It would also be ridiculous to deny the need of methodical, daily work. It is true that obsession will never replace talent and industriousness, but no one is maintaining this. Obsession and daily work are not mutually exclusive. But without obsession talent and industriousness remain a dead slab. Talents have existed always and everywhere— why then are there epochs of flourishing and periods of grayness? Obsession is neither extreme nor explosive. False emotions are more often explosive. The flame of obsession burns evenly and calmly. Self-immolation is not necessary. I, personally, am more inclined to accept the philosophy of

[19]Yevhen Sverstyuk (b. 1928): senior scientific worker at the Institute of Psychological Research in Kiev, member of USSR Psychological Association, writer, researcher, teacher; during the 1965 wave of arrests in Ukraine he was detained for a few months and released; wrote lengthy essay *Cathedral in Scaffolding* in 1968, which was circulated in manuscript form in Ukraine and then published in the West. Arrested in January 1972; tried in March 1973; sentenced to 7 years of severe regime labor camp and 5 years of exile.

[20]Mykola Shamota (b. 1916): literary critic noted for pro-Moscow stand.

Shveyk, who said: "A good soldier is not one who dies for the Fatherland, but one who compels his enemy to die for his Fatherland." Therefore, accusations of "Don-Quixotism" and lack of common sense are not addressed correctly. We are not against work, be it the dirtiest. Someone must make idiotic official speeches so that he may, in turn, use his official position to help a good cause; for the same reason, someone must write worthless jubilee poems to retain his post. But must it be Dzyuba? Not only must he not be that person, he has no right to be. For this, there are at least three reasons.

First, there has never been a shortage of people who wanted to love Ukraine a little and still retain a little comfort. There has never been a need to specially cultivate a Pavlychko[21]—he always grows by himself. No one claims that Pavlychko does not love Ukraine. Pavlychko sincerely loves Ukraine and wishes to do as much as possible for her—on condition that comfort is not sacrificed. He knows that this is a weak position and his conscience bothers him, but he knows well how to deal with it. Pavlychko has convinced himself that he is also a martyr, that he is persecuted, that he is looked upon with suspicion. In general, the more a person is afraid, the more he tends to see himself as a great martyr. And it is true that he who fears most suffers most. Pavlychko, of course, will never admit even to himself that the reason for his behavior is common, ordinary fear. No, he will rationalize. He consciously takes upon himself this ungrateful, unheroic role in order to serve the cause, you see. And so it has always been: the pettier a man's motives for action, the more grandiose and romantic he imagines them to be.

We know that Pavlychko will answer with a sceptical smile. But we also know that at the source of this scepticism are fear and fatigue. Dzyuba once well described these people who hide behind "melodramatic scepticism into which they

[21]Dmytro Pavlychko (b. 1929): Ukrainian poet, translator and critic.

eagerly and 'elaborately' escape from civic responsibility; they escape out of idleness, fear and blindness; behind this miserable scepticism is a sophomoric slave who, wanting to deceive himself and pretend that he is fascinated by the play in paradoxes, fails to notice the yoke on his neck." It always happens this way—a man first grows tired of adhering to a position and then begins to rationalize: "What is it all for; after all, this is not a position, but a theatrical pose; anyway, the time has come to end this 'Don-Quixotism'."

The obsessed and the sceptical are eternal antipodes. The exhausted, emaciated sceptic always looks upon the vigorous man as impractical, a Don Quixote. Tired by the burden of his erudition, the Roman philosopher could produce any number of "irrefutable" arguments against the Christian neophyte, and, in the shallow practical sense, he was right. The Christians did not completely change the world and did not build on earth the Kingdom of God. But, in trying to build it, they resurrected the moribund spirituality. And his opponent, the sceptic, has remained dead to this day.

Admittedly, there have been epochs when scepticism was most valued. But these were periods of mass psychosis, periods of artificially elicited fanaticism.

We live in different times, however. Today, the sceptic should be feared most in Ukraine. There is nothing in Ukraine that needs extinguishing, it is still necessary to kindle. Therefore, Dzyuba "regained his senses" and said farewell to Don Quixote somewhat prematurely.

No, special greenhouses are not needed to cultivate Pavlychko. Do not worry, HE will do it on his own and, at the same time, he will convince himself and his friends that he too, is a martyr, that he too, is a victim. We do not propose to proclaim Pavlychko an absolutely negative figure. *Pavlychkoism* is a complicated and contradictory phenomenon, encompassing both negative and positive aspects. Pavlychko, we admit, will do much for Ukraine. But this is beside the point. What matters is that there are always a hundred

Pavlychkos for one Dzyuba. It is, therefore, simply unreasonable to change Dzyuba into a Pavlychko—both from the point of view of the Don Quixotes as well as the point of view of the all-knowing piglets. Few people in Ukraine possess the spark of obsession that can ignite others. As another point, Pavlychkoism is an aggressive phenomenon. Psychologists know it well: he who finds himself in a quagmire wants (for the most part, subconsciously) to also drag in the one who stands on dry land. This desire makes Pavlychkos dangerous. It was on their whispered counsel that Drach wrote his article, and now Dzyuba his statement. Dzyuba acquiesced to the *Pavlychkos,* not the *Kozachenkos.*[22] It is easier to resist external pressure than corruption from within. And Dzyuba was found lacking.

As we can see, arguments taken from Dzyuba's own speech are sufficient for the first reason. They are also sufficient for the second reason. A few more selections from his speech in 1965:

"After all, most of the young poets and writers began and are beginning more or less on the same level as did Vasyl Symonenko, and they certainly have no less 'spontaneous talent'. Therefore, many of them could have reached his ultimate level, but only a handful did; the rest remained unchanged. Many a talent turned petty, banal, and declined before our very eyes! Why? When a person speaks loudly— his voice grows stronger. But when he trains himself to speak in a half-whisper—this half-whisper becomes his normal voice. Vasyl Symonenko spoke the truth as a man, and the truth made him ever greater and greater. In order to expand his talent a poet cannot limit himself. If he does limit his talent and does not constantly strain its limit, his talent, like the muscles, will grow weaker, his strength will decline, he will become feeble. There is a medical term 'idle heart'."

[22]Vasyl Kozachenko (b. 1913): Ukrainian writer, considered a staunch supporter of the Party line.

How dangerous it is to regulate one's voice so as not to be expelled from the Writers' Union.

How many talents became "petty, banal, and declined" because of this logic: Now I am writing for publication; the truth will come later. Life passed him by, however, and the truth was never heard.

No, we do not call to recklessness. It is not necessary to found "The Secret Union of the Sword and Eagle." Someone has to tailor his voice to the Writers' Union and the journal *Notebook of the Agitator*. Someone, yes—but not Dzyuba. There are too few like him in Ukraine. Endless hard times in Ukraine have given birth to a shallow, *one-dimensional* person. Obsession—that must be underground, anarchic. Practicality, on the other hand, must be without principles, slavish. Let us, at last, stop being so narrow-minded. The time has come for us to learn to live our prosaic, everyday lives *without losing the pure flame of obsession.*

And now, the third reason. It so happened that Dzyuba's book became the most important document of the present Ukrainian renaissance, its condensed representation. The world is learning about Ukraine "through Dzyuba." He became a symbol. He became an example—and he himself spoke to us about the importance of an example. An ideal is not enough; alone, it is bare and dry; what is needed is its living embodiment. The truth is known; what is lacking is *faith*. The poor Ukrainian fate has chosen Ivan Dzyuba; it has placed upon his shoulders the *burden of being the symbol*. To throw it underfoot, would not be honorable. Dzyuba has written and said too much to be handing now to Kozachenko written excuses.

Dzyuba has forgotten about the thousands upon thousands of people throughout Ukraine for whom he had become a god. Oh, I understand, I understand how ridiculous this sounds to some people: "god," "symbol." For him who "elaborately escapes into scepticism," all this is "primitive." But let us remember: these "primitives" number forty million! They form the Ukrainian nation. And as long as they remain asleep and frozen—there will be generals *without an army*. Who knows, maybe they are "primitive." But I do know this: *those who have a god* are happy! *"No God—no people."* I first heard this from a woman in Polisya; later I read the same in a work by a European philosopher. Dzyuba became a god for the people, and they believed in him. His statement was a chilling gust of nihilism on budding faith. Now we hear: "There was one man of principle in Ukraine, and even he has written a statement." This was precisely what they wanted: that Dzyuba poison the awakened faith and turn the people back into a state of dead nihilism. That is why they immediately published his statement and gave it wide circulation. Would it have seen the light of day if it had been in our favor, if it did not compromise us? Would Kozachenko and Korniychuk[23] have voted against his expulsion if he had not admitted to a mistake? Let us not be naive. . . .

Well then, let us suppose for a minute that the destiny of mankind depends on Dzyuba's staying in the Writers' Union, and that for its sake one can sacrifice principles. It appears, however, that he achieved nothing by having written his statement. His statement is being considered "merely as a first step," and his continued membership in the Union will depend on a second, third, fourth. . . . Is it possible that Dzyuba has yet to recognize this police tactic: he who has admitted to "A" is put under threefold pressure to admit to "B." Many a man has admitted "B" in these circumstances.

Ukraine expects more books from Dzyuba. But the first page written out of Demyan Byedny's key will again place on the agenda the question of his expulsion from the Writers' Union. In fact, it is already on the agenda. An "anti-Dzyu-

[23]Oleksander Korniychuk (1905-1973): Ukrainian playwright; held high positions in Party and Government.

bist" sequel by I. Bass in the latest issue of *Soviet Literature*[24] finds the *post-statement* Dzyuba the same "nationalist" as the pre-statement Dzyuba and impudently demands that he prove his innocence by more than mere "declarative statements" (p. 70). The ink has yet to dry on the spot where Dzyuba wrote "A," and they are already pressuring him to write "B." What, then, has his statement achieved? As we can see, the logic of the "obsessed" is more *realistic* than the logic of the "realists." He who reproached others for their "Don-Quixotism" has shown himself to be naive and impractical.

Ukraine has seen many who spoke and then retracted, spoke again and again retracted their own words. Maybe this explains the mass loss of faith; the people have seen the highest fall before their eyes. Pygmies have always licked the corporals' heels. But the world probably has never before seen a giant like Tychyna bowed to "sergeants with usurped generals' insignia." And—who knows—this may have inflicted the deepest wound on the people. What and in whom is one to believe when *everyone* renounces, when gods become footmen?

Ukraine has already seen Ostap Vyshnya,[25] who came out of prison and immediately announced that he had never been there and that "nationalists are lying." Ukraine has already had its Epik, who wrote in 1935:

"In preparing terrorist activities we, feigning innocence, assured the Party of our loyalty and honesty, and in the course of many years we played such roles which make highway robbery seem like an example of honesty and humaneness by comparison. I have come to understand that the most merciful verdict of the proletarian court would be to deal with me as people deal with a rabid dog, to destroy me as a

[24]*Radyanske literaturoznavstvo*, No. 1, Jan. 1970, pp. 61-70, "In a campaign against Truth." Monthly journal published in Kiev by the Ukrainian Academy of Sciences and Writers' Union.

[25]See fn. 45, p. 32.

horse sick with foot and mouth disease, to take me out of the body of society. The Communist Party has magnanimously believed in my repentance. In granting me my life, the Party has given me the greatest of all the possible earthly prizes— the right to life, to experience the joy of work."

Enough of this. Ukraine hungers for those who renounce nothing and make excuses before no one. We have a great number of people who, having said a good word about Ukraine, immediately make three curtsies toward Russia. They will never write "Shevchenko and Pushkin." For them it always come out "Pushkin and Shevchenko." It does not happen intentionally; it happens mechanically. The serf's feeling of being *second-rate* is already in their blood. They put an "and" before anything Ukrainian: Pushkin and Shevchenko and Franko, Nekrasov and Lesya Ukrainka. They could never get rid of their subconscious feeling that Ukraine is an *addendum* which must be preceded by something important and separated by the word "and." Some of them voted against the expulsion of Dzyuba from the Writers' Union. Many thanks for that. Perhaps, for the first time in many years, having mustered enough courage to defend Dzyuba, they felt like men. They may have talent and do a lot for Ukraine, but they will not thaw the Ukrainian winter. They have been vaccinated against the possibility of being infected by the spark of obsession.

The Ukrainian rebirth needs *people of a different quality— aristocrats of spirit*. We laugh at the word "nobility," having forgotten that "noble" comes from the same root. It is the greatest tragedy for Ukraine that endless bad times have made us a *nation of plebeians*. But the *constructive,* selective qualities are found only in the aristocrat. This was well known . . . Stalin assured us that the motive force of history was the "proletariat," but, for some reason, he destroyed our intelligentsia, our elite. When religion reigned and socialism was repressed, a decent person would not say a word against socialism even if he considered it unworthy of attention. He was an aristocrat. Now, when socialism reigns and religion is repressed, a decent person will not say a word against religion. He is an aristocrat of our time. Dzyuba has the right to view "nationalism" in any way he wishes. But to speak out against it when every decent person is called a nationalist (including Dzyuba)—that Dzyuba has never done before.

There were Jehovah's Witnesses in the Mordovian camps. Having observed them closely, we found them to be our worst potential enemies, the most susceptible agents of Russification, because in becoming a Jehovah's Witness a Ukrainian becomes hopelessly deaf to the national problem. Yes, we found them to be extremely unsympathetic. Yet, it would have been shameful to write against them on the camp wall newspaper whose exclusive contributors were informers. Dzyuba may evaluate the Ukrainian emigration in any way he likes—that is his own affair—but to write against it in the sergeant-major's newspaper with which Kozachenko cleans his boots, in the *Literary Ukraine*, which is edited like the wall newspaper of the district militia"[26]—this was not expected from Dzyuba.

"I do not accept the name 'nationalist' regardless of the meaning one may give it," writes Dzyuba and hastens to explain that in the nationality question he adheres to the "principles of scientific communism, as taught by Marx, Engels and Lenin." But it is difficult to believe. Absolute rejection of nationalism "regardless of the meaning one may give it" is a *Stalinist* and not a Leninist thesis. Lenin would not accept this. Lenin, as is known, viewed nationalism of an oppressed nation as something positive. Dzyuba differs here not only from Lenin, but . . . from himself. Five years ago, in his book *Internationalism or Russification?* he wrote:

"One has to know and respect Lenin a little, to know his direct instruction on the inadmissibility of a formal approach

[26]Dzyuba's own words.

to the question of nationalism 'in general,' his instruction on the two types of nationalism, on the fact that at the source of local nationalism is Russian chauvinism."

Five years ago Dzyuba opposed his present position—that is, he was against the rejection of nationalism "in general," "regardless of the meaning one may give it," and he strengthened his arguments by quoting from the 12th Congress of the Russian Communist Party: "Remnants of nationalism are a peculiar form of defense against great-power chauvinism" (stenographic report from the 12th Congress, p. 38).

Those who claim that Dzyuba rejected neither his book nor his positions are, apparently, mistaken. Perhaps they did not read his book very carefully.

Having rejected "nationalism," regardless of the meaning one may give it, a person can find himself in a position that is awkward as well as embarrassing. For then we have to reject Shevchenko, about whom Lunacharsky[27] wrote:

"Certainly, there is enmity in Shevchenko's nationalism, but only towards the oppressors. His nationalism, like his tender soul, is primarily filled with love. One cannot deny, however, that Shevchenko is both a national poet and a poet-nationalist. The question of the destiny of the Ukrainian nationality is foremost in his poetry. This is understandable from the political reasons that made Shevchenko's nationalism kindred with the nationalism of Mickiewicz, Foscolo, some Irishmen, as well as with the nationalism of the great folk poetry of the Serbs." (p. 19)

"I used to place Shevchenko alongside other poet-nationalists, but none of them, not even the greatest of the great —Mickiewicz—expressed his love of country with such emotion, with such unbridled force!" (p. 20)

"Shevchenko, the writer, supported Shevchenko, the citizen, in his nationalism." (p. 21)

[27]Anatoliy Lunacharsky (1875-1933): literary critic and writer. Moroz quotes from his *Velyky narodny poet Taras Shevchenko* (*The Great National Poet Taras Shevchenko*), Kiev, 1961.

"This democratic nationalism of Shevchenko does not contradict in any way the new socialist outlook." (p. 25)

". . . the noble nationalism that opposes violence and demands equal rights for all nations." (pp. 30-31)

"Therefore we, socialists, should support Shevchenko's form of nationalism, which has deep popular roots and is benevolent toward other peoples." (p. 26)

And here are a few more evaluations of nationalism:

". . . the spirit of freedom as the consciousness of a nation, as *nationalism*" (p. 106) ; "the force which can open the way to a better future is in the national consciousness, in nationalism" (p. 107) ; "Our nationalism should be positive, constructive" (p. 107) ; "Without nationalism there is no progress; without nationalism there is no nation." (p. 108)

No, I am not quoting from an emigre journal. All these quotes are from Sukarno's book *Indonesia Accuses,* published in Moscow in 1961. As we can see, such comments have been printed without explanations for a long time in the Soviet Union. Similar works had been published even before the 20th Party Congress. In Nehru's book *The Discovery of India,* published in Moscow in 1955, we read:

"In India nationalism has been and remains inevitable; it is a natural and healthy phenomenon. . . . Recent world events have shown the contention that nationalism will disappear under the pressure of internationalism and proletarian movements to be incorrect. It remains, as before, one of the most powerful motivating forces of a nation. . . . Meanwhile, as the bourgeois intelligentsia gradually drifted away from nationalism—or so it thought—the worker and proletarian movements, based on the principles of internationalism, were drawn increasingly toward nationalism" (p. 50) ; "the principle of nationalism has deeper and firmer roots; it does not appear obsolescent or meaningless for the future." (p. 51)

We can add Sun Yat Sen's comments from the abovementioned book by Sukarno: "Nationalism is the priceless entity that gives a nation the strength to strive for progress,

84

to defend its right to existence." (p. 103)

We can also quote Pavlo Hrabovsky:[28] "Nationalism is necessary for the progress of all mankind; not only the nation itself but all humanity suffers from the death of a nation."

Dzyuba rejects the "name 'nationalist', regardless of the meaning one may give it," at a time when even official brochures state that the term "nationalism" is also used in the meaning of "patriotism." Thus, in the quoted article by Lunacharsky, published in Kiev in 1961, there is an editorial footnote which states that "when the author writes of Shevchenko's nationalism, he is referring to Shevchenko's love of his country." (p. 19)

The most significant recent events—the national liberation movements in the world—came about under the banner of nationalism (meaning "patriotism"). Dzyuba rejects "the name nationalist, regardless of the meaning one may give it" instead of asking: "How long shall we remain the perennial laughing stock? How long shall we go on asserting that the earth stands on a tortoise? How long shall we consider as profanity a notion which the rest of the world accepts in the positive sense, which is a banner for half of mankind, and about which one of the outstanding Marxists—Lunacharsky—wrote that "it does not contradict in any way the new socialist outlook"?

Dzyuba also renounces the so-called "Ukrainian bourgeois nationalism"—that completely mysterious rebus. To renounce the so-called "Ukrainian bourgeois nationalism" is about the same as to renounce contacts with the devil in the Middle Ages, when godlessness was always "pinned" on an opponent. The Pope called Luther an atheist, and Luther called the Pope an atheist. Both considered Calvin godless, and all three believed in God. Who has not been a "Ukrainian bourgeois

[28]Ukrainian writer (1864-1902) persecuted by tsarist regime; died in Siberian exile.

nationalist"! Kostomariv,[29] Hrinchenko,[30] Oles,[31] Kosynka,[32] Mykola Kulish,[33] Ostap Vyshnya,[34] Antonych[35]—they all carried the label of "Ukrainian bourgeois nationalist." And then, without explanation, the label was removed. But never mind Hrinchenko; the list of "nationalists" even included those who with their own hands defeated Petlyura:[36] Skrypnyk,[37] Yuriy Kotsyubynsky[38]. . . . The so-called "Ukrainian bourgeois nationalism" is a label that was pinned on anyone marked for destruction—in the same way as the Nazis pinned a yellow patch on the backs of Jews. To renounce, after all this, the so-called "Ukrainian bourgeois nationalism," one has to be completely without any sense of humor.

Five years ago Dzyuba thought differently:

"They try to justify KGB violence with twaddle about 'Ukrainian bourgeois nationalism' (that is, any deviation

[29]Mykola Kostomariv (1817-85): historian, writer, journalist.

[30]See fn. 5, p. 12.

[31]See fn. 4, p. 12.

[32]Hryhoriy Kosynka (1899-1933): Ukrainian poet; arrested, tried secretly and shot for alleged participation in "terrorist" anti-Soviet activities; "rehabilitated" after Stalin's death.

[33]Mykola Kulish (1892-1942): Ukrainian playwright, accused of "Ukrainian bourgeois nationalism" in 1933; died in prison camp.

[34]See fn. 45, p. 32.

[35]Bohdan Antonych (1910-1937): Ukrainian poet whose works, until recently, had been banned.

[36]Symon Petlyura (1877-1926): Head of the Directory and Commander-in-Chief of the Armed Forces of the Ukrainian National Republic in 1919-21; assassinated in Paris in 1926.

[37]Mykola Skrypnyk (1872-1933): Ukrainian Communist, a friend of Lenin, one of the leaders of the opposition to the Ukrainian National Republic; held high Party and Government posts and tried to carry out a policy of "Ukrainianization" in Ukraine. Having failed, he shot himself in 1933.

[38]Yuriy Kotsyubynsky (1895-1937): Ukrainian Communist leader, son of famous Ukrainian writer Mykhaylo Kotsyubynsky; sided with the Bolsheviks against the Ukrainian National Republic; promoted a policy of Ukrainianization; arrested for "Ukrainian bourgeois nationalism" and shot.

from the Russified standard)"—*Internationalism or Russification?*, p. 223. He reiterates this point several times in his book (pp. 109, 224).

Why should Dzyuba worry that some emigre newspaper called him a leader of an underground in Ukraine? Who said that Dzyuba must be held responsible for this? What if tomorrow someone called him a counterfeiter, an Eskimo, a Dalai Lama? Will he have to write another statement? For goodness sake, who would have thought that I would have to argue with Dzyuba about something so ridiculously obvious!

Dzyuba, moreover, had no right to forget that his statement places others in a more difficult position. For the fewer the numbers of those who refuse to write statements, the more pressure they will have to endure. In six months Opanas Zalyvakha[39] will be set free. Could we look him squarely in the eye if we had written such statements? If we, enjoying freedom, consider it proper to write statements *under duress*, then Zalyvakha should have an even greater right to write them and renounce "nationalism." Yet, he has not written a single statement nor renounced anything.

To allow one's position to be dependent *on pressure* is very dangerous logic. If this is justified, then Levko Lukyanenko[40] has the right to become an informer.

Zalyvakha will soon be free, but Lukyanenko will still remain in prison a great number of years. Are we not ashamed to complain of pressure, knowing the situation in which this man finds himself? Are we not like the fat lady in the comedy movie who loved to tell everyone how "awfully unhappy" she was? We are, after all, men. Let us at least show some

---

[39]Ukrainian painter (b. 1925), arrested in 1965 and sentenced to five years of imprisonment in severe regime labor camp for protests against the policy of Russification in Ukraine.

[40]See fn. 18 above.

shame before those women[41] who are sitting out their 25 (!) year sentences without even once complaining of pressure.

Have we not grown too contented and forgetful, joining those whose enthusiasm lasts about five minutes, and who, after the first taste of unpleasantness, then renounce their own signatures under petitions and for the rest of their lives hold in account those who suggested such a "reckless adventure" as signing a petition. Dzyuba must have really grown in their eyes; how much wiser and more serious he has become; how gratifying and uplifting they must find his statement! Their retreat, they now believe, was no retreat at all; there was no flight in panic. Now, solemnly and joyfully, they carry Dzyuba before them. They now carry an idol, and a procession with an idol in the lead cannot be flight. Their retreat, they now believe, is no weakness at all, dictated by irresolution and fear, but clever strategy. And they will tear anyone's throat who would dare to oppose his statement.

I was also told the following: Dzyuba's statement is bad, but . . . "the pill must be swallowed"—so that's that. No, a thousand times no. Ukraine has swallowed enough of these pills! She has poisoned herself with them, and she is still sick. It is very difficult to understand those who had thought his statement bad and were against its publication, but said nothing to Dzyuba . . . could it be out of tactfulness (?!). How they advise us to stay silent . . . could it be out of love for Dzyuba (?!). Forgive me, but this is not love. This is *false love*: to lick and wipe tears. And that is what these people did to Dzyuba. True love is active. Love is not always warm compresses; a cold shower is often better. Chekov was not ashamed to admit that he was *squeezing the slave out of*

[41]Moroz is referring to Kateryna Zarytska, Odarka Husyak and Halyna Didyk, who were sentenced in 1947 and 1950 to 25 years of imprisonment for their Red Cross work in behalf of the Ukrainian Insurgent Army, fighting against Soviet occupation of Ukraine. They were kept in Vladimir Prison and in Mordovian camps. Zarytska and Didyk have served out their terms, and have been released.

himself drop by drop. And we must help one another to free ourselves from the plebeian burden. I regret that during my first interrogation I had no one near me who would look me in the eye and tell me the bitter truth when my behavior was found lacking. Drach was luckier—there were people around who reacted sharply and decisively to his article and thus helped him to see his mistake. There are such people also at Dzyuba's side. But does he listen to them? This will depend on Dzyuba himself—on whether he can muster enough strength to examine himself critically, to overcome his ambition and petty egoism. The ability to recognize one's own mistakes is a mark of a strong personality.

Even if Dzyuba's statement were good in itself, he would have to protest against the "framework" in which it was presented. Some think that Dzyuba should now quit the Writers' Union in protest. Others are not so radical. I, for instance, am among those who think that Dzyuba, in one way or another, must renounce his statement in order to neutralize the tremendous harm already inflicted by it. Common ethics demands this.

No one is passing "a death sentence" on Dzyuba, as he states in his letter. People do not die from truth. They die from "realism," from the cold scepticism which gave birth to Dzyuba's statement. We do not want Dzyuba to die. We want Dzyuba to rekindle with *pure flames of obsession*—for this is the greatest asset of the presently *frozen* Ukraine.

February 1970

A CHRONICLE OF RESISTANCE

A WIDE nest between mountains—Kosmach. . . .

Like the resounding echo of cymbals, the Hutsul[1] houses are flung upon the forested slopes.

The endless patchwork of fences, the dark firs and the blue contour of mountain peaks loom on the horizon. An ancient pagan tryptych: the gurgling stream, the sporadic jingle of cow bells, the distant barking of a dog.

> I stop by in Kosmach,
> I wouldn't miss it for my life;
> To Kosmach, to my lovely,
> To my good friend Stephen's wife.

Kosmach—the name itself evokes something gloomy and foreboding, primevally ominous, as a peasant's sheepskin coat turned inside out during a thunderstorm. Wild bears still roam the surrounding woods. Perhaps from this we get the name Kosmach. (In Ukrainian, *kosmaty* means furry, grizzled, hence Kosmach—Trans.) Earlier, during the time of Dovbush,[2] houses were sparser and the forest thicker. Mighty doors and hinges hung on a stout beech frame, and behind them the dark eye of a flintlock rifle and the wide

---

[1]Hutsuls: ethnographically distinct Ukrainian inhabitants of a region of the Carpathian Mountains; subsist from agriculture, breeding of cattle and sheep, forestry; known for original architecture, wood-carving, brass work, weaving, ceramics.

[2]Oleksa Dovbush (1700-1745): leader of Ukrainian rebel groups called *opryshky* that fought against oppression and exploitation in Hutsul and neighboring regions of Ukraine in a "Robin Hood" manner of robbing the rich and giving to the poor; glorified in folk songs and legends.

smirk of a *bartka*[3]—not just a decorative display piece; they were once of pure steel. The bartka became an ornament only later. Then it was a weapon. *Law, then, was determined by the axe.* . . . There are legends about giants that left us the "Written Rock" near Yaseniv. Legends tell us that the credo of their faith was the axe. Their god was the mountaineer's hatchet.

> If I only had an axe,
> Forged from powerful iron,
> I would not have any fear
> Of the Pole or German.

"At night, the priest of Utoropy, Ioan Stupnytsky, was attacked by the *opryshky*[4] shooting through the windows, but Father Ioan shot one to death and wounded two. The *opryshky* scattered, dropping their tar and candles in front of his house" (*Hutsul Chronicle* by Petro Stupnytsky, 19th century). However, the Hutsul past is not interesting for this —the cult of the axe. Remarkable is the fact that during these times when the axe was god and law, when priests handled the rifle better than the cross—even in these conditions the Hutsul land did not become uncivilized, it did not become a spiritual wasteland. On the contrary, it retained that which the rest of Ukraine had lost, and surprised the world with its talent, its astonishing power of self-preservation. The Hutsul "lyubasuvannya"[5] did not become debauchery (as it did elsewhere); the *opryshok* did not become a bandit, although he could have! Yet elsewhere it did happen.

"To all stout young men, men willing to travel, to people capable of anything, to thieves and bandits! If you want to dance on the warpath with the great leader Kondrat Bulavin, wander across the virgin prairie, drink and eat your fill and ride good horses, you should come to the black peaks of Sa-

[3]Light Hutsul axe, used in defense against wild animals and robbers as well as a walking cane.
[4]See fn. 2 above.
[5]Hutsul courting.

marsk." (S. M. Solovyev, *History of Russia from Earliest Times,* vol. XV, p. 180.)

A Hutsul never joined the *opryshky* to "eat and drink his fill." Even when he had no clear national or social ideals— even then he became an *opryshok* to *"really live."*

> Oh, three policemen shot,
> With pistols they shot at me.
> So I, I hid behind a tree,
> Behind the leaves so green.
>
> > O, I hid behind a tree,
> > Behind its greenery—oh,
> > So they would not shoot me,
> > A lad so young, so young.

"To really live"—a pure Hutsul expression that cannot be understood; it must be felt. *"To really live"*—to scratch your way through the fat of the everyday, mundane life to pure ecstasy, to a world of light, where the spiritual begins . . . where creativity begins. "I'd like to *imagine* that which the world has never seen."

> Oh, I came into the church,
> And stood in the rear,
> Where the candle burnt so sad,
> For my love was not here.
>
> > But when my loving darling,
> > My handsome eagle came,
> > The candles flickered bright and high,
> > And set the altar aflame.
>
> My darling is like the light of day,
> And I, a blooming tree;
> I'd never stand under a thatch,
> Lest it catch fire from me.

Even among the *opryshky* there were wayward people of Bulavin's type. But they do not exemplify the essence of *opryshky.* Mostly, people with a high sense of dignity became *opryshky*. Under the conditions of feudal despotism, they had two choices: become a slave or take to the woods. Sometimes they built churches. But, no, they did not go into *opryshky* to "eat and drink their fill." They were not thieves. Thieves robbed churches. These people built them.

The Uniate[6] movement, having attained control of the cities, gradually spread, defeating opposition in the most remote parts of the country. The Hutsul land was still experiencing a fierce struggle between the Orthodox and Uniate churches during the middle of the 18th century. Ukrainian Orthodoxy, having lost the major cities, was building bastions far in the mountains. Skyt Manyavsky[7] became such a bastion of the old faith.

The year 1735. Ivan Chupirchuk built a church in Kosmach all by himself with an axe, a saw, but not a single nail. This was a clear challenge, for a Uniate Church already stood nearby. Far away in Lviv and in Kiev a polemic war was being waged between Smotrytsky and Potiy.[8] Here, among the beech trees, in the shadow of Hoverlya,[9] the war was not on paper. Here, the opponent was not destroyed by a figure of speech, and blood was spilled instead of ink. Chupirchuk, sentenced by the Stanyslaviv court, died in jail.

The year 1740. Oleksa Dovbush contributed a large sum of money for a new church. From that time on it was called Dovbush's Church.

The year 1741. Six people of Kosmach went to Stanyslaviv with three yoke of oxen to buy bells for their new church. Two were sentenced to death; four, headed by Ozhynyak, were forced to flee and become opryshky. The list of martyrs

[6]Refers to those Ukrainians who, as a result of the Union of Brest in 1596, recognized the Papacy and joined the Catholic Church, while retaining the Eastern Rite; the Ukrainian Catholic Church of today.

[7]Carpathian monastery.

[8]Meletiyus Smotrytsky and Ipatiy Potiy: two 17th-century religious polemicists.

[9]Highest peak in the Ukrainian Carpathians, elevation 6,800 feet.

does not end here. The priest sent to the new church from Skyt Manyavsky was poisoned.

The year 1773. The church was reconsecrated Uniate, but this no longer had its previous meaning. There had been a change in the order of priorities. Halychyna[10] became a province of Austria. Polish rule was ended. The Uniate movement grew into the living body of Ukrainian spirituality and became national in character. Struggling with it ceased to be a national matter. The same happened with the cause of defending Orthodoxy. In fact, the roles were reverse. Before long, Russia made Orthodoxy a tool of Russification of Ukrainian lands taken from Poland. The Uniate reconsecration of the church was a formality now. The church remained Dovbush's.

Then came the twentieth century. Dovbush was placed on a pedestal. Kosmach was invaded by artists and art scholars. No longer were people sentenced for the possession of antique pistols; they were paid considerable sums of money for them.

The year 1959. The Executive Committee of the Kosmach Village Council passed a resolution for the establishment of a Dovbush museum in Dovbush's Church. At long last the forefathers who paid with their blood for the preservation of the sanctuary found grateful descendants. A golden age had come.

But the devil has many faces. Sometimes he even dons the mask of a man of culture.

The year 1963. Representatives of Kiev's Dovzhenko cinema studio borrowed the iconostasis[11] from Dovbush's Church for the filming of *Tini Zabutykh Predkiv* (*Shadows of Forgotten Ancestors*).[12] The people of Kosmach

[10]Halychyna or Galicia; refers to Western Ukraine.

[11]Wall of icons, separating the altar from the rest of the church in the Ukrainian Orthodox and Catholic Churches.

[12]*Tini zabutykh predkiv* (*Shadows of Forgotten Ancestors*): award-winning Ukrainian film, based on a novel by the same title by Mykhaylo Kotsyubynsky (1864-1913), depicting Hutsul life.

received a receipt with a detailed list of all borrowed items (altogether 29) and a promise to return the iconostasis within five months.

The year 1964. Five months had long passed, and the very upset people of Kosmach began to demand the borrowed items. After much chicanery they were told: the iconostasis had been given to a museum of Ukrainian art in Kiev! How?! On what grounds? What about the note? And common decency? As yet, no one has answered. The people of Kosmach still do not know what to think. Why, they had dealings with people of culture. They thought that these people of culture would also treasure their holy relics. Of course the people of Kosmach have become used even to those who call the whole town "Banderovshchyna."[13] (Some "comrades" from the Kosiv Art Institute, seeing these Hutsul artifacts, said, "get rid of this 'Banderovshchyna'.") But these were not the same. . . . . These had nice, well-trimmed old fashioned beards and spoke without vulgarities. The Hutsuls could not believe that it could simply be that their objects would not be returned. They still do not believe it today—even after writing more than ten appeals to all possibly concerned: to the Ministry of Culture, to the Society for the Preservation of Historical and Cultural Relics, to the Moscow Patriarch, to the prosecutor, to the committee dealing with religious matters.

Writing letters did not bring any results, but it did surface some interesting facts. The iconostasis was given to the museum according to directives from the regional representative dealing with religious matters for Ivano-Frankivsk, Atamanyuk! About the ethics of certain cinema personnel we shall talk later. Now let us analyze something else: What business did Atamanyuk have with a non-functioning church, a church which a number of years ago had been

[13]Another Soviet term for Ukrainian nationalism, derived from Stepan Bandera (see fn. 16, p. 14).

turned into a museum? Also, how could Atamanyuk, of Ivano-Frankivsk, give directives to Kiev? Something is wrong here. . . . Anyone who is even slightly familiar with bureaucratic logic knows that things like that do not happen. Someone more powerful must stand behind Atamanyuk. . . .

The initiator of the Dovbush museum, Vasyl Babyak, had a discussion with the assistant director of the Kosiv Regional Executive Committee, with Atamanyuk and with a representative of State Security. The conversation began in this manner: "What right did you have to write?" "I took the iconostasis and I'll take the church." Soon after this the conversation became concrete: "You are being riled up by nationalists from Lviv. We know your Kosmach; there was a whole regiment of Petlyura's[14] troops there." We shall not bother with Atamanyuk at this point. . . . How was he to know that Petlyura's troops never entered Western Ukraine. He must have attended the wrong high school. He became an expert in ecclesiastical affairs . . . after working with the KGB. We shall not bother with Atamanyuk anymore if only for the reason that he is no longer among the living. After him, the man responsible for church matters in Ivano-Frankivsk became Derevyanko. He also served in security, but something unpleasant happened there, and he was switched to church affairs. Such is the tradition of Ivano-Frankivsk: church matters are administered by the least important members of security. Let's leave them in peace. . . . We can only sympathize: it is difficult to take care of church affairs without having any theological education. But is it only a lack of theological education?

A few words about Babyak. We were sitting in his home, talking . . . looking at photographs. . . . Here is one from before the war: Hutsuls with a red flag, with red arm bands. The year was 1939: liberation, popular militia. Vasyl Babyak hides this photograph modestly, finding it uncomfortable. He

[14]See fn. 36, p. 86.

was a member of the popular militia, fought for Soviet rule, and here he is accused of being a "nationalist." He was an activist, a deputy of the village Soviet. He was, but is no longer. He has no regrets. But he will not rest until the stolen iconostasis is returned. Such people are disliked. Only those are liked who follow the "official" line. But he does not care. "They can't change me," he laughs.

He showed me a letter from the "nationalists" in Lviv. There was an autograph of the historian Hrabovetsky, the author of the monograph, *Hutsul Opryshkivism.* "To the initiator of the establishment of the Oleksa Dovbush Museum in Kosmach, a true Hutsul, fervent lover of his native Hutsulshchyna." There was another letter from the patriarch of the Lviv artists, Hebus-Baranetska.

There were also letters from the Kiev "nationalists." For instance, the Laureate of the Lenin Prize Oles Honchar[15] writes: "The incident with the iconostasis is downright revolting."

A very revealing list of "nationalists." This is a new meaning of the word "nationalist." Previously there was a linguistic criterion. A "nationalist" was anyone to whom the fate of the Ukrainian language was of any importance. (In Eastern Ukrainian cities it was much simpler: anyone who spoke Ukrainian was labeled a "nationalist.") At Vasyl Babyak's house I saw the matter in a completely new light: a "nationalist" is anyone who has any concern about Ukrainian culture.

It is very symptomatic that Oles Honchar, the author of *The Cathedral,* found himself among the "troublemakers." As a matter of fact, here we have a classical example of "poaching," so brilliantly depicted in *The Cathedral,* with an added example of absolute spiritual deafness. Here is Atamanyuk's reply to the citizens of Kosmach: "We have received and studied your claim and we consider it ill-founded. *There*

[15]See fn. 56, p. 47.

98

are not and have never been any historical relics in the village of Kosmach." There are none and have never been any. How about Kosmach itself—a unique village, a rare flowering of talent? A mind-boggling concentration of talents—mind-boggling even for Hutsulshchyna, which is so generously endowed with talent. The most artistic pysanky[16] are from Kosmach; the most delicate embroidery, the most elaborate sheep skin coats, as well as the most talented musicians—they all come from Kosmach. How about Novakivsky,[17] or Smolsky,[18] or Moroz?[19] They are part of Kosmach. Since the village became a Mecca for Ukrainian artists, how many new talents has the village inspired? At the entrance to the village there should be a plaque calling for its preservation: "Kosmach is an historical monument. Protected by law."

As far as Atamanyuk is concerned, it feels awkward to give so much attention to such a petty bureaucrat. Most likely, these bureaucrats never give due consideration to the full meaning of their work. All they know is that they have to liquidate a church. The fewer iconostasis there are in their region the better. (Once the director of a school near Kiev told me proudly: "Do you know that in our region there are no churches left?") It is true that Atamanyuk did not ruin any church by himself. This war against culture is fought by even pettier personnel. They get 25 rubles for bringing down a cross. Judas' occupation is being devalued; they once paid 30 pieces of silver. I wonder from which budget is this money being deducted? The economists who set up the budget are not interested in having the crosses knocked down. Is it possible that the person who gives the order pays out of his

[16]Traditional Ukrainian Easter eggs decorated with multicolored geometric designs, dating back to pagan and early Christian times.

[17]Oleksa Novakivsky (1872-1935): noted Ukrainian painter.

[18]Hryhoriy Smolsky (b. 1893): Ukrainian artist noted for Hutsul, Carpathian themes in his work; born in that area.

[19]Mykhaylo Moroz (b. 1904): Ukrainian artist noted for landscapes; now residing in USA.

own pocket. Our deputies to the Ukrainian parliament should inquire into this. But where will we find such deputies? So far, we have none who would inquire.

The distribution of power is very "symbolic." The people who defend the church are ready to sacrifice for the sake of an ideal. They are few, but fighters were always few in number; however, they do the work. Atheism utilizes trash, willing to knife anyone and anything for 25 rubles. This is truly a struggle between light and darkness, as the atheistic pamphlets proclaim. But which is the light and which is the darkness?

Perhaps Atamanyuk never gave much thought to his "kulturkampf," but you cannot say the same about his superiors. V. Lyubchyk knew very well what he was doing when he was burning the works of Boychuk,[20] Archipenko,[21] Narbut,[22] as well as century-old Ukrainian art. This was followed by the burning of libraries in Kiev, Tartu, Ashkhabad, Samarkand, but not a single one in Russia. For some reason, Ukrainian, Estonian, Uzbek and Turkman artifacts are flammable. . . . They say it was an accident. All right, let us assume it is true. We will assume that the Lviv Museum of Ukrainian Art also *accidentally* established a special section for "ideologically harmful art" where all the articles collected were assigned to be destroyed (a kind of death row). We might believe that it was *accidental* that it was composed exclusively of Ukrainian classics, and that Lyubchyk *accidentally* received orders to prepare lists of items to be destroyed, and that the commission to review these lists also fell from heaven. In all seriousness, however, there was only one

[20]Mykhaylo Boychuk (1882-1939): Ukrainian artist and teacher; his icons brought him into official disfavor; arrested in 1937, died in Soviet labor camp.

[21]Alexander Archipenko (1887-1964): Ukrainian-American sculptor of world fame, noted innovator in that art form.

[22]Yuriy Narbut (1886-1920): Ukrainian graphic artist; his works banned under Stalin, later "rehabilitated."

accident in "Lyubchyk's story": the letter from the artist Kryvonis, from Paris. Leaving the country at the outbreak of the war, some artists left their works to be stored in the museum. And so, Kryvonis asked about his stored works. If he had lived in Kosmach, Atamanyuk would have simply *had a talk* with him. But he lived in Paris, and this was already after the 20th Congress. The comedy had to run its course: Lyubchyk was sentenced to ten years as . . . a Ukrainian bourgeois nationalist. Within half a year, Lyubchyk was set free. (Now he has a position on the faculty of the Lviv Art Institute.) At last the truth is revealed: Ukrainian culture is being destroyed . . . by Ukrainian nationalists. Among the items that were destroyed were articles with a trident. These are strange nationalists who destroy their own symbol. As a matter of fact, a "nationalist" in Western Ukraine is a synonym for a "saboteur." The "saboteur" is also responsible for all the insanities of Stalin and Khrushchev. Whenever there is not enough bread, or when hogs die on the collective farm, the "saboteur" is responsible. All evil in Western Ukraine (even the flood of 1969 in the Carpathian Mountains) is caused by "nationalists." The worker from Donbas, transformed into a robot by enormous doses of liquor and inhumanly hard work, believed in the "saboteur." He still believes in him. However a person from Western Ukraine, not having completed the process of cultural genocide and demoralization, does not believe in Lyubchyk's "nationalism." Lyubchyk is known widely, and there are poems about his accomplishments.

VASILIY LYUBCHYK

"Why was I sentenced to die"
—Vasyl Symonenko "Herostrat"[23]

You live, it seems, in God's own bosom,
With merits and services, you deftly slither away.
Of course, you lecture now, and at after-dinner toasts
Your good deeds are mentioned, time to time.

Once you used to send flames to lick at
Kholodny's immortality,
Archipenko—he too crumbled in your hands,
Flames that crackled from one canvas to another;
From dust it came, to dust it will return!

If you're a Little Russian—return to the weeds,
And sow your buckwheat amid the chicken coops,
Even the devil can't stop you now,
Lyubchyk, our darling, you bastard.

(Ihor Kalynets)

It is also important to note for posterity the name of Lituyeva—the former curator of Stanyslaviv Regional Museum. Coming to Western Ukraine in the role of a "culture disseminator," Lituyeva had specific instructions—as did Lyubchyk. In 1953 she destroyed unique objects—the works of Bakhmetyuk[24] and those of the Shkriblyaks.[25] And here a real scene was performed: exactly the same way as in Lviv. No, she did not do these things on her own—just as no

---

[23]See fn. 5, p. 65.
[24]Oleksa Bakhmetyuk (1820-1882) : Ukrainian master ceramist.
[25]Shkriblyak, Yuriy (1822-85), Vasyl (1856-1928), Mykola (1858-1920) : master wood-carvers in Carpathian area.

corporal would have dared on his own to order the mass execution of the Kobzars[26] in the 1930's.

Lituyeva destroyed everything with "crosses." Generally speaking, the easiest way to destroy the foundation of a nation is to do it under the pretext of fighting the Church. The Church has rooted itself in the cultural life so deeply that it is impossible to touch it without damaging the spiritual structure of a nation. It is impossible to imagine traditional cultural values without the Church. It is ultimately necessary to understand that an attack against the Church is an attack against culture. How many times has the nation been saved by the Church? This was especially important when a change in faith meant a change in nationality. There were a number of villages near Kholm where Ukrainians spoke Polish. But they remained Ukrainians as long as they adhered to the Ukrainian faith and Church. Similarly, a Polish family in a Ukrainian village in Podilya would remain Polish for generations without knowing the Polish language as long as the family remained Catholic.

In Eastern Europe the Church was the only power independent of the authorities. Let us take the Ukrainian revival in Halychyna,[27] how trivial was the role played by the teacher as compared with the priest! The teacher was a state employee afraid of losing his job. The priest did not know this fear. The majority of the people working for the Ukrainian cause came from the clergy. "The Reverend" was often justifiably criticized, but it is also important to remember that it was he who kept the Ukrainian movement alive. Halychyna did not turn Polish because of the Ukrainian Church. In this and similar cases we can equate the Church and the nation—just as we can equate the Church and spirituality, in general.

We often hear: "The Church always sided with the ex-

[26]Bards; author refers to execution of Ukrainian writers in the 1930's.
[27]See fn. 10 above.

ploiters." We hear it so often, in fact, that we accept it as a matter of fact. But facts give us a different story.

Early Sunday morning
All the bells were pealing,
We were driven to our toil,
By overseers with whips.

Oh, no, my good neighbor,
There'll be no church today
Take your shovel and thrasher
Go, beat the golden grain.

The first of all our pain—to work our bitter serfdom,
And the second pang—to toil three full measures,
But oh, we'll work our serfdom—all three measures,
if only we could go to church and pray.

The exploiters, as we see, drove the people from church with whips. Would they do this if the Church were really on their side? And the people were willing to work any kind of serfdom—just so they were not forbidden "to go to church and pray." People know instinctively that under certain conditions the Church is their only hope for spiritual self-preservation, their only guarantee from becoming a beast of burden. The master also understood that it is impossible to break people and make slaves of them until you have robbed them of their holydays, ruined their traditions, trampled their temples.

It is not always necessary to chase people away from temples with whips. Sometimes the devil is more sly. The treacherous sorcerer in the Estonian epic promised the giant Kalevipog everything, if only he would give him one useless item: an ancient book, chained in a storeroom. The simple-minded hero, who exercised his muscles but not his brain, agreed. Later, he was extremely sorry, but it was too late.

104

This was the Testament of the Lord God. Our Ivan also frequently gives away without thinking. The classical swindle: declare the spiritual riches of a nation "useless superstitions," "opium of the people." All that remains then is to find a plebeian like Lyubchyk, who will burn and destroy whatever he can for 25 rubles.

Enter . . . the instinct of self-preservation—the cornerstone of *Resistance*. The same *Resistance* that sustains a nation and its spirit. A man has already "been convinced" that these are "superstitions," but somehow he does not fully surrender —as the workers in Honchar's novel. They know from "the cradle" that the cathedral is "unnecessary," they do not even notice it, but something prevents them from giving it up for destruction. During the massive Norman invasion, when all of Ireland was in flames, the Irish first of all hid their sagas. During the battle no one would dare touch the Irish bard with his sword, even though his songs frequently decided the outcome of the battle in favor of the opponent. The same privileges were bestowed on the bards of the Cherkess.[28] Instinct dictated that the carrier of spirit had to be preserved.

Nowhere in Ukraine is this instinct so strong as among the Hutsuls. Maybe this formed the Hutsul character: proud, suspicious of anything alien and, most of all, independent. Hutsuls do not like to crowd their houses together. They would rather have them tower on the wooded hillsides. One must always be *cautious*. The devil has many faces. The devil is sly. One must live by his wit and hold on to everything dear. A Hutsul always accepted something new with great caution, and only that which blended well with the old. So it was with Christianity. The Christian holydays were matched to older, pagan holidays. Therein lies the art of national self-preservation: to accept the new without destroying the old, to incorporate the new into age-old structures. Otherwise, the soul of a nation will be built on fragments and be

[28]Nationality in southern RSFSR and Turkey.

based practically on nothing. The Georgians have mastered this art. How very Georgian and national they have made even very recent phenomena such as the cinema and jazz! The secret of their success is fanatical attachment to their cultural heritage. The Georgians have songs with ancient, undecipherable words, and yet they sing these songs, without a word being understood.

The Hutsul region is known by all. Every Ukrainian west of the Zbruch River[29] is called a Hutsul. Why a Hutsul? Why, if the Hutsul region is only a small part of Western Ukraine? Why is he not called a Boyko, a Polishchuk, or a Podolyak?[30] Because the Hutsul land is the most distinctly individual in all of Ukraine. Age-old political boundaries divided the Boyko and Lemko[31] lands. Transcarpathian Boyko lost all feeling of a mutual identity with the Halychyna Boyko. The same is true of the Lemkos in Pryashiv;[32] they do not call themselves Lemkos. Only the Hutsul land was not destroyed by boundaries. Living for hundreds of years within the boundaries of three states—Romania, Poland and Hungary—the Hutsuls retained a strong feeling of identity.

The ability to preserve—therein lies the secret of Hutsul identity. Inside the Church of Dovbush there is a Crucification scene depicting next to the hands of Christ the sun and the moon. The same is on Hutsul candleholders: on one side is the Christian God, and on the other the sun. The Hutsul did not discard the old god for the sake of the new God. The faces on Hutsul candleholders are not Christian. With their pagan, warlike appearance (perhaps even bloodthirsty) they are more akin to Polynesian wooden sculpture or North American Indian masks. This is a Christian deity—power

[29]Zbruch River, used as boundary prior to World War II, dividing Western Ukraine (under Polish rule) and Eastern Ukraine (under Soviet rule).

[30]Ethnographic inhabitants of Western Ukraine.

[31]Same as fn. 30 above.

[32]South-eastern part of Czechoslovakia.

106

that is divided into God and Demon, a deity that comprises both Good and Evil. The Hutsuls greet the lowering of the cross into the river on Epiphany with powerful blasts from their trembitas[33] and horns, as they once greeted their former gods, Yarylo and Khors. (This unusually beautiful spectacle is now impossible to see. The blessing of water in the river is forbidden—an accomplishment of the *Kulturkampf!*)

High cultural attainment is possible only through uninterrupted tradition. Lose nothing, and keep adding layer upon layer. Only in this way can spirituality grow. It cannot be built according to a Five-Year-Plan, as could a canal during Stalin's time.

The people of Kosmach who built the church and, risking their lives, brought bells, thought of it as something more than just a church. It stood for a nation, for spirituality, without which man becomes a mere working animal. In those days there was no lack of shrewd demagogues who tried to convince the people that the old faith had outlived its age.

But the illiterate Hutsul understood that behind the dogmatic discussions between the Uniates and the Orthodox stood something more basic: on one side—the fangs of "Polonization"[34] which had already devoured the cities, and on the other side stood Resistance of the Ukrainians. His descendants also understand that the fight for iconostasis—is *Resistance!* Resistance to the leveling, dehumanizing force that strips a man of his national and cultural identity and makes him a working machine of one-half horsepower.

The individuality of Kosmach and its people is striking even in the Hutsul land where every town is unique. It is impossible to confuse a decorated Easter egg or an embroidery from one town with that of another.

[33]Hutsul wind instrument; long (up to three yards in length), thin, made of wood.

[34]A process, similar to Russification (Russianization), of forced cultural and linguistic assimilation; Polish in this case.

Forces that threatened to erase the uniqueness of Kosmach and make it gray and average were always there. But the greatest trials that Kosmach suffered came in the 20th century.

First came the trial by tourists—esthetes and epicureans of art. They smothered more than one flame of originality in many parts of the world. They were followed by the spirit of commercialism; the climate of the unrepeatable was lost as was that certain aura. Artists began to produce on order from wealthy connoisseurs. Their work deteriorated into mediocrity. Kosmach lived through and withstood this.

The second test was Siberia. It happened that after the war half the citizens of Kosmach ended up on the Siberian taiga. Why this happened is hard to say. No invented class theory can explain it. According to the class theory, rich exploiters should be deported. Is it possible that the exploiters can comprise half a population? Particularly in a small mountain village where few people had more than five acres of land. Really, the class approach explains nothing. However, if you view the whole matter in the light of nationalism, then you begin to understand. Stalin was very upset with the Ukrainians; he thought there were too many of them. He could not deport them all as he did with the Chechens,[35] but he tried. Stalin sent Lituyeva and Lyubchyk westward and trainload after trainload of Hutsuls eastward. There, behind barbed wire, in "camps" and "special settlements," deprived of all their traditions, among thieves and bandits, they had to become like Lituyeva. According to the plan, if the Hutsul did return, he would be culturally broken, and his land, where Lituyeva, Lyubchyk and Co. had enough time to do their work, would be culturally devastated as well.

Assimilation is not simply robbing a nation of a set number of individuals. Assimilation is the destruction of traditional

[35]Moslem population north of the central Great Caucasus; fought against Russian expansion in 19th century; after World War II resettled throughout USSR for alleged collaboration with the Germans.

structures—a process that is far from mechanical. It is rather a delicate chemical process of extracting the cement that binds a nation. If a nation is broken into one-tenth of its strength, but its soul is left intact, then it is still not fatal. One can grow a meadow from a healthy willow twig. This has happened to the Armenians, the Hebrews and, in our times, the Chechens. They were not only exiled, but scattred throughout all of Kazakhstan; still, hardly any of them became Russified. On the other hand, the Mordovians were never sent into exile, and this nation is being Russified with hardly any resistance. At some time, the spiritual identity of this nation must have been damaged. It is obvious that at some crossroad in their history Mordovians had lost their instinct for resistance. It is certain that Mordovian patriots would willingly accept the Chechen fate with its purely arithmetic losses, if they could also get their national strength.

Stalin borrowed a method proved successful by the Romans. Historians are puzzled to this day at the speed with which the Romans Romanized their subjugated nations. Their secret was intermixing. When a Gaul, an Egyptian and a Syrian were brought together, they were compelled to talk in Latin. The son of an Iberian and a Frank born in Sicily became a Roman just as the son of a Byelorussian and Chuvash born in the virgin lands becomes a Russian. And so, a German, a Ukrainian and a Kazakh in a frontier state farm must speak Russian with each other.

There is a German town in Kazakhstan where for ten years the local authorities tried unsuccessfully to settle some Kazakhs. Everyone was shocked at the "backwardness" and "racism" of the Germans. They could not understand why the Germans were against the "fraternization of nations." The Germans themselves were not aware that they were guided by the power of *Resistance,* which prevents the disappearance of a nation. The Germans explained their unfriendliness on the level of everyday life: Kazakhs are "dirty," "uncivilized." That is how it usually is: complicated subconscious motives (too complicated to be raised to a logical plane) manifest themselves through the mundane, the concrete, through "prejudice." Prejudice is also an element of the traditional structure. The "prejudiced" German collective farmers did not *understand*, but *sensed* that, *by* accepting Kazakhs and Ukrainians into their village, their German atmosphere and character and all that constitutes their national identity would be lost. Denationalization means *deculturalization*. A nation grasps this through the instinct of spiritual preservation which keeps a man from turning into an ape when he is faced with hardships.

And so the man from Kosmach returned from Siberia. He came back a Hutsul. Even though he had to go through the nine pits of hell he did not lose his traditions. He still sings the same songs, paints the same Easter eggs, and he has not forgotten the customs of a wedding ceremony. Using the official expression of the *Kulturkampf*, the great Stalinist plan of transforming human beings "with respect to the village of Kosmach" was not achieved. Kosmach proved to be too tough a nut even for Stalin's teeth.

Having returned home, the Hutsul thought that he had bid his last farewell to Siberia. But he would see it more than once. In Kosmach the Hutsul found a phenomena called "mass unemployment" in the West; in Ukraine, because of the absence of unemployment, it is called "temporary job shortage." (Actually, even socialist countries like Yugoslavia now use the term "unemployment.") Six months at a time (if not longer) the Kosmach citizen has to spend away from his village, working on temporary jobs. This has traumatic effects, and the wooded northern regions of Russia can serve as an example. This part of Russia became a land of ghost towns, a land of boarded windows. A Russian poet once wrote: "I am sitting in a house that is exquisitely constructed, a masterpiece of a house. However, it is empty; its master is far away in a restaurant, shouting drunkenly: 'Lidochka, honey, some more cognac!' " What tragedy: a masterpiece, but his last. Even if the master does come home, he will be unable to construct another like it. He has been wasted *incorrigibly*.

In Kosmach there are no boarded windows. From Kosmach they leave en masse, but they return. And what is most important, the man from Kosmach comes back a Hutsul.

One experiment follows another. . . . The devil keeps changing his mask. This time he came back as the movie director Paradzhanov.[36] Yes, yes, the same Paradzhanov. . . . *Shadows of Forgotten Ancestors* . . . international film festivals. . . . It is hard to believe: Lyubchyk, Atamanyuk, KGB and . . . Paradzhanov—all in the same company! But they are. It appears that Paradzhanov has the icons from Dovbush's church, but he has covered his tracks so well that the people still do not believe it. Everyone accuses Atamanyuk, because he gave the order to relinquish the iconostasis to the museum. True, the iconostasis did go to the museum, but on the way it was stripped by Paradzhanov. Paradzhanov hid behind Atamanyuk—what an unnatural, fantastic union. And yet, all this is based on fact.

"Semi-education was the misfortune of Old Russia; it is the misfortune of Soviet Russia, as well," wrote Masaryk.

Semi-education results when a person is first deprived of his traditions and then educated. *Semi-education* results when culture does not develop naturally, but is stuffed into a person according to a Five-Year-Plan, or some other accelerated program. *Semi-education* is manifest when people recognize the value of the Kosmach icons, but see no wrong in stealing them.

I do not know if Masaryk was right to treat semi-education as an exclusively Russian phenomenon. Maybe it once was. Now it is universal. Better still, it is a universal illness. In

[36]Serhiy Paradzhanov (b. 1924): Armenian-born film director, winner of sixteen international prizes for *Shadows*. Was one of signers (total 139) of a letter, protesting the wave of arrests in Ukraine in 1965-66. Arrested in December 1973, released in January 1974.

the West it is known as "mass culture." Lyubchyk has not yet passed into history—he is still teaching at the Lviv Art Institute—and already a new figure looms over Kosmach— the ominous spectre of *Chuvak.* Outwardly, this figure is not ominous but comical, sometimes even witty when he is criticizing dogma. Everyone is fond of criticizing dogma—and in our situation this is understandable—but in this pleasant task no one noticed that the main danger had become the person *without any dogma* who believes in nothing. Enter *nihilism,* the product of mass culture. It sweeps away all creativity in its path and leaves on everything its stamp of *mediocrity.*

This is how one Muscovite who proudly considered himself a *Chuvak* explained this term to me: "A man who adopted the higher American culture." *Chuvak,* for short. This is curious, and yet symbolic. America is a chaotic mixture of many cultures. America is the deculturalization of all elements who find themselves in its melting pot. Russia, which is so unlike the United States in all other respects, here goes hand-in-hand with it. Russia is also eclectic.

Masaryk said that the history of Russia after Peter I was a methodical destruction of Russian culture through the forcible introduction of Western influences. As in the United States, so also in Russia, a person with no roots does not consider himself lacking in respectability; on the contrary, he is proud of his detachment from tradition and "open-mindedness." A person who is attached to some definite traditions, both here and there, is considered "backward." The sooner an Italian immigrant becomes Americanized (in other words, forgets his language and traditions), the greater are his chances of being considered "respectable." And so it is here: if you want to prove that you are "progressive," you should forget your ancestry and become a "universal" person (in effect, a Russian).

———————

Just as the whole world is reflected in one droplet of water, so are all the misfortunes of Ukraine reflected in the story of Dovbush's iconostasis. Actually, not so much in the story itself, as around it. If it were only a matter of Paradzhanov alone, it would not be worth writing an article; a statement would suffice. The reason for writing about this was the dull indifference with which our intelligentsia reacted to Paradzhanov's actions. The prevalent logic seems to be: "Well it's obvious that he stole it, and that's bad. But is it worth troubling him for it? After all, he is Paradzhanov."

Herein lies the source of our Ukrainian tragedy. To the intelligentsia, our national heritage has yet to become a treasure that is more valuable than any of the accomplishments or talents of Paradzhanov, no matter how great they might be. There are even some second thoughts on Paradzhanov's accomplishments. Some attribute the success of *Shadows of Forgotten Ancestors* to Yakutovych (in Uruguay the film did get a medal for *color*), Ilyenko and Skoryk. Some observers feel that the parts where Paradzhanov's stamp is most evident are the weakest in the film. They say that Paradzhanov is not the director of *Shadows*, but rather a talented impressario, an able producer who successfully gathered the right people for the film. I should emphasize again, however: this is beside the point. I wonder whether the Armenians would let a Ukrainian film director (even if he were a genius!) get away with stealing their icons from Echmiadzin or the Tatevsky Monastery? Or would they stand in shameful silence because of his accomplishments.

Armenia no longer has the threat of Russification hanging over her. That is all in the past, and Armenia is not only formally but actually Armenian. Ukrainians explain it thus, "It's a small nation . . . they're permitted to. . . " This is an argument of the weak! No one *permits* anyone anything. Everything must be *asserted*. Mordovia is also a small nation. So what? The reason of Armenian success lies in the way they value their heritage. Our fate can turn, as it did in Armenia, but only when we stop being indifferent spectators to the destruction of such bastions of Ukrainian Resistance as Kosmach. In the meantime, Ukraine will remain the proving ground for experimentation by such people as Paradzhanov and Solntseva,[37] who are not necessarily without talent, but their talents are wasted, for they never really felt Ukraine. To them the icon from Dovbush's Church will always be an *artifact,* but never a *relic.*

Everyone grazes on Ukrainian pastures. Working under the Rivno Regional Art Fund there is only *one* Ukrainian among twenty artists. The rest were "borrowed" from Omsk, Tomsk, Khabarovsk. . . .

The Armenians would not have permitted them into the same room where national treasures are created. Not because they are "horrible nationalists," as the Russian carpetbaggers who failed to land on the Armenian payroll so loudly complain, but because they believe that Armenian culture should be created by Armenians. Otherwise, the distinctness of Armenia will become blurred. Armenians understand this well; Ukrainians have yet to realize it.

The art plunderer has always been around. But during the period of our mass culture, he became a mass phenomenon. Even a special title was created for him: "collector-poacher." Paradzhanov must be cited here, if only for the fact that he is the classic example of a collector-poacher. He was known for his stealing. . . . He would borrow an antique object from some Hutsul "only for a few hours" and then disappear. The name Paradzhanov to a Hutsul became synonymous with "thief." ("Ah, you are from Kiev? Why don't you tell Paradzhanov to return my valuable antique belt.")

The poacher even developed a "theory" that valuable objects are lost in the remote parts of the country, while he is saving them. But this is not exactly how it is. The poacher only endears himself to such people as Ivan Hon-

[37]Yuliya Solntseva (b. 1923): Russian actress and director, widow of noted Ukrainian film director Oleksander Dovzhenko.

char,[38] who zealously tries to save valuable objects of cultural heritage from being forgotten and destroyed. The poacher does not trouble himself with searching for bits and pieces. He thrives on whatever has already been collected. Paradzhanov knew very well that Dovbush's Church was to be turned into a museum. The people of Kosmach probably expected that this guest from Kiev with his authority and influence would help to get the project off the ground. And Paradzhanov certainly did: he stole the main exhibit. Paradzhanov did not steal just from a future, not yet established, museum. Paradzhanov also did not leave with empty hands from the already existing museum, which had been active for a number of decades and was known far beyond the borders of Ukraine: the collection of the artist Sahaydachna in Kosiv. Stealing there was even easier than in Dovbush's Church. Anyone could steal from this half-blind woman. But not everyone could bring himself to do so. . . .

Paradzhanov set a record. And how many followers he has! Vasyl Babyak complained, "It's almost impossible to find a real *opryshky* pistol in Kosmach anymore." Everything has been scattered, and no one has asked himself: Will Kosmach remain Kosmach if everything is taken from it? Will it not disappear as an artistic phenomenon? Will this unusual flower grow if the air it breathes is taken away? It does not matter if the Easter eggs or the embroidery which is produced now is taken away from Kosmach. But is it necessary to take away to Kiev Dovbush's iconostasis from the 18th century—even if it were whole and not dismembered by Paradzhanov? This is a classic example of the logic of bureaucratic centralization: everything valuable must be located in the center; the peripheries must be satisfied with the leftovers.

The administrative concept of centralization, however, does

---

[38]Ivan Honchar (b. 1911): Ukrainian sculptor, curator of a semi-private museum-archive in Kiev.

not coincide with the concept of culture. Is it possible, from the artistic point of view, to call Kosmach or, for that matter, Yavoriv or Opishnya, provincial? These are the real cultural centers of Ukraine, the springs without which Ukrainian art would wither. This is, in fact, the most authentic part of Ukraine. This is where the artist from Kiev or Lviv can truly experience the essence of Ukraine. National self-realization without such centers is impossible. If a Ukrainian is to look for holy places, they would be in Kosmach, and not in Jerusalem. Stealing from holy places was always severely punishable. Ukrainians, however, have permitted the looting of national relics from their Mecca to go unpunished. They even steal from their own. Enslaved, materialized, devastated and lulled into a state of slumber, today's Ukrainian does not react even to heavy blows. The apathy with which the Ukrainian intelligentsia accepted the plundering of Dovbush's Church is proof enough.

Even nations with a fate more fortunate than ours do not have the pure springs and mighty bastions with the instinct for resistance as Kosmach. Those that do exist are carefully guarded, because they are both invaluable and educational. You can travel through many parts of Ukraine and find that the oldest architectural monuments are tea houses from 1948, plastered in gray cement of the classical Stalinist renaissance!

De-Christianization, collectivization, industrialization, mass migration from villages into cities—all this brought about the unprecedented ruin of traditional Ukrainian structures, the full catastrophic results of which have yet to be felt. But, even now one can see the product of this destruction:

> Open up, blue ocean,
> Open up in half,
> Hide a girl with her child
> Into your depths.
> . . . .

Marusya, oh, Marusya
Open up your eyes.
Marusya answers,
Don't bother me, I am dead.

This is an example of "spontaneous poetry." There is also
an organized form called "self-creativity." Lately there has
been an attempt to *create* new traditions. This brought about
word abbreviations and combinations—one more ridiculous
than another: "Building of Happiness," "the Holiday of
the Workers' Spring. . . . "

The *creation* of traditions is just as ridiculous as the pro-
motion of cultural revolution. "Culture" and "revolution"
are incompatible, contradictory concepts. Culture represents
centuries of *maturation*, a process that is impossible to speed
up. Any form of revolutionary interference is destructive.
You cannot create traditions. They are *created by themselves*
through the centuries. You can call everyone to a clubhouse
and proclaim some idiotic Holiday of Swineherds or Milk-
maids instead of Easter, but it will never become a true
holiday. It will just be one more collective farm meeting
with another booze party afterward. A holiday must have
spiritual *meaning*, an *atmosphere* that evolves through more
than one lifetime. The atmosphere of Christmas and Easter
in a Ukrainian village has been crippled and defamed. It is
even hard to remember what Christmas stands for . . .

The creator of History—the people
play dominos 'til dawn.
(*Mykola Kholodny*)

Now they want to fill the vacuum with commercialism:

Christmas, Christmas, Christmas song,
the cows have calved,
the cows have calved on the farm
and the calves have been born.
We will take care of these calves
to the farmer they're his wealth,

117

to the kolhosp it brings new revenue,
to the people it brings meat and butter too.

(*Shchedrivky*, Kiev, 1968, p. 299)

This is truly cattle folklore, and this *bovine* character permeates everything. All you have to do is look at the grotesque presentations of amateur singing or drama clubs in their Ukrainian costumes.

You have to travel a bit in this structureless Ukrainian wasteland in order to understand the true value of the unspoiled orderliness of Kosmach. You have to see and compare holidays (weddings, birthdays) that have degenerated into drunken brawls in order to understand what a treasure a Hutsul wedding truly is with all the traditional rituals. In the present state of confusion, Ukrainian folklore is being changed after every newspaper headline. The Kherson amateur group sings the same song as the group from Chernihiv, while we passively observe the destruction of the village of Kosmach, a village with its own face and character, perhaps the most distinct and the most individual in all of Ukraine.

Lyubchyk is still alive. In 1968 in Zhydachiv, near Lviv, during the construction of a gas station, the oldest Ukrainian wooden Crucifix, dating back to the 15th century, was thrown from a height of eight meters. Every year during the spring fair in Kosiv, bands of "activists" destroy Ukrainian Easter eggs (they even wrote about it in the *Komsomolskaya Pravda*). For 25 rubles these bands also go around destroying the remaining crosses which can be found at the crossroads in Western Ukraine. These are Crosses of Freedom erected to commemorate the abolishment of serfdom. In November 1969, three unknown persons wearing police uniforms entered the Uspenska Church in Lviv, carried out some very old books and burned them in the churchyard. Again burning, and again of Ukrainian treasures. Who were these people? It is impossible to find out. The report about the burning was locked in a safe by the Chairman of the Lviv

Branch of the Society for the Preservation of the Historic and Cultural Monuments, Kudin. Not even the workers of the Society were allowed to see these reports. What a strange Society . . . it is not clear whether it protects historic treasures from pyromanicas, or pyromaniacs from public wrath. Moreover, the leaders of this Society were selected on the same basis as the people who were made responsible for Church matters in Ivano-Frankivsk. One gets the impression that they are not as interested in cultural monuments as they are in the people who are interested in cultural monuments. They are not concerned about drawing up lists of the national relics, but the lists of persons interested in these cultural monuments have been drawn up a long time ago. . . . This Society has a very large budget; however, only a meager sum is being spent on the restoration and preservation of monuments.

Yes, Lyubchyk and Lituyeva are still alive, while over the Kosmach mountains hangs a new shadow—that of a mass culture. *Confusion* is setting in. Songs on radio are the same in Japan and Brazil. One must always be *wary*, for the devil is sly. He keeps changing masks. One must always be ready to resist and not believe in gilded trinkets. A Hutsul does not believe in a God who is differentiated into Good and Evil. In real life they are both one. There is nothing wrong with mass education or mass medicine. However, with them came mass culture. Instead of the heaven that the Utopians promised us, came deculturalization, alienation, dehumanization, and the loss of one's roots. There is an English bank, but there is no English folklore. People are hypertrophically developing the technical at the expense of the spiritual, and for some reason they call it progress. Never before has there been such an urgent need to learn and mobilize the Resistance, and to use as arms that which has more than once saved nations from losing their identity. Every nation must find these means in its own heritage and form its own antidote against disease.

Ukrainians must seek this in Kosmach.

The people of Kosmach have written everywhere. Nobody helped them from Ukraine—the same Ukraine that boasts of 100,000 scientists and more college students per capita than England. In that case, the people of Kosmach have the right to appeal to the world community. There also is the UN and UNESCO. Kosmach is a cultural treasure not only in Ukraine, but of the world. The Easter egg from Kosmach became known world-wide a long time ago.

During the 11th Session of UNESCO general conference, the Ukrainian delegation supported the "basic agreement of mutual recognition of art valuables." This delegation declared: "Ukraine, just as the other Socialist countries, has great experience in the organization of education, science and culture, and would gladly share the knowledge with all." We cannot call this a lie, but neither is this the truth. This is a half-truth—the product of semi-education. Let the Ukrainian delegation share its knowledge in UNESCO—the knowledge of semi-education, that is, education based on destroyed traditions. Let the delegation explain that folklore in Ukraine is safeguarded only where the atheistic "Kultur-kampf" was unable to reach. Let the delegation tell about the oldest crucifix in Ukraine which was destroyed by being dropped from a height of eight meters, about artists that burn paintings, about the movie director who steals from museums, and about the Ukrainian intelligentsia that could care less. And, of course, let them also know about the Lyub-chyks who burned museums during the days of Stalin and now burn books in the Uspenska Church.

A wide basin between the mountains, and in it lies Kosmach, unlike any other village. Having seen and spoken with the people, I understood: Kosmach will always be different, it will always be distinct. These people will never be destroyed by materialism. Materialism was never important to them—neither when they built homes, when they became *opryshky,* nor when they go for seasonal work into distant lands. The people in these mountains exhibit a tremendous ability to give spiritual value to everything around them. Miserly pay, eternal wandering through seasonal jobs—one would think that from such a life Dovbush's Church would be forgotten forever. But in Kosmach everyone talks about it. I first heard about the stolen iconostasis on a bus from Kolomyya to Kosmach, and later I heard in every home: *"We have been orphaned!"*

There are millions of people with higher education that know everything, but hold nothing sacred. Is it necessary to prove what a great spiritual treasure we have in the citizens of Kosmach, who feel orphaned without their Dovbush iconostasis?

Their income is miserly, but no one rejoiced when an oil derrick was erected in the middle of the village. Everyone prays to God that no oil will be found. No, Kosmach cannot be bought with materialism. Here the right of the first-born cannot be bought with a bowl of lentil soup.

We forbid the riding of motorcycles within a national forest in order to preserve an atmosphere that is conducive for the existence of some rare birds. Nothing can be changed within the preserve. When will we understand that Kosmach is also a national preserve, only a thousand times more valuable? We should also forbid any changes in Kosmach that might disturb the unique atmosphere in which the Kosmach artistry developed. Destroyed Kosmach Easter eggs for a few tons of petroleum? How can we allow ourselves to even talk about any industry in such unique places as Kosmach, Yavoriv, or Brustury?

The oil derrick is there, even though nobody in Kosmach wants it, and the art artel which the Kosmach citizens have requested a long time ago is not. In fact, there is nothing. Kosmach embroiderers spend more time looking for thread than they do embroidering. The art artel was promised for 1972—no, not its construction, just the technical permit. Why it takes three years for it to be drawn is a mystery. (It was promised in 1969.) One would imagine that this was a project for an American spaceship flight to Saturn.

The Lyubchyks managed to get a lot done. Of the things collected from Dovbush's Church, very few are left. The document of the Village Council on the opening of a museum has been destroyed. The people of Kosmach receive help from only a few enthusiasts. But the people of Kosmach have not grown indifferent and have not given up. They are all ready to remodel the church—all they want are the materials. For this, they are told, there are no funds. True, there is the Society for the Preservation of Historic and Cultural Monuments, and with large sums of money in its budget, but Atamanyuk, evidently, is sitting there and he feels that "in the village of Kosmach" there are no cultural treasures, "now or ever." All are ready to turn over to the Dovbush Museum their own family relics, if given a guarantee that they will not disappear again. And all are ready to continue demanding the return of the stolen iconostasis, in spite of the threats of "nationalism."

The year 1969. A wedding party wends its way along a mountain path—the mellow jingling of bills, horses hung with copper *shelests,* and up front, on the first horse, a rider with a branch. The branch is so thick with leaves that you cannot see the rider. Behind him rides the groom in an immaculately white outfit with a bartka in his hand.

The branch represents the Tree of Life, the symbol of immortality. The one holding it is not a young man. Indeed, this is the symbol of *his* immortality. He traveled halfway around the world; he saw hell beyond the Arctic Circle, but did not lose his identity; he did not become Chuvak, but returned a man of Kosmach. And here he is again, holding the branch—as did his ancestors at the time of Dovbush. He does not let go his Tree of Life.

This is KOSMACH.

I will return once more into these mountains to gather

strength, to study Resistance, to find myself, to search for the answer to the question "Who am I?"

We must, however, do everything possible so that we may have a place to return to, so that Kosmach will live—the bastion of Ukrainian Resistance.

January 1970

P.S.—Not even two months have passed since I wrote this article, and the problems cited in it have already been compounded. An employee of the Lviv Regional Society for the Preservation of Historical and Cultural Monuments, Pavlo Chemerys, was released because of a "staff cutback" (without the agreement of the union committee). He reminded Kudin too often that the Society for the Preservation of Monuments does indeed have to care for the preservation of monuments.

According to a decision of the Kosiv Regional Executive Committee, some thirty citizens of Kosmach were fined fifty rubles apiece for Christmas caroling. Under this pretext, close to 100 persons were interrogated (at the village and regional level). Father Romanyuk, of the Kosmach Church, was suspended from performing his duties for one month. That was the decision of the Commissioner of Church Affairs in the Ivano-Frankivsk region. What is this phenomenon called the Russian Orthodox Church, in which neither the bishop nor the metropolitan, but a government representative suspends a priest from his duties, a representative of the same government that, according to its constitution, separated the Church from state affairs and does not interfere in its internal affairs.

Why was Father Romanyuk punished? Because in his sermons he urged people to wear their traditional Hutsul clothes, to refrain from selling antiques to collectors like Paradzhanov and to preserve their traditions.

"What is wrong with caring for Hutsul traditions?" Father

Romanyuk asked. "It reeks of nationalism," the Commissioner for Church Affairs answered.

Everything Ukrainian reeks of nationalism. The *Kulturkampf* continues.

March 1970

MOSES AND DATHAN[1]

THE author deals with the question of national inferiority complex in analyzing the article by Yevdokiya Los. In contrast to other "internationalists," who conceal their lack of national dignity if only with a thin curtain of smoke, Yevdokiya Los openly declares that, in spite of her love for Byelorussia, it is "not national patriotism" that guides her. Byelorussia is to her a "second Moscow": "Our meadows are the same, our snows are the same, and even both languages are almost idential (Byelorussian—Russian). Minsk is Moscow, Pinsk is Moscow, and also the modest Ushachi."[2]

The author contends that with such feelings of *inferiority* with respect to Russia a Byelorussian cannot have genuine Byelorussian patriotism. He is convinced that Yevdokiya Los's Byelorussian patriotism is purely provincial and local: "You stopped thinking of Byelorussia as a nation long ago; you use the phrase 'Byelorussian people' by force of habit. The Byelorussian *nation* is not indispensable for you; a Byelorussian *province* suits you fine. You dispense with Byelorussia as you do with an old fingernail."

[1]Written by Moroz in response to an article in *Literary Gazette* (No. 36, 1969) by Byelorussian poetess Yevdokiya Los, titled "The Impotent Simplicity of Blindness: An Answer to the Radio-Liars of Munich." Only a resume of Moroz's essay reached the West.

[2]Presumably the inhabitants of the Ushachi valley in the border region between Vitebsk and Smolensk.

The author contends that between the emigres in Munich, who once served the fascists, and Ye. Los, who criticizes them, there is amazingly much in common: "You sincerely hate them—I know. But you are not *adversaries*—you are *rivals*. For you, Byelorussia is a 'second Moscow'—for them, Byelorussia is a 'second Berlin'. The absence of their own Byelorussian values had turned these people into mercenaries."

In ridiculing the Russifying theory of the "inevitability of the fusion of nations," the author says: "How boring the world would become if your rosy schemes really were 'an historical inevitability'! What would be left for humanity if progress was *inevitable*, if the future was a guaranteed paradise? And all of this—is known ahead of time? Would man still be a human being, an autonomous entity, who alone in the world has the capacity to *choose*?" Man is the antipode of automatic programming. . . . There is no guaranteed progress. Man is human because of his constant struggle against ever-present evil, because of the unprogramability of history, because of the opportunity to change the world in conformance with his goals.

The author believes that only those who have a deep consciousness of nationality can build universal human values: Nationality is a truth as concrete as goodness, truthfulness and beauty. It is universal, but with a million facets, and every facet is assigned to a specific nation. The mission of a nation is to find that one side which no other nation can find, and to enrich mankind with it." "It is not enough to bring Marx to Byelorussia. If he is to become alive for you, it is necessary to see him with Byelorussian eyes, to discover him in a Byelorussian way. If you think that Marx can be simply borrowed from Moscow, ready-made, you are deeply mistaken. If you consider yourself a Marxist, then your duty before Marx, if you want it, is to 'discover' him in a Byelorussian way. Marxism (or any *ism*, for that matter) brought into Byelorussia is but the comb that must still be filled with Byelorussian honey."

126

The author maintains that in a person fully devoleped spiritually, the nation, the Fatherland, should be a thing treasured above all: "I do not know for what purpose Byelorussia exists in the world. But I know for sure that a Byelorussian who says, 'Why do I need Byelorussia?' is already a dead man. 'What is Byelorussia good for?'—for such questions there is no answer. Where sacred things are concerned, logic has no meaning. . . The nation is something most holy. The nation is the synthesis of everything spiritual in man's realm. The Christian Shevchenko placed the nation above God (the formal, dogmatic God; the real living God is the nation):

> I love her so, I love so much
> My destitute Ukraine,
> That I would curse the Holy God,
> And lose my soul for her.

In the same context the author later writes: "There is no progress that automatically guarantees a nation the right to existence. A nation lives only when there are people ready to die for it; when there are Byelorussians who do not ask: 'What is Byelorussian good for?'; when her sons believe that their nation has been chosen by God and their people are the highest product of history. I know that all people are equal. My mind tells me this. But along with this I know that my people are singular, the best. My people—are the pride of the earth. My people—are the arrow from God's bow. That is how my heart speaks. It is unwise to bring the voices of the mind and of the heart to a common denominator. The voice of reason is indispensable. But a person whose reason has eaten away the heart is a shell without a core. Mental superiority does not always indicate spiritual superiority."

The author is of the opinion that a Byelorussian who has feelings of inferiority with respect to Russia can neither love nor be a friend of the Russian people. "But is it really love, that which you accept as love? Love . . . between whom?

Between the hunter and his dog? Love, friendship are possible only between equals. I can love Russia, because I do not have a feeling of inferiority before a Russian. . . . You cannot love Russia, for you look up at Russia from below."

Stating that the national consciousness of the contemporary Byelorussian is asleep, the author writes: "But hypnosis does not last forever; the effect of hypnosis is shortlived. In a Byelorussian soul, the Byelorussian being has been crystallized by a thousand years of suffering. It is impossible to destroy it, just as it is impossible to put out a volcano by stuffing it with trash. You can cover it, but at the time of the mighty eruption, when mountains tremble, the trash will dissipate. It won't even burn, it will vaporize. . . . "

The author concludes with these words: "The Byelorussian may become friends with a Russian. He may—but only when he has developed his full national consciousness. He may—but only after he has stepped over You!"

From the PRELUDE Collection

Ukraine

Sunny redness, heavy blackness—
your hues

curved lashes of flying poplars—
your song

intertwined scepters of trihorned gods—
your signs

nocturnal whisperings of the gray steppe—
prayer

sunny dispersion in a blue sky—
banner

Bowstring

Trumpets the wind, Svaroh's gray grandson,
like a jarl's horn that calls into the ocean,
through black clouds' tangle silver blues the bottom,
and the moon races through mist like a deer.

The sail drones into the night, tautened by the wind,
through the chaos of clouds—the blueness of the silver horn.
The greyhound-moon speeds along, the bow-string's copper
    resonance.
Diana's taut bow. The furious run rages.

Sleep's ceiling sags. An arrow quivers on the edge.
My skiff flies into the night through a wadding of clouds.
Strain's taut bow will tear the gray curtain
and a squall of power will break through sleep's blank wall.

A late flight

In the sinews—the rumble of wanderings.
Beyond the naked forests
winter's steel bell
drones over the world again.
Wild honey rages.
Alarm's muffled drum
drives us bewildered
in pursuit of the sun.

The days have matured.
Through the naked rustle of tops
October whispers
its final note.
It's time, it's time!—
Winter's silvery fox
already breathes snow,
grabs at the wing.

Prelude

Among the oaks, on land newly grubbed,
longhaired forefathers sowed millet,
rains bleached the emblem above the gates—
a horse's skull on an ashen spear.

The strong-toothed power of the forest world
surrounds the homestead from four sides,
by evening Blud shines in the rushes
with blue night-lamps for the late guest.

With boundless chaos the primeval forest flourished,
wolves multiplied in great overgrown swamps,
a green-eyed goat shook his beard
in a thicket of hops on the playground of the rites of spring.

Summer was going off into September's circle,
the Sun's golden crown cooled,
and from a far-off kingdom Kolyada was on her way,
a full-faced girl—Dazhboh's daughter.

Lutsk

Lyubart-prince, silverbearded knight,
the sycamore psalteries of your minstrels have gone dumb,
princely majesties on moldered parchment have faded
and your name has blackened on jagged steel.

I will gather the square gold coins of forgotten words,
from prophetic silver I'll forge an enchanting chain,
from the silt I'll lift Dazhboh's great wooden altar
and I'll comprehend the proto-Ukrainian spirit of our
      testaments.

Stolpye will put its wall into the earth, beyond the swamp
      Sedlyshche will settle,
melodious Zaborol will gleam with the white of birch bark,
like a sharp-eared wolf lustful Khotomel will peer out,
and Bila Vezha will rise up like a bear's head.

The hooves of Ratno will thunder, Voynytsya will shine
      with its shields,
to the four corners Rozhyshche will sound a bison's horn,
with meads Lupno will entertain—the great hollow tree,
and Hordlo will snuggle within its walls beyond the
      narrow Buh.

Owls gathered above the great castle's parapet,
ashen wings frighten off the gray twilight,
and slanting slabs on Karayim graves
scare the heathens with mysterious characters.

THE FIRST DAY

THE FIRST day in prison is eternity filled with pain. Everything—sounds, smells, dimensions, words—everything is written in pain.

The first day in prison is a man without his skin. Every memory a scalding drop, every thought a hot coal.

The first day in prison is a world severed in two. Every nerve rent down the middle. The origin of every human *I want* is found here, but the roots that tie it to life are severed and remain . . . out there. Normal *I want*s flow through normal channels and inevitably arrive at the point of severance. And every time . . . more pain.

The first day is a plant with its roots in the air, unable to imbed themselves in the emptiness. And this brings on the greatest suffering, for it is in the nature of the root to take root.

Nothing is more shocking than to daydream. Then, oblivion joins the freshly severed parts, and the *I want* is satisfied. But the sudden awakening breaks the thin thread, and the pain, which began to subside, flames up again.

* * * * *

The strong find it difficult. All their *I want*s are great—those that put them behind prison bars and those that call them to freedom. No, this is not a struggle between *I want* and *I must*. This is a struggle between two satanic *I want*s —both brawny and furious, with a strong, distinct pulse and an insatiable hunger for life; both fed by a firm, full-blooded organism.

The weak find it easier. Their *I wants*, small and languid, do not overcome complacency. Sometimes even they hear the voice of their *I want*, but, hypnotized by the fear of prison, they silence it forever. Afraid of the bitter, they will not drink from the goblet to the very last drop. They will never know *taste*.

The time will come when new roots will sprout from the wounds; they will imbed themselves in new soil and draw new nourishment for the insatiable human *I want*. The pain will thicken and turn into a constant, lasting yearning, heavy and dark like pitch. With every passing day the pitch will grow brighter and harder until it solidifies into a *crystal of expectation*. Freedom is most alluring when seen through its cloudy mass.

The axe of time strikes the crystal gates, and suddenly you are outside and free again. But this is not the freedom which for countless days shone through the crystal wall. You have your freedom; you are drunk, confused and . . . again without skin. It is impossible to pass through prison bars—going in or coming out—without leaving your skin on them. Though it be a hundred times, prison always takes its toll.

Afterwards there will be reminiscences, stories, countless facts—amusing and shocking, disgusting and touching. But prison is not made of facts. Prison is a man without his skin on the first day. Whoever can describe this can describe a prison.

> But you cannot describe it . . .
> And yet, you will try.
> That will come later . . . later . . .
> For today . . . is the first day . . .

Ivano-Frankivsk, KGB Prison.

PART TWO

The Case of Valentyn Moroz
Documents

Chapter I

First Imprisonment

1

VALENTYN MOROZ

VALENTYN YAKOVYCH MOROZ was born into a peasant family
on April 15, 1936, in the village of Kholonovo, Horokhiv district, Volyn region. After graduating from secondary school,
he enrolled in the Department of History at Lviv University.
As an active member of the historical circle, he often delivered research papers. After graduating from the university in 1958, he worked in his native Horokhiv district of
the Volyn region as director of studies in a secondary school
and as a history and geography teacher in the school for
working youth. He lectured at pedagogical conferences in
Lutsk and delivered lectures on historical subjects in the
villages of his district. From February 1964, he taught
modern history at the Lesya Ukrainka Pedagogical Institute
in Lutsk, and from September 1964, modern history in the
Pedagogical Institute at Ivano-Frankivsk.

While working in the villages, he prepared, without any
assistance, his dissertation on the subject: "The Lutsk Trial
of 1934: An example of revolutionary collaboration of the
Polish and Ukrainian peoples in their joint struggle against
the Fascist regime in bourgeois Poland." He did not defend
this thesis due to his arrest.

He is married and has a five-year-old son.

Towards the end of August 1965, he was arrested, and in
January 1966 he was sentenced by the Volyn Regional
Court on charges of anti-Soviet propaganda and agitation to
five years in severe hard-labor camps. He was kept in camp
No. 1 (Sosnivka) of the Mordovian camp complex for polit-
ical prisoners; at present he is in camp No. 11 (Yavas). In
December 1966, together with M. Horyn, M. Masyutko, and
L. Lukyanenko, he was sentenced to six months in the camp
prison.

139

2

PUBLICATIONS

1. "The Lutsk Trial of 1934," Collection of Theses presented at the Ivano-Frankivsk Pedagogical Conference on December 27-28, 1964.

2. "Western Ukrainian Rural Population in the 1936-37 Strike Movement in Poland," from the same collection.

3. "The Solidarity of Ukrainian and Polish Workers in Fighting Fascism in Spain (1936-39)," Collection of Theses presented at the Ivano-Frankivsk Pedagogical Conference on June 26-27, 1965.

3

FROM LETTERS TO HIS WIFE

I FEEL much better here. You understand—after the cell, especially after being in the company of criminals; it was loathsome, not only to talk to some of them, but stay in the same place with them.

They say here that Drach[1] died on July 15. A notice appeared in *Literary Ukraine* of July 22. I haven't seen the paper yet myself. That's how it goes. You think the man is alive, yet he is already dead!

July 29, 1966

I'M now very interested in the problem of individuality. I see that it is one of great importance in the development of humanity. Inanimate nature represents unity, similarity, lack of individuality. With the appearance of a live being, there appears an individual, but only in the physical sense. For, in the spiritual sense, there is absolutely no difference between one monkey and another. Human beings had their beginning in the dissimilation of the spirit, in the appearance of a spiritual world of their own, original and unstandardized. . . .

October 1966

WELL, that's how I live. My work is as simple as mooing: lift up, put down. That's good—it leaves my mind free. I'm reading Cicero, Hobbes, Alberto Moravia. . . .

November 1966

[1]Moroz is not referring to the poet's physical death, but to a change in his position.

I haven't yet received the Kant and Russell you wrote about. Recently, I finished reading Hobbes. . . .

December 1966

THE German language now reigns. I have more time for it now, although even before I used to devote some time to it every day (except Sunday). I intend to make my final effort to end the course in the next six months. Even now I can always make out what I read in the paper. Next, I'll start on English. This place is full of teachers! . . .

I've started reading Kant now. . . .

January 1967

4

**To Petro Shelest,[1] First Secretary of the CC CPU
From Political Prisoner Valentyn Moroz**

STATEMENT

THERE is an elementary political wisdom imperative for every social force that wishes to stay on the surface of life and not fall under the wheels of history. It must solve the eternal problem of survival: it must throw its ballast overboard and rid itself of the tendencies which keep dragging it under; it must absorb the new trends proposed by life.

It is not even a political, but a biological fact of life. The organism eliminates products of decay—everything that reduces its chances of survival and deprives it of perspective. Dinosaurs became extinct because they failed to rid themselves of biological hereditary traits which became a ballast and dragged them under. Mammals survived because they made this necessary adjustment.

The question of life and death for a political organism is how to free itself from the forces of the past that masquerade as friends and defenders of the existing order, but are, in reality, a time bomb; sooner or later they will destroy the one who failed to throw them out.

The KGB is preparing a new campaign. Again the false words: "In the name of the Ukrainian SSR. . . . " This is a lie. The interests of the political organism called the Ukrainian SSR do not demand a new act of lawlessness. In the

---

[1] Since replaced by Volodymyr Shcherbytsky and removed from the CC CPSU at its Plenum on May 26-27, 1973. Western Sovietologists at first considered him a victim of a confrontation within the Politburo between the proponents and opponents of Leonid Brezhnev's policy of "detente." More recently, many of these experts have taken the view that Shelest was removed for his inability, or unwillingness, to deal with the revival of Ukrainian nationalism.

Report from the Beria Reservation there is not a single word against Soviet rule or Communist ideology. The document is directed against violations of legality. It cites crimes. And still the document has been declared not only "anti-Soviet" but even "subversive." It is finally clear: I was not tried for anti-Soviet activities; on the contrary, the violators of the law carry out reprisals against those who expose their crimes.

The document clearly states that it is specifically directed against those who compromise (and thus undermine) socialist order; yet, the document has been labeled subversive. He who has been robbed is proclaimed a thief!

The forces that have instigated this reprisal have outlived their time; they would have liked to eternalize the Stalinist era. But they cannot destroy me physically today as they recently destroyed millions of Ukrainians. They have only half their teeth left, and, without doubt, the inexorable march of history will also pulverize the rest. But, for now, they still bite. They drape themselves with the interests of socialism. And what is most important, regrettably, they are still successful in covering up their deeds with the name of socialism, while, in fact, they *undermine its position.*

The CC CPU is constantly faced with the same problem: to discern whom it is sheltering under its banner. Read thoroughly the documents you sign. They say that a supervisor signed (without reading) a memorandum which stated that he was promoting himself to a higher position.

There is nothing unusual in the fact that chauvinists are imputing anti-Soviet activities to us. It is an old tactic to declare one's opponent an enemy of the existing order and prevalent ideology. Even Thomas Aquinas, the father of Christian theology and a canonized saint, was accused of atheism by his opponents. . . . Russian chauvinism has always imputed to Ukrainian patriots a hostile attitude toward the prevailing doctrine. At one time, they labeled them "socialists," when socialism was considered subversive. Now,

144

they label them "enemies of socialism."

Whoever considers as anti-Soviet a document directed against chauvinism, Stalinism and lawlessness, in effect, equates Soviet rule with chauvinism, Stalinism and lawlessness. Whoever persecutes an individual who exposes crime takes the criminal under his protection. *Could the most bitter anti-communist have conceived of a more effective way of undermining the position of Communism in its ideological conflict with the West?*

Escalation of an *ideological* conflict with an adversary does not mean swinging a club in front of his nose more vehemently. An *ideological* struggle can only be won with ideological weapons. Court sentences will not help here; on the contrary, they are a hindrance. Whoever defends his point of view in a discussion with his fists, only proves that he has lost. To "counterattack" against an ideological attack of the opponent is not the lexicon of the anointed. Whoever brandishes a club against an idea hammers the last nail into his own coffin, hangs a millstone around his neck. A political force that wishes to have a future must take a good look at such a stone; sometimes it may look, on the surface, like a laurel wreath.

Throughout Northern Europe monarchies have survived; in the South, they vanished. Does this phenomenon indicate that Northern Europe is backward? On the contrary. What is, then, the point? The point is that the Northern European monarchies found within themselves the strength to part with circles and tendencies which were dragging them under. They were able in time to throw their lot in with new tendencies and currents, ignoring the howling of those to whom change meant death. They knew how to throw the lethal ballast overboard and replace it with new sails. The monarchies of Southern Europe acted differently: they cast their lot with those who advised them to "hold on, not to let go," to crush all opposition. Who proved to be the stronger? Not he who with eyes shut, oblivious to reality, raved about his

145

own "invincibility." (This method is perhaps useful for suppressing one's own fear.)

"Not to let in" a new tendency is impossible; it will penetrate nonetheless, but in alien dress, as an argument in the hands of an adversary. Not to allow a spring stream to flow into its own riverbed is to divert it into the mill of another. Not to forge for oneself a weapon from a new trend is to surrender it into the hands of the enemy.

In the center of the ideological duel between East and West is the issue of freedom, the issue of human rights. Under such conditions, to try an individual for expressing his views —when the Constitution of the Ukrainian SSR and the Universal Declaration of Human Rights guarantee freedom of speech—is to saw the tree limb on which you sit. In an ideological struggle, the one who thinks up more semicensored expressions does not win. He wins who opens his floodgates to forces which have future prospects, and not to forces which are on the wane.

Today, reality has confronted Ukrainian communists with the identical problem Lenin faced fifty years ago: national rebirth. Then, too, there was no lack of Artems and Patakovs who screamed that "Ukrainianization" died with Petlyura.[2] But Lenin understood that to accept this view meant to direct a mighty stream (the national factor) into the mill of the adversary.

Will Ukrainian communists today be able to renew at last the Leninist policy of Ukrainianization and to declare all-out

[2]Symon Petlyura (see fn. 36, p. 86). After the Bolshevik takeover of Ukraine in 1921, Ukrainian Bolsheviks, ardent communists but with a Ukrainian consciousness, instituted policies of Ukrainianization of the country's cultural, political, educational and social institutions which had been Russified under the tsarist regime. This period of Ukrainianization ended in the late 1920's with a bloody purge of the CPU. The "Ukrainianization" referred to here was tolerated by Stalin as a form of Ukrainian nationalism which served to neutralize the anti-Communist form of Ukrainian nationalism of which Petlyura was the embodiment.

war on Russian chauvinism in Ukraine? The successful outcome of the ideological conflict with the West depends precisely on this. But as long as people continue to be tried for protesting against chauvinism, solemn oaths proclaiming that Leninist norms with regard to the nationalities question have been fully restored in Ukraine will not be very convincing. The communists of Czechoslovakia are demonstrating to the communists of all countries the necessity of throwing overboard that which has become a ballast and opening the sluices to those forces which guarantee a future. *Will the communists of Ukraine succeed, in their own interest,* in mastering this lesson?

National rebirth is the most powerful force today, and it is ludicrous to shield oneself from it with a piece of paper called "verdict." This wave will wane of itself but only

> When into a gaping grave will fall
> The last chauvinist on this planet.

(Vasyl Symonenko)[3]

New ideas open doors without knocking. "To allow" or "not to allow" national rebirth (or any new movement) is beside the point. The point is: he who comes to terms with it will survive. He who ignores it will find himself under the hooves of history.

The KGB is preparing new reprisals. Basic human rights will again be trampled even as humanity marks the Inter-

---

[3]Vasyl Symonenko (1935-63): the leading poet in the group called "poets of the sixties" that revived Ukrainian literature and began the movement for national self-preservation. The lines above are from his poem "To the Kurdish Brother," in which he exhorts the Kurds to continue resisting with arms "those who came to take away your freedom and your land." In 1968, Mykola Kots, a lecturer at an agricultural college, was sentenced to seven years in a labor camp and five years in exile for circulating seventy copies of this poem, in which he replaced the word "Kurd" with the word "Ukrainian."

national Year of Human Rights. Again the West will receive a powerful argument in its ideological conflict with Communism.

Whose interests does this serve?

Is it possible that once again the Central Committee of the Communist Party of Ukraine will fail to stop those whose actions are undermining the position of Communism? Is it possible that individuals who consider political wisdom their profession will fail to comprehend this basic fact of life, that of self-preservation?

Kiev, KGB Prison   *Valentyn Moroz*
May 15, 1968

5

To the Prosecutor of the UkrSSR
From Political Prisoner Valentyn Moroz

PETITION

ARTICLE 60 of the UCC stipulates that individuals conducting an investigation are subject to removal from the case "when they or their relatives have a personal interest in the results of the case." The KGB, which is investigating my case, has indeed a personal interest in its results, inasmuch as the content of the *Report from the Beria Reservation* is directed against violations of legality by agents of the KGB (and not against socialist and state order, as they allege). In connection with this, I request that *the investigative organs of the KGB be removed* from my case.

Article 97 of the UCC stipulates that the prosecutor, the judge and the investigative organs be obliged to press criminal charges within three days of being informed about the crime, or to examine the facts of the crime within ten days. The *Report* . . . exposes an entire series of crimes committed by agents of the KGB, including the most serious crimes, such as homicide and attempted homicide.

In contradiction of the law, the Prosecutor of the UkrSSR failed to react in any way to this information; otherwise, 1 would have been questioned in this matter. Moreover, the Prosecutor of the UkrSSR made it possible for the organs of the KGB to launch a *campaign of revenge* against those who expose their illegal acts.

I direct your attention to the fact that failure (on the part of those whom the law obliges to react to such information) to act on information about a crime is *in essence* the harboring of those who have committed the crime.

Kiev, KGB Prison   *Valentyn Moroz*
May 16, 1968

149

6

To the Chairman of the KGB at the
Council of Ministers of the UkrSSR
From Ukrainian Political Prisoner Valentyn Moroz

DEMAND

THE *convicted* Doctor Spock makes public appearances *at liberty*. The arrested Reverend Abernathy writes a letter of political content immediately after his arrest, and this letter passes freely beyond the prison confines. (It would be great if every KGB agent had such a photograph under glass on his table. Maybe then he would get used to the concept of human rights.) Even the Greek junta twice allowed Red Cross representatives to visit the imprisoned activist Elihu.

I do not demand such liberties for myself. I understand that the citizenry of Ukraine will not gain such rights for Ukrainian prisoners soon. (Not soon, but it will gain them, although some cannot even comprehend how this could happen. The wheel of history does not stand still.)

I refer to something else. More than seven months have passed since I last saw my family. The regulations for the investigatory isolation cell allow the convicted prisoner one visit every two months. Even in Vladimir Prison visits are granted twice a year.

I know your answer: the investigative organs may deny a prisoner under investigation all visitations. That is true. But an investigation which has been proceeding for a year and has consisted of only three interrogations is not an investigation. It is an abuse of the investigation procedure. The prisoner is deliberately kept in a state (of being investigated) that allows for the denial of all his rights.

I demand my right to have visitors, which, according to law, has long been due me.

August 1, 1968   *Valentyn Moroz*

150

7

To the Prosecutor of the UkrSSR
From Ukrainian Political Prisoner Valentyn Moroz

STATEMENT

MORE than seven months have passed since I last saw my family. The organs of the KGB have simply not replied to my written request. My wife and six-year-old son, who a few days ago demanded to be allowed to see me, were turned away.

I know that I am a prisoner under investigation and that I am allowed visitors at the discretion of the investigators. But may the organs of the KGB abuse this right? And what if the investigation should last two or three years?

Where are we? In the jungles, or in the most humane state in the world? In the year 1938, when the sole privilege a political prisoner could hope for was to remain alive? Or is it 1968, five minutes before the Promised Land, in a society which is five minutes from Paradise and very close, within twelve years (see the Program of the CPSU) of reaching the shores of Communism, from which all blessings will flow "like a full stream," in which there will be absolutely no coercion or violence? Is this the society whose leader, a dedicated Leninist, promised three years ago (Don't blame me, that is what the newspaper wrote!) that in 1965 he will show the last prisoner on television?[1]

Could not the organs entrusted with the protection of legality (i.e., the Prosecutor) construct at least a small levee against the stream of abuses of the KGB which flows torrentially upon my head? Could they not guarantee me human rights—not those of a future paradise, but the real rights of today that have long been guaranteed by law?

August 9, 1968   *Valentyn Moroz*

---

[1]Nikita Khrushchev promised in 1965 that he would have himself photographed with the last prisoner.

8

To the newspaper *Eleutheria Patrida,*
organ of the Greek anti-dictatorship forces,
London, England.

ALLOW me on this day, a Greek national holiday, to express
through your paper my solidarity with all those Hellenes who
have not capitulated to the dictatorship, who have not laid
down their arms, who stand fast by their "No." I firmly
shake the hand of a man who remains free even while in
prison, whom it is possible to kill but not conquer, who believes that freedom is indispensable for all. I firmly shake
the hand of all those who have dedicated their lives to the
struggle against all juntas, gangs and mafias, against every
kind of totalitarian regime, no matter under what phrases
or masks they may hide.

October 28, 1968   *Valentyn Moroz*
Kiev, Ukraine,
KGB Prison.

9

To the Association of Jurists of the UkrSSR

I SALUTE all Ukrainian jurists on the Day of Human Rights, on the twentieth anniversary of the issuance of the Declaration that guarantees these rights. One official in the Mordovian camps, touching upon the subject during one of the "political indoctrination sessions," explained: "The United Nations—but that's for Negroes." It seems to me that the Universal Declaration of Human Rights by the United Nations is not only for Negroes, but for Ukrainians as well. And as long as I live, I will strive to convince others of this.

Kiev, KGB Prison   *Valentyn Moroz*
December 10, 1968

10

MOROZ RELEASED

VALENTYN MOROZ was released on September 1, 1969. He had been arrested in 1965 in Ivano-Frankivsk and sentenced by the Volyn Regional Court to four years of imprisonment under Article 62 of the Criminal Code of the UkrSSR for disseminating anonymous *samvydav* articles on the state of affairs in Ukraine, for having his works published abroad, and for "oral agitation." In 1967, while in Mordovia, he wrote an essay, *A Report From the Beria Reservation,* which was widely disseminated in the Ukrainian *samvydav* and in the Russian *samizdat.* In 1967, the remainder of his term was changed from camp to prison confinement. However, he was not held long in Vladimir Prison, but was transferred to the investigation prison of the republican KGB in Kiev. There they questioned him as a witness in the case against Chornovil, but Moroz refused to give any testimony. At the beginning of 1968, they brought charges against Moroz under Article 62 of the Criminal Code of the UkrSSR for writing and disseminating the *Report.* Moroz completely boycotted the inquest, which lasted almost two years. The case was handled by investigator Kolchyk. He searched and questioned a number of persons in Kiev, Lviv, Ivano-Frankivsk, and Moscow, as well as several political prisoners.

Due to insufficient evidence, the investigation of Moroz was halted in March of 1969. This is one of the very few cases in which the KGB fully adhered to the letter of the law. V. Moroz was sent to complete his term in Vladimir Prison, from which he was later released. He now lives in Ivano-Frankivsk and is unemployed.

Chapter II

Taste of Freedom

11

To the Prosecutor of the UkrSSR
To Comrade Shelest, First Secretary of the CC CPU
To Comrade Nikitchenko, Chairman of the KGB of the
Council of Ministers of the UkrSSR

STATEMENT

On April 26, 1970, I was in the village of Kosmach of the Kosiv district, Ivano-Frankivsk region, attending Easter services along with scores of tourists who had come to see the Kosmach Easter, with its unique Easter eggs, traditional dress and songs. While tape-recording the Easter liturgy, I was approached by three strangers, reeking with the stench of cheap alcohol. Without any introduction or presentation of credentials, the drunkards insisted that I go with them. (I later learned that one of them was the principal of the local school and the other two were officials of the Kosiv District Committee). When I refused, the hooligans tried to use force. The surrounding crowd of faithful became indignant and called upon the hooligans to behave. This incident took place on church grounds during the consecration of the Easter bread. Thus, the people were deprived of the right of exercise of religious rites which is guaranteed by law.

I returned home on April 29. A few hours later, I was visited by KGB officials Pryhornytsky, Basysty, Baranov, and Ostrolutsky; following "fresh tracks," they came to search my apartment. The level of the search can best be judged by the fact that the confiscated items included Ivanychuk's *Hollyhocks* and the children's fable *Tomcat Murko* by Iryna Stasiv.[1] They took most of the older edition books and

[1] Iryna Stasiv-Kalynets (b. 1940): writer, college instructor; in July 1972 sentenced to six years of labor camp and three years of exile for "anti-Soviet agitation and propaganda"; wife of poet Ihor Kalynets (b. 1939), who in November 1972 was sentenced to nine years of hard-regime labor camp and three years of exile. They have one child.

magazines, irrespective of the content, and also poems by Symonenko, Lina Kostenko,[2] Vinhranovsky, and Drach. (This literature had "survived" three previous searches, but was now found to be seditious.) Seeing in a notebook of my son, a first-grader, the words "a Mauser pistol and eight cartridges," the provincial Sherlock Holmeses in all seriousness(!) demanded the pistol and eight cartridges. At great length I explained that the scribbling was in my son's handwriting, but, it seems, I never did convince them.

When I pointed out that according to search regulations only anti-Soviet works were subject to confiscation, I was told that they had the right to confiscate anything they deemed necessary.

During the search, the literary critic Volodymyr Ivanyshyn came to my apartment. He also was searched, in spite of his protests and without a warrant. They released him, but afterwards stopped him again on the street and took him to KGB Headquarters. In the process, they tore his suit and demonstrated a degree of brutality unusual even for KGB agents. This took place in the street to the indignant shoutings of a crowd. Even passing auxiliary policemen stood up for the unjustly apprehended man.

It is difficult to assess the danger to our government from "ideological diversions" from abroad about which the radio screams day and night. But I am convinced by what I have seen with my own eyes that the authority of the government is undermined by the "guardians of the law" and by drunken "cadres" from the District Committee who confiscate *Hollyhocks,* who search for weapons in children's notebooks, and who, by their marked disregard for legality, cause street riots.

May 2, 1970   *Valentyn Moroz*

[2]Lina Kostenko (b. 1930): considered the first of the "poets of the sixties"; one collection of her poems, printed in 1962, was immediately destroyed for political reasons; signed numerous protests against repressions; unpublished in UkrSSR since 1968.

158

12

To the Prosecutor of the UkrSSR
To the Chairman of the State Security Committee of the
Council of Ministers of the UkrSSR
From Citizen V. M. Ivanyshyn

COMPLAINT

I APPEAL to you in connection with the open assault and detention to which I was subjected by KGB officials in the city of Ivano-Frankivsk.

On April 29, 1970, I visited in Ivano-Frankivsk an acquaintance of mine, Valentyn Yakovych Moroz. At his apartment I came upon officials of the Ivano-Frankivsk KGB—Basysty, Ostrolutsky, Baranov and a fourth person whose identity I do not know—conducting a search. They also made an illegal search of my person. Although they found nothing on me, they demanded, without presenting any warrant, that I go to the KGB Department of Investigations, ostensibly to clarify some matter. I categorically refused and protested. After two hours, I was allowed to leave. . . . I promised Moroz that I would return in a few hours.

When I returned, the search was still on and they would not let me into the house. Basysty, one of those conducting the search, led me out into the street and again demanded that I go to KGB Headquarters. I again protested that this demand was unlawful. Then Basysty and Ostrolutsky resorted to force and twisted my arms behind my back. I freed myself and walked off. On Mateyko Street I was overtaken by a Volga. There were four of them in the car, including the driver. They all jumped at me, trying to knock me off my feet; the driver kept shouting vulgar abuse. A crowd gathered. Those who tried to intervene in my behalf were chased away by agents waving KGB credentials. They scratched my arms and legs and ripped the buttons and sleeves on my suit and shirt. Several times I asked why they were taking me, but without so much as a word, they grabbed at me and twisted my arms until they threw me into the car.

For any person to be detained and searched, well-founded suspicion and proper authorization are needed. The above-mentioned KGB officials violated these precepts of Soviet legality, they vulgarly insulted my human dignity, for which they should be held accountable.

It became clear at the KGB regional office that there were no substantive charges against me. The KGB officials Cherkasov and Kovalchuk demanded that I write a statement explaining the purpose of my trip to Ivano-Frankivsk and my visit with V. Y. Moroz. They also demanded that I surrender my passport, which I had already shown as identification at Moroz's apartment. I refused to submit it to them on the grounds that they were not competent in this matter (it was a question of updating the passport to indicate an extension of the residency permit).

On Cherkasov's orders, a police detachment transported me, as they would a criminal, in a regular police vehicle (the "Raven") to the police station in order to confiscate my passport. I was finally released at 10:40 p.m. All told, I had spent seven and one-half hours at the KGB office and the police station.

In our country, where the Constitution guarantees to everyone the inviolability of his person, what happened to me must be considered a street mugging in broad daylight.

Please see to it that the above-mentioned KGB officials and the driver are made to answer for their actions. Persons who abuse their authority during the performance of their duties should be punished.

May 1, 1970 *Volodymyr Mykhaylovych Ivanyshyn*
Village of Duba
Rozhnyativ District
Ivano-Frankivsk Region

13

KGB SEARCH REV. ROMANYUK'S[1] HOME

IN the beginning of May 1970, agents of the district and regional KGB searched the home of Rev. Vasyl Romanyuk in Kosmach, Kosiv district of the Ivano-Frankivsk region. They were looking for "anti-Soviet" documents and essays by V. Moroz; they found none, but did confiscate several old books, among them a pre-Revolutionary edition of a *History of Ukraine.* The search was apparently linked with the above-mentioned incident with Moroz, or with the fact that Rev. Romanyuk had a number of guests for Easter from Ivano-Frankivsk, Kiev and other cities.

---

[1]Rev. Vasyl Romanyuk (b. 1922): in June 1972 sentenced to seven years of hard-regime labor camp and three years of exile for "anti-Soviet agitation and propaganda"; currently in Vladimir Prison.

14

"AMID THE SNOWS" IN "SAMVYDAV"

Samvydav is circulating two works criticizing the now well-known statement of I. Dzyuba to the Ukrainian Writers' Union, which was published on January 3, 1970, in *Literary Ukraine.*

Vyacheslav Chornovil, in the introduction to his collection of polemical notes *What B. Stenchuk Defends and How He Does It* (aimed at Stenchuk's[1] book *What Y. Dzyuba Defends and How He Does It*), calls Dzyuba's statement "without a doubt, a wrong move." He, however, considers this a singular act, as compared to all of Dzyuba's previous works and actions, and he considers it unnecessary (and even counter-productive) to speak of a change in I. Dzyuba's position, of his demise, etc.

Valentyn Moroz, in his essay *Amid the Snows,* delves further into this matter. He analyzes the reason for the emergence of the "poets of the sixties" in Ukrainian literary and civic life as well as the current processes within their midst. In this context, he sees Dzyuba's statement as a natural outcome of their loss of *obsession,* which earlier had been part of their character.

A certain portion of the public (even some who find fault in Dzyuba's statement) considers the above-mentioned open criticism of Dzyuba unnecessary. They argue that the text of Dzyuba's statement is not conclusive enough for one to state that there has been a change in principles, but that it can be viewed as a tactical compromise, be it successful or not.

---

[1]Bohdan Stenchuk: pseudonym; author unknown.

Chapter III

Second Arrest

15

ANOTHER CAMPAIGN AGAINST
VALENTYN MOROZ IN PROGRESS!

ON June 1, 1970, Ivano-Frankivsk KGB agents again arrested the Ukrainian civic activist, historian and publicist Valentyn Moroz. The name of Valentyn Moroz is known to the Ukrainian public; therefore, we will only briefly retrace the course of his life.

Valentyn Yakovych Moroz was born on April 15, 1936, in the Horokhiv district, Volyn region, into a peasant family. After completing his secondary education, he studied at the Department of History at Lviv University. After graduating from the university, he worked as a teacher in his native district and afterwards lectured in history at the Lutsk and Ivano-Frankivsk teachers colleges. He was also working on his dissertation on the revolutionary struggle of the workers and peasants of Western Ukraine against the Polish bourgeois regime.

On September 1, 1965, Valentyn Moroz was arrested in Ivano-Frankivsk and sent for preliminary investigation to Lutsk. He was charged with "anti-Soviet propaganda and agitation aimed at subverting or weakening the Soviet rule" (Art. 62, Sec. 1 of the Criminal Code of the Ukrainian SSR) for reading and distributing *samvydav* articles and foreign publications (I. Koshelivets, *Contemporary Literature in the Ukrainian SSR*; articles "Concerning the Trial of Pohruzhalsky," "The Answer to Vasyl Symonenko's Mother," and others). Disoriented by the unexpected arrest and the investigation methods, V. Moroz confirmed the testimony of a number of people and partly admitted a certain element of crime in his actions. But he did not refute his views, and at his trial in Lutsk in January 1966 (the trial was open), he defended them. He was sentenced to four years of imprisonment in hard-labor camps and sent to Mordovia. During his imprisonment, he openly protested against his conviction and against the actions of the prison-camp authorities, and was punished for it several times. Moroz spent only several months as an ordinary prisoner in the concentration camp. The rest of the time he spent in penal solitary cells, strict-regime barracks and prisons.

During imprisonment, Valentyn Moroz crystallized his convictions. This is reflected in his work, *A Report from the Beria Reservation* (dated April 15, 1967), which was smuggled out of the camp and widely disseminated in the Ukrainian and Russian *samvydavs*.

In autumn 1967, V. Moroz was transferred from Vladimir Prison to the investigation prison of the Ukrainian KGB in Kiev, where he was kept for a time as a witness in the case of V. Chornovil and later as one charged with writing and disseminating the *Report*. V. Moroz did not cooperate with the investigation, which lasted more than a year and was closed in the beginning of 1969 due to the lack of evidence of authorship. V. Moroz was then sent back to Vladimir Prison, from where he was released on September 1, 1969.

V. Moroz was unemployed from the time of his release to his new arrest. He tried to find a job (as an apprentice wood worker, meteorological assistant, etc.), but obstacles were always put in his path. He was permitted to work as a construction worker, which he refused.

From his very first day of freedom, V. Moroz became active in civic life, attempting to either revitalize those national forces which had appeared in the mid-sixties, or form new ones. He wrote three essays (*Moses and Dathan, A Chronicle of Resistance* and *Amid the Snows*) in which he touched on the acute problems of national existence and national ethics.

Well-written and substantive, Valentyn Moroz's articles gained popularity and evoked lively and often sharp debate among the Ukrainian public (this is especially true about *Amid the Snows,* written on the occasion of I. Dzyuba's letter to the Presidium of the Writers' Union of Ukraine). Prior to

166

his arrest V. Moroz had started to write a major work about the national outlook of Lesya Ukrainka (on the occasion of her 100th anniversary).

In April 1970, during Easter holidays, a provocation was staged involving V. Moroz in the village of Kosmach, in the Hutsul region. Obviously following instructions from above, representatives of the local authorities wanted to arrest V. Moroz merely because he recorded Easter songs near the church, but the inhabitants of Kosmach prevented the arrest.

Here we bring in the statement to the Prosecutor of Ivano-Frankivsk region, signed on behalf of the community by several Kosmach residents. We have retained the style of the account.

STATEMENT

We, the citizens of the village of Kosmach, Kosiv district, Ivano-Frankivsk region, turn to you with our grievance with respect to what occurred in our village and church grounds on Easter during the blessing of the *paska*.[1]

When the priest had blessed the *paska,* a great commotion arose among the people. They started to yell. Some say that they're hitting people, others say arresting. The people were greatly alarmed. There was a man standing among the people and by him stood our school principal, Comrade Didukh Mykhaylo Andriyovych, and with him still two more comrades. Didukh started to pull this man by the hand because we, the choir members, had asked this man to record on his tape recorder a church song; that is why these comrades started to pull the man by the hand. Then this man said—"What evil have I done to you people that I am being arrested?" The people started yelling—"Why do you drag the man from the people and ruin the people's good mood and persecute religion?" Then Didukh summoned Hrebenchuk, a village official, and he followed this man down the

[1] Easter bread.

167

street, but all the people followed him and didn't allow the man to be taken; we said that he was not to blame, since we had asked him to record our song.

This is why we ask you, the Prosecutor, to investigate our complaint, to look into everything; can it really be like this, for us to have our good dispositions ruined near the Church and for religion to be persecuted.

Our school principal Mykhaylo Didukh and the Chairman of the Village Council, Comrade Ivan Vasylyovych Klaptsunyak, sit in our teahouse every day over shotglasses, and don't look out for order in the village, for the fact that we have no bridges, that it's been a year since the waters took them away, and no one pays any mind so that roads would be constructed, so that there would be order, a road, and bridges in the village.

Up until this year, we never had such a thing happen here, that people should be pulled from the church grounds.

We ask you to act on our request. We, the people of Kosmach.

Olena Knyshchuk   *Dmytro Klaptsunyak*
Hanna Bervenychuk   *Vasylyna Polyak*
Yurko Lyndyuk   *Petro Polyak*
Anna Senchuk

(As could have been expected, as a result of the statement all of the signers were called in for questioning, at which time demands were made of them to retract their signatures and to name the "instigator.")

As soon as Valentyn Moroz returned home, a group of KGB functionaries from Ivano-Frankivsk Regional Headquarters (Maj. Baranov, Capt. Pryhornytsky, Capt. Basysty, Sen. Lt. Ostrolutsky) came to his room at the Teachers College dormitory, where he lived with his family, and searched it. They took many old editions (all of them had been in his room during three previous searches in 1965, 1967 and 1968, but had not been confiscated), letters, notebooks, work diaries with various excerpts and rough notes (most of them from the period of imprisonment, already checked by the KGB of the Ukrainian Republic), as well as tape recordings of folklore material. Of *samvydav* material, the following were confiscated: Vira Vovk's speech in Kiev at the Society for Cultural Ties with Ukrainians Abroad, excerpts from O. Poltoratsky's article, *What is Ostap Vyshnya*, I. Dzyuba's speech at an evening for Symonenko at the Ukrainian Writers' Union in January 1965, and an article by the political prisoner Masyutko about the letter "g,"[2] which was sent out of Vladimir Prison through legal channels. Among confiscated literary works were typescripts of poems by Symonenko (mainly reprints), by I. Drach, Lina Kostenko, I. Kalynets,[3] H. Chubay,[4] children's fables by I. Stasiv, a humorous piece by an unknown author, *I Saw Mohammed*, etc.

During the search, one typescript copy each of V. Moroz's articles, *A Chronicle of Resistance* and *Amid the Snows*, as well as a number of letters and notes, privately passed to V. Moroz, in which his articles had been mentioned, were also taken away.

As it became clear later, a case against V. Moroz had already been initiated at that time, and an investigation started, although Moroz himself was unaware of it.

In the middle of May, a search was carried out at the home of the Rev. Vasyl Romanyuk, the parish priest of Kosmach, in connection with V. Moroz's case. Notebooks with various chance notations and a great number of items of religious literature (mostly published prior to the Revolution) were taken from him, and have not yet been returned. Nothing

---

[2]The letter "g" was eliminated from the Ukrainian alphabet in the 1930's by the Ukrainian Academy of Sciences allegedly in the interest of linguistic reform. The "g" sound, however, remains in the spoken word. This action is considered by some Ukrainians as a conscious effort at Russification.

[3]Ihor Kalynets: husband of Iryna Stasiv-Kalynets (see fn. 1, p. 157).

[4]Hryhir Chubay: young poet and artist.

relating to V. Moroz was found at Rev. Romanyuk's.

On June 1, 1970, Valentyn Moroz received a summons to appear at the regional office of the KGB, where he was arrested. This happened exactly nine months after his release. . . .

Simultaneously with the arrest of Moroz on June 1, searches were carried out in Kiev, Lviv, Ivano-Frankivsk, at the residences of former political prisoners Lyubov Lemyk[5] (Ivano-Frankivsk), Oksana Meshko[6] (Kiev), Iryna Senyk[7] (Ivano-Frankivsk), Vyacheslav Chornovil (Lviv). Searches were also made in the little town of Yaremche, in the Hutsul area, at the homes of Moroz's acquaintances, where he sometimes spent his holidays, as well as at the house of the parents of the literary critic Volodymyr Ivanyshyn in the Rozhnyativ district (Ivano-Frankivsk region). Another search was carried out at V. Moroz's flat, and all notes made during the month since the first search (especially the notes relating to the article about Lesya Ukrainka) were confiscated.

While in Kiev and Lviv the KGB agents behaved reasonably politely during the searches, in Ivano-Frankivsk, where former members of the Organization of Ukrainian Nationalists movement were searched, they behaved in a rough manner and resorted to threats and verbal abuse. For example, KGB agents Andrusiv and Zavhorodniy, who carried out the search at Lyubov Lemyk's home, used foul language (particularly Zavhorodniy), addressed her in a rude manner, and even had body searches made on the people present;

[5]Lyubov Lemyk (b. 1915): sentenced in 1947 to imprisonment and exile for Red Cross work for the Ukrainian Insurgent Army fighting Soviet occupation. Released from prison camp in 1957; from exile in 1963.

[6]Oksana Meshko (b. 1905): served same term in Stalinist labor camp as L. Lemyk, above; writer of numerous protests, especially in the case of Moroz.

[7]Iryna Senyk (b. 1925): poetess; served same sentence as Lemyk and Meshko (fns. 5, 6, above); in 1972 sentenced to seven years' labor camp and five years' exile for "anti-Soviet agitation and propaganda."

Lyubov Lemyk, her sister Mariya and her niece Daryna, as well as a complete outsider, Oksana Popovych, who happened to come to see L. Lemyk during the search, were made to undress completely. The brutal procedure of the body search was carried out with professional skill by a certain Anastasiya Lavrentyeva, who had been brought in specially by the KGB and later identified in the search records as a "witness."

The KGB behaved in a similarly brutal manner at Iryna Senyk's home.

During the searches, old editions of books, notebooks, manuscript notes, typescript material of a completely neutral character (poems, linguistic and literary studies, etc.) were taken away; at V. Chornovil's even an old icon was confiscated. Nothing forbidden, not one article by Moroz or anything relating to his case was found on the premises of those searched (papers and other items, in some cases partially, have already been returned to some of them).

A few days after Valentyn Moroz's arrest, it became known that he was charged under Art. 62, Sec. 2 of the UCC, which calls for a term of imprisonment of from three to ten years. The case was conducted by an investigations officer of the Ivano-Frankivsk Regional KGB, Baranov, assisted by Pryhornytsky. It is known that Baranov has been working for state security organs since the time of Beria. In 1949, for instance, he conducted the case of a group of students of the Polytechnical Institute in Lviv and teen-age pupils from Zolochiv district, Lviv region, who were charged with attempts at anti-Soviet propaganda. On the basis of his investigation, the three-man OSO (Special Conference) sentenced the students to twenty-five years of imprisonment and the teenagers to ten years.

In 1965-1966, Baranov conducted the case of the painter Panas Zalyvakha, subsequently sentenced under Art. 62 ("anti-Soviet propaganda") to five years' imprisonment. The sentence given to P. Zalyvakha for the "crime" uncovered by the investigation is regarded as being exceedingly cruel even when compared to the severe sentences given out then. Baranov was also one of the investigations officers who conducted the case of the Ukrainian National Front in 1967 which also ended with very severe sentences (from six to fifteen years of imprisonment).

The indictment against V. Moroz originally made much use of the articles *Moses and Dathan, A Chronicle of Resistance* and *Amid the Snows,* as well as the humoristic story *I Saw Mohammed,* whose authorship has been ascribed to Moroz by the KGB without sufficient evidence. But in so far as it would have been difficult to classify the above-mentioned works as "anti-Soviet" and to assemble sufficient proof as to their "dissemination," the KGB did what, from the legal point of view, was very doubtful and, from the ethical point of view, inhumane and cruel.

Without any new incriminating evidence or testimony regarding the *Report from the Beria Reservation* at their disposal, the KGB nevertheless reversed their previous decision to close the case against Moroz for writing the *Report,* adopted in the spring of 1969. There are those who believe that the KGB thus smacked itself in the face and signed its name under an admission that it did not recognize any guarantees of justice and the inviolability of the individual. It seems that it would have been perhaps "more humane" and "more decent" to convict Moroz for his *Report* in 1969, than to close his case, entice the man with short-lived freedom, and then to throw him again behind bars on the identical charge. Some people connect this decision with a change in the leadership of the KGB in the Ukrainian SSR (Nazarchuk replaced Gen. Nikitchenko, who was dismissed in the summer of 1970).

About 30 people were questioned in connection with the Valentyn Moroz case. Testimony given by Volodymyr Ivanyshyn and O. Meshko (Kiev), O. Antoniv and Sheremetyeva (Lviv), D. Voznyak, M. Voznyak,[8] L. Volynyuk, L. Lemyk, R.

[8]Mariya Voznyak (b. 1913) : served same sentence as Lemyk (fn. 5) and Meshko (fn. 6), above.

Moroz (Valentyn's wife), O. Popovych, I. Senyk (Ivano-Fankivsk), V. Babyak and V. Romanyuk (Kosmach) and a number of other persons, have been more or less similar. All of them denied ever reading Moroz's articles or hearing about them. O. Antoniv, R. Moroz, and L. Sheremetyeva, who were again questioned about the *Report*, stated that they could not add any new testimony to that given in 1968.

Testimony by Antonenko-Davydovych, A. Horska,[9] M. Plakhtonyuk, Yevhen Sverstyuk (all from Kiev), by V. Chornovil (Lviv), whose letters or notes had been taken away from V. Moroz, and also by Ivan Dzyuba, to whom the article *Amid the Snows* had been addressed, differed somewhat. The artist Alla Horska stated that lines from her postcard mentioning "a flower amid the snows" had been misinterpreted, and they did not mean that she was acquainted with the essay *Amid the Snows*. Similarly, Mykola Plakhtonyuk, a medical doctor, denied any knowledge of Moroz's works, saying that he had used several general phrases about these articles in a note so as not to offend the author's pride by admitting to Moroz that he had not read them. Literary critic Yevhen Sverstyuk explained that in a letter to Moroz he had discussed Moroz's appraisal of Dzyuba's statement, but had not touched upon *Amid the Snows*, which he had not read. Vyacheslav Chornovil explained his letter in a similar way. He too refused to give new testimony about the *Report*, saying that he stood by his statements in 1968-69. For several months before, V. Chornovil refused to give any testimony at all until his papers

[9]Alla Horska (1929-1970) : artist; born into a family that was completely Russified; became "Ukrainianized" during the national revival period in the 1960's; circulated *samvydav* materials; wrote letters of protest, defending arrested intellectuals; in 1964 was commissioned, along with three other artists, to create a large stained-glass window for the main entrance of Kiev University; the window, depicting the poet Taras Shevchenko, was judged nationalistic, destroyed, and Alla Horska was expelled from the Artists' Union of Ukraine. Alla Horska was brutally murdered on November 28, 1970, under questionable, and so far unexplained, circumstances.

and effects, unlawfully taken from him during the search of June 1, were returned to him.

Only the critic Ivan Dzyuba and the writer Borys Antonenko-Davydovych confirmed that they were acquainted with some of the works by Moroz. I. Dzyuba testified that V. Moroz gave him a copy of *Amid the Snows*, because it had been written on the occasion of Dzyuba's statement and was, in fact, addressed to him. B. Antonenko-Davydovych testified that V. Moroz gave him the unfinished versions of *Amid the Snows* and *Moses and Dathan* and asked him to give his writer's opinion, which he later did in a letter to Moroz.

Characteristically, all those questioned denied that Moroz's writings or conversations had any anti-Soviet bias. V. Chornovil, in particular, insisted that his own written statement on this matter be included in the record of the questioning; this was done. B. Antonenko-Davydovych called Moroz's ideas erroneous, but denied that they were anti-Soviet. He also protested against the attempt to interpret the fact that Moroz turned to him for literary advice as evidence of "dissemination." None of the questioned persons admitted that he had read or even heard of the work *I Saw Mohammed*.

Thus the investigation, which ended in the middle of October 1970, failed to assemble any new evidence that V. Moroz was the author of the *Report from the Beria Reservation*, nor did it establish who was the author of the humoristic story *I Saw Mohammed*. It is not clear how the investigation managed to prove that the articles *Moses and Dathan*, *A Chronicle of Resistance*, and *Amid the Snows* had an anti-Soviet bias. The fact that V. Moroz showed two essays which in one way or another touched on the literary process to two members of the Writers' Union of Ukraine is absolutely insufficient grounds for asserting that he personally "disseminated" his articles. Nevertheless, without even having collected formally sufficient evidence of guilt, the KGB found it possible to hand over his case to the court.

It is known that during the investigation Valentyn Moroz

conducted himself in a steadfast, manly and dignified manner. Immediately after his arrest, he demanded that the investigation be transferred from Ivano-Frankivsk, basing his demand on the incompetence and prejudice of the Ivano-Frankivsk KGB personnel. His demand was rejected. V. Moroz then refused to take any part in the investigation. He departed from this principle only when B. Antonenko-Davydovych's testimony was read to him. He disagreed with it, but nevertheless did not sign the record of the questioning. Afterwards, an eye-to-eye confrontation was arranged, during which V. Moroz again denied that he personally gave his articles to Antonenko-Davydovych. V. Moroz did not sign the record of the confrontation.

It is known that during the investigation, V. Moroz wrote a letter to P. Yu. Shelest, in which he stated that his arrest was without any grounds, that it was the expression of the powerless rage of reactionary forces of society doomed to collapse. The letter was sharp and uncompromising, and without any requests by Moroz to lighten his personal lot.

The Valentyn Moroz "case" has now been handed over to the regional court. The date of the trial is not yet known. Moscow lawyer Kogan (who conducted Sinyavsky's case in 1966) will defend V. Moroz. At first, the well-known attorney V. B. Romm (Moscow) agreed to defend Moroz, but soon afterwards he was forbidden to take part in any political trials.

16

To Comrade O. P. Lyashko, Chairman of the Presidium
of the Supreme Council of the UkrSSR
Cc: Comrade V. F. Nikitchenko, Chairman of the KGB
Comrade B. E. Paton, Member of the Supreme Council
of the UkrSSR

STATEMENT

ON JUNE 2, 1970, KGB agents searched my apartment without providing reasons for doing so.

They were looking for letters from Valentyn Moroz, for anti-Soviet literature and for "other objects banned from general use." Nothing was confiscated; nothing compromising was found.

It is difficult to understand, however, what literature is considered to be anti-Soviet, what objects are subject to confiscation; no list drawn-up and approved by appropriate authorities, which would clearly state what books, articles, etc., were banned and subject to confiscation, was presented to me before the search.

I find just this fact itself very deplorable.

But most of all I was upset by the news of the arrest of Valentyn Moroz.

I know Valentyn personally. I talked with him several times when he had returned to freedom after four years of imprisonment. He was worn-out and exhausted, but spiritually lucid and humane, attractive in his selfless concern for the good and justice for all mankind.

I heard about Valentyn Moroz as far back as 1965; then he was tried for the first time in Lutsk, not on a charge of tangibly proven crimes, but essentially for his convictions.

He spent only nine months at liberty, unemployed, in an atmosphere poisoned by the surveillance of that Ivano-Frankivsk institution which had prevented him from finding employment in his own profession, which followed at his heels wherever he went, which provoked the incident in the village of Kosmach, where he had been recording Hutsul Easter folk traditions.

What has he ever seen of the world?

Straight from the student's desk, he taught for several years; then came the sham trial of 1965 and four years of imprisonment and concentration camps.

After his release in September 1969, was he permitted enough time to take a close look at our reality? Was he allowed to develop freely the creative force of his uncommon intellect?

I myself experienced all the horrors of concentration camps of the cult period when I was sentenced for no reason at all to ten years of imprisonment; the eventful finale—rehabilitation and apologies. . . .

I cannot remain indifferent to the violation of legality in our socialist Fatherland.

I consider it my moral duty and my right to rise in defense of Valentyn Moroz, who committed no crime—he is incapable of crime.

I am appealing to you who have been given official power and delegated authority and am asking you to deal with the case of Valentyn Moroz in such a manner that it will be judged fairly and constitutionally.

June 17, 1970   *Oksana Yakivna Meshko*
16 Verbolozna
Kiev 86

17

To O. T. Honchar,
Chairman of the Writers' Union of Ukraine,
Deputy to the Supreme Soviet of the USSR

Dear Oles Terentiyovych,

WE believe it to be our duty to inform you, a writer and a member of the highest agency of our country, that Valentyn Moroz, a talented publicist and former history instructor at the Ivano-Frankivsk Pedagogical Institute, was arrested again on June 1, 1970.

He returned to Ivano-Frankivsk in the fall of last year after four years of imprisonment and was hardly able to take a good look around or even find a job.

His highly controversial writings, with which some of us were able to become acquainted in manuscript form, show only an unusual literary talent. It is impossible to ascribe to them the anti-Soviet character of which (as may be seen from the preliminary investigations) he is accused of today. Moral and cultural problems, national and ethnic problems, human spiritual development in line with the writings of Lesya Ukrainka—these are the things he has dealt with recently. We shall not attempt a value judgment of his work—evaluations may vary, if only because of the consciously controversial character of his articles, but is it possible that these important current world problems fall within the competence of the security agencies?

We are appealing to you, Oles Terentiyovych, to raise the question of the fate of Valentyn Moroz with appropriate authorities and to help ensure that it is decided in accordance with the needs of our society. What we need today are wholesome and honest forces capable of perception and with the civic courage to raise pertinent questions, who become unselfishly involved in today's issues of national importance.

Yours truly,

I. Dzyuba
I. Svitlychny
Z. Franko[1]
V. Chornovil
E. Sverstyuk

---

[1]Zinoviya Franko (b. 1925): linguist; granddaughter of Ukrainian literary giant Ivan Franko; interrogated in the spring of 1972; recanted; currently writing pro-regime articles for Soviet periodicals aimed at the West.

18

To Oles Terentiyovych Honchar,
Chairman of the Writers' Union of Ukraine,
Deputy to the Supreme Soviet of the USSR

Dear Oles Terentiyovych,

I AM writing to you on a matter not customarily discussed in our country, even though it concerns the most fundamental premises of life in our society.

I have learned that Valentyn Moroz, a history teacher by profession, who was sentenced in 1965 to four years of imprisonment and has served his term, was arrested again on June 1st of this year in Ivano-Frankivsk and is now on trial.

He is now charged with the same crime against our republic as on the previous occasion: attempts to weaken (if not to overthrow) the existing social order (Article 62 of the Criminal Code).

I do not know whether the prosecution in Ivano-Frankivsk has grounds for such charges. I am convinced, however (in part because of my personal experience), that prison cannot be regarded as a suitable place for "the corrective rehabilitation of enemies of the people." Prison invariably means grief, sorrow, misfortune. This is even more applicable when you speak not of habitual criminals, murderers and spies and saboteurs who are marked for solitary confinement, but of people employed in intellectual pursuits.

I also know that prosecuting agencies are fond of creating the appearance of a threat to society from people having the courage to openly express their views on certain aspects of our life. I still remember the mass arrests of young Ukrainian intellectuals in 1965 (even for reading an article or a book considered undesirable). Were these arrests really necessary? Was it not possible to avoid them? Can we really claim with certainty today that these arrests bore some positive results? Were these people really so harmful that it was imperative to use such drastic methods on them? I am convinced that any unprejudiced person confronted with the available facts will conclude that these arrests did nothing but harm to our society. They did us no good. On the contrary, they multiplied our problems. This is true even if we were to ignore the question of guilt or innocence of the people arrested, but what if we do indeed cast doubt on their guilt?

Under these circumstances, arrests of young Soviet intellectuals for expressing critical thoughts about what they believe to be shortcomings in our society appear to me simply as obtuse cruelty on the part of certain representatives of our law-enforcement agencies who occupy positions of trust and should therefore temper their passions.

It is said that Valentyn Moroz is a talented writer and publicist. In all fairness, it is also said that the tone of his journalistic writings is quite sharp. (But what else can you expect from a talented, strong-willed individual after four years of imprisonment?)

But let us consider something else, while there is still time. To what extent is this latest arrest justified? Will anything be gained from it? (I am personally convinced that the answer is No). Does the prosecution in Ivano-Frankivsk have sufficient grounds to hold Valentyn Moroz responsible for the seriousness of the charges under Article 62?

These questions torment me. I find it very risky to leave their solution entirely in the hands of the prosecution.

I, therefore, appeal to you, Oles Terentiyovych. I appeal to you because you are a writer and a man highly respected by our people. I also write to you because you are the Chairman of the Writers' Union of Ukraine and a member of the Supreme Soviet of the USSR.

It is your official duty, your duty as a writer and as a human being to take interest in the fate of Valentyn Moroz. The deciding of his fate must be placed under the effective control of the people. Be assured that our society can only gain from it.

Dubova 32
Lviv 27

Truly yours,
Mykhaylo Kosiv

181

19

To Comrade Oles Terentiyovych Honchar,
Chairman of the Writers' Union of Ukraine,
Deputy to the Supreme Soviet of the USSR

Dear Oles Terentiyovych,

ON JUNE 1, 1970, in Ivano-Frankivsk, the city bearing the
name of one of the most freedom-loving representatives of
Ukrainian culture, Valentyn Moroz was arrested. The victim's wife informed me of this sad event. On the basis of
preliminary interrogations, it is apparent that Valentyn
Moroz is accused of having been motivated by anti-Soviet
feelings in his sharply controversial and well-written articles.
These articles reflect the kaleidoscopic issues of contemporary
Soviet life in the areas of national relations, education, ethics,
honor and pride of our citizens in the national and cultural
heritage and artistic traditions of the great and talented
Ukrainian people.

The diversity of Valentyn Moroz's subject-matter, the
topical and controversial nature of his writings and their
fiery style aroused those among the intelligentsia who, in one
way or another, became acquainted with the literary output
of Valentyn Moroz to heated discussions on the need to carry
on the glorious traditions in the arts and in social action of
the industrious and freedom-loving Ukrainian people.

These are the themes, Oles Terentiyovych, which, it seems
to me, distinctly and loudly pulsate in your own recent works,
particularly in the novels *The Cathedral* and *The Cyclone*.
Even such problems as the scattering and huckstering of
Hutsul folk art ring in both your own writings and those of
Valentyn Moroz. And this is the most eloquent proof that
Valentyn Moroz is a young, socially sensitive writer who sees
the important problems of today—the same problems which
cause you pain and concern; you, a talented writer respected
and honored by our people, our teacher and leader.

Dear Oles Terentiyovych!

I am not a personal friend of Valentyn Moroz. I even disagree with some of his controversial ideas and rash generalizations. But I am, after all, the same age as Valentyn Moroz. I am hurt by the thought of the moral face which our Fatherland—mine and yours—presents to the world when it ruthlessly isolates from our society people to whom courage and expression of individuality have become the guarantees of honesty in social involvement.

I appeal to you, a member of the Supreme Soviet of the USSR, to do everything to assure that the fate of Valentyn Moroz will be placed under the effective control and protection of our community. Through the strength of moral authority and prestige we must insist:

1. That Valentyn Moroz publicly declare that he is not being beaten and that he is not being subjected to any psychological pressure;

2. That the texts of Valentyn Moroz's articles, which have been declared anti-Soviet, be made public;

3. That an objective and unbiased commission of the most qualified writers be formed, and that this commission provide a true, and not ordered, analysis and evaluation of the writings of Valentyn Moroz;

4. That the case of Valentyn Moroz be made a matter of public record.

In the name of humaneness, in the name of our native Ukrainian culture and literature, in the name of socialist legality.

July 7, 1970   Respectfully,
Lviv   *Mykhaylo Osadchy*[1]

[1]Mykhaylo Osadchy (b. 1936): writer, university professor; sentenced in September 1972 to seven years of hard-regime labor camp and three years of exile for "anti-Soviet agitation and propaganda"; previously imprisoned for two years (1966-68); married; two children. His autobiographical novel, *Bilmo* (*Cataract*), has been published in French (*Cataracte*, Fayard, Paris, 1974).

20

To the CC CPU,
To the KGB at the Council of Ministers of UkrSSR.

EVERYONE today realizes that we are living on the eve of great change. This is discussed in *samvydav*, in speeches made at plenary sessions of the Central Committee, in conversations among commuters and around the family table.

The last decade was marked by a nearly systematic deterioration in both our material and spiritual lives. The overall devaluation of standards—from the value of the ruble to many economic, political and ethical concepts—continue.

I am convinced that A. Solzhenitsyn and Yu. Andropov, V. Nikitchenko and V. Moroz, V. Kozachenko and I. Dzyuba, I. Svitlychny and M. Shamota[1] feel almost the same degree of need to solve many of today's problems.

The need for a wholesome dialogue grows. We need a referendum on many questions. Unfortunately, healthy discussion of many problems is forbidden. True, these problems are discussed, but in abnormal circumstances: either at closed party meetings, or in *samvydav* literature. The abnormality of the circumstances makes it impossible to arrive at the truth and leads to a situation where even the truth, when and if discovered, becomes abnormal, because it exists only for a few individuals and, being a "secret," a "mystery," it understandably evokes resistance of the people.

The lack of this vital dialogue creates a fertile ground for escalation of disagreement and discord. Each participant of a silent discussion is seen as if through a magnifying glass. A person assuming a different position is regarded by the opposite side as . . . the enemy!

Here is an example of a situation where abnormal condi-

[1]An antipodal grouping of names.

tions quite logically create "enemies of the people" and lead to extreme polarization.

A person "V" addresses an agency "N" with concrete proposals and suggestions and receives no reply. "V" writes again and once more—no reply. Then "V" becomes indignant. He writes again, but in a sharper tone, even though the sharpness of his tone is merely a reaction to the deafness of the agency "N," whose duty it is to respond. And what happens next? "V" is asked to report to another agency and is threatened or, worse, is placed for a long time behind bars.

This is the undesirable result of a lack of dialogue; both agencies are well aware of the fact that "V" is right, but "V" is put in jail, because the time is not yet ripe for speaking of the problems raised by "V". True, both agencies will be discussing the problems raised by "V" some ten years from now (and are talking about them privately even now!), but before these problems become general knowledge, the unfortunate "futurologist" will have served his sentence and will return as a convinced enemy of both agencies. And he will be right; his only "crime" was being born ten years before his time!

Simply and obviously—a man is born in order to live. And when a society accuses a man of having been born before his time, it deprives him of the right to live. This society becomes a murderer.

It is sad to note that by forbidding people to take an individualistic stand in life our society assumes the responsibility for their spiritual or physical death. Such a society cannot be called humane.

It is dreadfully painful and embarrassing to think of the fate of Valentyn Moroz, who was arrested two months ago for writing a few controversial articles. This is a clear example of a man being denied the right to live. For think of what it means to deny a human being the right to think and to express his thoughts! Valentyn Moroz is undoubtedly an unusually talented writer. He is a kind, humane writer, sometimes harsh and angry, but never vicious. His sharp tone and anger stem from his desire to help people, not from any inclination to shame, humiliate or insult them. It is no accident that he is interested in the problems of culture, people, honor. His writings are permeated with pain for the violated soul of the individual, of culture, of the nation. This is a human being of the highest ethical order, a valiant, brave and honest man.

In normal circumstances it would have been possible and necessary to argue with him. But how unconscionable such arguments would be now, when Valentyn Moroz is being summarily persecuted.

He is being dealt with by people least capable of honest and open discussion!

In my opinion, to demand that the charges against Valentyn Moroz be dropped is a matter of conscience and honor for every human being in the USSR who values the good name of his society, his country, his native soil.

And I appeal to you to do everything to assure that the possible trial of Valentyn Moroz does not serve to dishonor us again.

Respectfully,

July 28, 1970   *Vasyl Stus*[2]

[2]Vasyl Stus (b. 1938) : poet, literary critic; sentenced in September 1972 to five years of hard-regime labor camp and three years of exile for "anti-Soviet agitation and propaganda."

21

To the Chairman of the Council of Ministers of the
UkrSSR
To the First Secretary of the CC CPU
To the Chairman of the Committee on State Security of
the UkrSSR
To the Chief Prosecutor of the UkrSSR

STATEMENT

WITH this statement we express our protest against the arrest of Valentyn Moroz in Ivano-Frankivsk. We live in a
country where there should be no political prisoners among
our citizens, since freedom of speech is guaranteed by the
Constitutions of the UkrSSR and the USSR. Everyone has
the right to take interest in national matters and to express
personal opinions about these matters openly and frankly.
An enemy, if he is truly an enemy, never reveals his face and
is secretive. We are certain that Valentyn Moroz could not
have concealed anything. He probably was, however, painfully concerned, as are all honest men, about current problems
pertaining to the preservation of the arts, culture, learning
and traditions.

An enemy, if he is a real enemy, gains by his actions. What
did Valentyn Moroz gain? After four years of totally unjust
imprisonment from 1965, he knew only unemployment, and
then was arrested once more.

On what grounds was Valentyn Moroz arrested? For
having openly expressed his thoughts, which should have
been discussed in the press? Or perhaps because he gave top
priority to problems of human dignity and honesty? Or
maybe because he was unemployed? (In this event, it would
have been better to arrest those who prevented Moroz from
finding employment.) Or could it be that Valentyn Moroz
actually did something which led to his incarceration? The

187

very fact that he was arrested requires immediate and full clarification. His imprisonment evoked consternation in a large segment of our society. And no one doubts that this imprisonment is unjust.

And one more thing: there was a time when V. Symonenko's writings were regarded as hostile; there was a time when V. Symonenko's writings were not published; finally, the time came when a collection of V. Symonenko's poems lay at the bedside of every lover of poetry. But how much damage malicious tongues had caused in the meantime!

Valentyn Moroz did not conceal his views, as would no honest poet or scientist, convinced that he is right. Valentyn Moroz longed for an open exchange of views, for their widest possible discussion. He can, therefore, be judged in just such an open dialogue or discussion. And so long as the materials used in charges against him are not published in the press, none of us has a right to regard Valentyn Moroz's arrest and imprisonment as lawful.

Iryna Stasiv (Lviv)   *Nina Strokata[1] (Odessa)*
Ihor Kalynets (Lviv)   *Olena Antoniv (Lviv)*
Lyudmyla Sheremetyeva (Lviv) *Yaroslav Kendzyor (Lviv)*
Mariya Kachmar-Savka (Lviv) *Yuriy Shukhevych[2] (Nalchyk)*
Stefaniya Hulyk (Lviv)

[1]Nina Strokata (b. 1925): microbiologist; sentenced in May 1972 to four years of hard-regime labor camp for "anti-Soviet agitation and propaganda"; wife of writer Svyatoslav Karavansky, who was sentenced in 1944 to 25 years of imprisonment for treason; released under general amnesty after sixteen years; re-incarcerated in 1965 without trial to serve the remainder of his original term after he protested against the Russification of Ukrainian schools.

[2]Yuriy Shukhevych (b. 1933): son of commanding general of the Ukrainian Insurgent Army, which fought Soviet occupation; began his first sentence of twenty years' imprisonment as a fifteen-year-old youth in 1948; released in 1968; married; two children; sentenced again in September 1972 to five years of prison, five years of strict-regime labor camp and five years of exile for "anti-Soviet agitation and propaganda."

22

To Comrade Shelest, First Secretary of the CC CPU
To Comrade Hlukhov, Prosecutor of the UkrSSR
To Comrade Fedorchuk, Head of the KGB in the
Council of Ministers of the UkrSSR

FROM day to day I await with apprehension the end of the investigation and trial of my husband, MOROZ Valentyn Yakovych, charged under Art. 62, Sec. 2 of the UCC for "anti-Soviet propaganda and agitation." Before it is too late, I beg you to intervene in his case and, setting aside any prejudice, to consider well who will benefit from this trial. Will the condemnation of a person for openly expressed convictions, even if differing on many points from yours, contribute in any way to the strengthening of the authority in our society, the authority of socialist democracy?

I am a wife and a mother; you may consider my opinions biased. Therefore, I do not express them. But I know that my husband's arrest did not go unnoticed. As his wife, I have been informed about a series of collective and individual statements in his defense, addressed to various official bodies. It is likely that there have been more, but I do not know about all of them. It means that a segment of society, those who signed the protests (these people, after all, do not live in isolation; they express not only their own opinions), regard Valentyn's arrest illegal and even harmful to the moral well-being of our society. Is it worthwhile to throw away their opinion from the scales of justice?

Finally, I have been greatly alarmed by the fact that the investigations division of the Ivano-Frankivsk Regional KGB, having failed, of course, to find anything of an anti-Soviet nature in Valentyn's writings since his release, has again included in the indictment the *Report from the Beria Reservation*. After all, Moroz had been under investigation for a period of more than a year regarding the authorship and dissemination of this work. His case was then in the hands of the investigation department of the Republican KGB, which

189

in the beginning of 1969 decided to discontinue the investigation. But now, however, although the investigative organs of the KGB do not have any new information about the *Report,* they—as has been stated to me—have included this work in the indictment. Can this not prompt every objectively thinking person to conclude that there are no permanent guarantees of justice and legality in our country, and that a man's fate depends only on what trends take the upper hand at the given moment among those ruling or investigative agencies, or even on changes in the personnel among the functionaries of those organizations?

Are you also aware that foreign propaganda has already been exploiting the very fact of Valentyn's arrest and, without doubt, will exploit the fact of his conviction a hundredfold? Will the authorities also see in this my huband's guilt, as well as a reason for dealing with him more severely?

For four long years I waited with our small son for our husband and father to return from imprisonment, the justification of which still seem problematical to many people. And we were able to spend only nine months together. If one takes into account the Article of the Criminal Code under which Valentyn is charged, long years of separation await us again, and prolonged physical and mental tortures await Valentyn.

Is this really necessary for building the most just and the most humane society in the world?

Because statements in defense of my husband have been addressed to various official bodies and may be unknown to you, I have decided to collect at least some of them and to send them to you.

Again and again I appeal to your objectivity, sense of justice, and humaneness.

October 8, 1970   *Rayisa Moroz*
Ivano-Frankivsk,   *wife and mother*
14 Naberezhna Street, Apt. 85.

23

LETTER WRITERS QUESTIONED

As far as is known, none of the letters and statements have been answered. Instead, for the first time in many years the KGB has officially called in for questioning persons who signed protest statements and recorded the interrogations. L. Sheremetyeva (Lviv) was called in for such questioning in Ivano-Frankivsk, without being informed of the purpose of the interrogation. She was questioned by the same agency which was cited in the letter of protest from Lviv. She was asked: Who initiated the statement? Who wrote the text? etc. L. Sheremetyeva told them that, since she had signed the statement, they could consider her as one of the initiators and authors; she refused to answer further questions.

Chapter IV

Second Trial

24

A SHAMEFUL TRIAL IN
IVANO-FRANKIVSK
(Valentyn Moroz sentenced to 14 years)

THE previous issue of the *Ukrainian Herald* reported in detail about the second arrest of the historian and publicist Valentyn Moroz on June 1, 1970, in Ivano-Frankivsk, about the gist of the charge, and the course of the investigation. Also mentioned were the protests that came from the public in connection with the illegality of V. Moroz's arrest. Therefore, we report below only about the trial itself.

The trial was preceded by "preventive" measures, never before applied, against persons who, in the opinion of the KGB, may have wished to attend the trial at Ivano-Frankivsk.

In Kiev, the critic and translator Ivan Svitlychny was summoned to the militia on the day of the trial for a talk about his "idleness"; teachers were sent to a hospital to check on the ill teacher, O. Serhiyenko;[1] at the tuberculosis sanitorium where M. Plakhtonyuk worked as a doctor, a meeting was hastily called, and everyone was warned that no one was to leave anywhere the following week, or even become ill, under threat of dismissal from his job (!) The same warning was given N. Karavanska[2] in Odessa.

In Lviv, shortly before the trial, a group of people (it is known that among them were writer-journalist M. Osadchy, poets I. Kalynets, I. Stasiv and H. Chubay, artist S. Shabatura,[3] teacher O. Horyn, and others) sent a phototelegram to

[1]Oleksander Serhiyenko (b. 1932): art teacher; sentenced in June 1972 to seven years of hard-regime labor camp and three years of exile for "anti-Soviet agitation and propaganda."

[2]Nina Strokata-Karavanska (see fn. 1, p. 188).

[3]Stefaniya Shabatura (b. 1938): artist; sentenced in July 1972 to five years of general-regime labor camp and three years of exile for "anti-Soviet agitation and propaganda."

the Prosecutor's Office of the UkrSSR and to the Ivano-Frankivsk Regional Court, demanding that they be admitted to the trial of V. Moroz and that they be informed of the date of the trial. On the following day, they were summoned by the management of the institutions where they were working. They were threatened and warned that a trip to Ivano-Frankivsk would mean dismissal from their jobs. Precisely on November 17th, the artist Oleh Minko was summoned for an auto inspection (he has his own car), from where he was taken, against his will, to the KGB for interrogation.

In Ivano-Frankivsk, several days before the trial, Mariya and Dariya Voznyak were summoned to the KGB for the purpose of intimidation. The artist Panas Zalyvakha,[4] who is under police surveillance in Ivano-Frankivsk, was officially forbidden to appear on the street where the Regional Court is situated, for the duration of the week.

They behaved particularly brutally in the town of Dolyna (Ivano-Frankivsk region) with the nurse Mariya Yukysh, who, after receiving information about the date of the trial, was to have passed it on to a Kievan woman, O. Meshko. In order to prevent this, the KGB immediately sent a "doctor" to her flat, and he "discovered" that her completely healthy two-month-old baby had a sprained leg, and forcibly took the mother and the baby to a hospital. M. Yukysh was kept with her baby for an entire week among people ill with infectious diseases in a general (not even a children's) ward, and was not allowed to use the telephone. Doctors and nurses who were informed about the entire matter at first wondered why a healthy baby was kept in the hospital, for it could have caught an infection from other patients. Later they found out, and someone among them quickly informed the worried mother that her baby was all right and that a "sick" KGB

[4]Panas Zalyvakha had been released from the Mordovian camps, where he spent five years.

agent, who watches here every move, had been admitted in the next ward.

Despite these measures, a group of people from Lviv and its outlying region, as well as persons from Moscow and Kiev, came to the trial. Several residents of Ivano-Frankivsk also came. (For greater authenticity we are describing the trial using combined material supplied by three persons who were present.) On an average, there were about 20-30 people present at the entrance of the courthouse during the two days of trial.

On the morning of November 17th, a group of people made personal applications and sent telegraphic requests to the Chairman of the Ivano-Frankivsk Regional Court for admission to the trial of V. Moroz, in order to be able to see for themselves whether V. Moroz had, in fact, committed any offense against Soviet laws. The requests stated that if specially selected people would be escorted into the courtroom, while the friends and acquaintances of Moroz who came from various towns would not be admitted to the trial, such a trial could not be termed open. However, the KGB and judges were afraid to let even tested people into the courtroom. Contrary to the Soviet Constitution and Soviet laws, the trial was closed. Even the guards were selected from among non-Ukrainian soldiers; they were mainly from the Caucasus, and understood poorly both Ukrainian and Russian.

Besides troops, many KGB personnel, even from distant regions (Lviv people recognized several of their own "guardians"), were summoned for "the preservation of order." According to sources, there were no less than ten "guardians" for each person present near the courthouse. No one was permitted beyond the main entrance. During the two days, the public was admitted neither to the court, to the office of the Lawyers' Guild, nor to the notary's office, situated in the same building.

Valentyn Moroz was tried by the Judicial Board for Criminal Matters of the Ivano-Frankivsk Regional Court, consist-

197

ing of Judge Ivan Ivanovych Kachylenko and Assessors Galkin and Bazhaluk. The Assistant Prosecutor of the region, Horodko, acted as the state prosecutor. (We draw your attention to the fact that this Horodko "supervised" the investigation in Moroz's case on behalf of the Prosecutor's Office, was present at the interrogations and, to a certain extent, directed the course of the investigation, while the defense lawyer was allowed to see the material of the case only after the conclusion of the investigation.) The accused was defended by Kogan, a lawyer from Moscow. (In 1966 he defended the Russian writer Sinyavsky).

We remind that the investigation in Moroz's case was conducted and the indictment prepared by the Ivano-Frankivsk KGB: regional director, Colonel Holda; chief of the investigations department, Colonel Dolgikh; case investigator was senior investigator Major Baranov, who was assisted by senior investigator Captain Pryhornytsky. The arrest warrant was issued and the indictment prepared by the KGB, and appoved by the Regional Prosecutor Paraskevych (known from his illiterate conduct of the case against M. Ozerny[5] in February 1966).

A linguistic examination of Moroz's writings in order to confirm his authorship was conducted by members of the Institute of Philology of the Academy of Sciences of the UkrSSR, Masters of Philology H. Yizhakevych (granddaughter of the famous Ukrainian painter) and A. Hryshchenko.

Called as witnesses in the case were: writer B. Antonenko-Davydovych, literary critic I. Dzyuba, critic and journalist V. Chornovil, and a villager from Kosmach in the Hutsul area, V. Babyak, who did not know anything about the essence of the case.

On the basis of oral reports it has been possible to recon-

[5]Mykhaylo Ozerny (b. 1929): teacher and writer; sentenced in February 1966 to six years of labor camp; later, sentence halved on appeal.

struct the following picture of the trial.

The trial began at about 10 o'clock in the morning on November 17, 1970. In order to confirm the presence of the participants of the trial, the witnesses were brought into the courtroom, where only the accused, judges, prosecutor, defense lawyer, secretary to the court and several armed soldiers were present. The identity of the accused was ascertained in the presence of the witnesses. In answering the question about his allegiance, V. Moroz said that he was a citizen of the Ukrainian Soviet Socialist Republic (but, as is known, in the USSR there is only an all-Union citizenship). To the question of whether he had been tried before, he said that he had been unlawfully sentenced to four years' imprisonment for propagating the secession of the Ukrainian SSR from the USSR, which is permitted by the Constitution of the USSR. To the question about his wife's place of work, he replied that he was not certain whether she had a job at all, because in our country it has become customary to take revenge on the family of persons arrested on political grounds. To the question of whether the accused had any objections to the make-up of the court or the prosecutor, he replied that he had enough grounds to challenge them, but that he would not do so because his fate had been decided without his "trial," and the procedure now taking place was of no significance.

After the witnesses had been led out and the court session resumed, Valentyn Moroz made a declaration of protest against the unlawful closed trial and demanded an open hearing of his case. The defense attorney supported the demand of the accused. The court rejected his motion without giving any justification.

The indictment was then read, and the accused was given the opportunity to answer the substance of the accusation. To this Moroz made a statement, the gist of which follows: a trial *in camera* is unlawful; therefore, he refuses to give any explanations at such a trial or to answer any questions from the judges or the prosecutor who sanction this lawlessness.

199

However, he reserved the right to raise protests or motions as well as to answer the questions of the defense attorney. So that his decision would not be interpreted as an unprincipled and cowardly attempt to deny the authorship of the works with which he had been charged, Valentyn Moroz said that he was at the same time declaring that he was the author of the articles *A Report from the Beria Reservation, Moses and Dathan, A Chronicle of Resistance,* and *Amid the Snows,* but that the humoristic story *I Saw Mohammed,* ascribed to him by the investigating organs, was not written by him. He would not give further testimony at such a "trial." Nevertheless, he was asked several questions to which he gave no reply.

I. Dzyuba was the first witness to be called into the courtroom. Instead of replying to the questions posed by the prosecutor, he stated that he would not answer any questions for two reasons: First, one of the articles for which V. Moroz was standing trial had been polemically aimed at him, I. Dzyuba, and therefore it was unethical to place him in the role of a witness against Moroz. Secondly, he could not take part in an illegal trial, because on the basis of Article 111 of the Constitution of the USSR, Article 91 of the Constitution of the UkrSSR and Article 20 of the Criminal Procedure Code of the UkrSSR, the trial of V. Moroz could not be held *in camera.*

The next witness, B. Antonenko-Davydovych, also stated that in view of the utter illegality of a closed trial he would not give any testimony. After all, twice in his life he himself had been tried in closed courts, as a result of which he was cruelly punished (once he was even sentenced to death) on the basis of the most ridiculously fabricated charges. He, therefore, considered it unthinkable for him to take part in such a "trial," because he did not wish to bear, along with the judges and the prosecutor, the responsibility before posterity for participating in overt high-handedness.

After a prolonged recess, caused, no doubt, by the court's

confusion over the behavior of the witnesses, Vasyl Babyak was called as the next witness. He answered completely irrelevant questions—how many more schools are there in Kosmach at present than there were under Polish rule; was it really true that a geological exploratory derrick in the middle of the village was a nuisance, etc.

Witness V. Chornovil, called last, refused to give any testimony for two reasons. First, any trial for openly expressed convictions undermined the foundations of socialist democracy and Soviet order. Second, a closed trial was a violation of the Soviet Constitution and of laws governing courtroom procedure.

Left without witnesses, the court decided, after a conference and despite a protest by the defense attorney, to read testimony given by witnesses during the preliminary investigation. They read V. Chornovil's testimony, in which the witness denied familiarity with the three latest articles by V. Moroz and stated that, having received *A Report from the Beria Reservation* from Mordovia, he—on his own initiative —sent it to deputies of the Supreme Council of the UkrSSR. This was one of the reasons for his conviction in 1967.[6] To the judge's question of whether Chornovil confirmed this evidence now, the witness refused to answer on the grounds that the trial was closed.

Witness I. Dzyuba, called for the second time, listened to his own previous testimony and stated that if it were not for his attitude towards the illegal closed trial he would have brought up some essential points to make it more precise. He said he would still do so if the accused and the defense attorney gave their permission. Having received this permission, the witness said that he was indignant at the blackmail to which the investigator, Baranov, had stooped during the preliminary investigation. Using deceit, he extracted from I. Dzyuba evidence that did not entirely corre-

[6]See fn. 59, p. 48.

spond to reality. As a matter of fact, I. Dzyuba never received a written text of the article *Amid the Snows* from Moroz, but only discussed this subject with him. After the trial, I. Dzyuba stressed that his statement did not negate his boycott of the closed trial, because it was made at the request of the accused; he did not answer any question of the judges or the prosecutor.

Previous testimony by B. Antonenko-Davydovych was also read in the presence of the witness, who had stated during the investigation that V. Moroz showed him unfinished drafts of the articles *Moses and Dathan* and *Amid the Snows,* seeking literary advice. Having listened to this evidence, Antonenko-Davydovych said that he could introduce essential changes into his testimony, since the investigator distorted his statement, but he added that he would not permit himself to do so, because it would mean that he recognized the legality of a closed trial.

The trial was in fact hamstrung by the lack of cooperation on the part of the accused and witnesses. The court had no opportunity to deal with any evidence. Nevertheless, the court session continued.

The next day, the court heard the experts, who diligently upheld the assertion *that Moroz was in fact the author of the four articles* quoted in the indictment. (The experts' testimony is not as innocent as it appears at first. During the preliminary investigation, V. Moroz refused to give any evidence; it was, therefore, impossible to produce an indictment against him and to bring him to trial without the findings of the examination.) It seems that the conclusions of some sort of an ideological assessment were read, giving an evaluation of the contents of V. Moroz's articles. Who offered this "expertise," which defined even the article *A Chronicle of Resistance* as anti-Soviet, remains unknown.

The full text of the closing speech by State Prosecutor Horodko is not known. It is known, however, that the prosecutor called the entire activity of V. Moroz and all his articles anti-Soviet. The prosecutor emphasized that the articles *A Report from the Beria Reservation* and *A Chronicle of Resistance* had been published abroad, seeing in this an aggravating circumstance. The prosecutor also cited the fact that Moroz was being tried for the second time for "anti-Soviet propaganda and agitation." He demanded the maximum punishment of 15 years permitted by Section 2 of Article 62—ten years' imprisonment and five years' exile. The prosecutor demanded the most severe conditions of imprisonment—in a special prison—so that Moroz could not write anything or pass anything to the outside.

The defense attorney, Kogan, in his concluding remarks attempted to prove the absence of the *corpus delicti* in V. Moroz's activities, as covered by Article 62, Section 2 of the Criminal Code of the UkrSSR, i.e., "agitation and propaganda for the purpose of undermining or weakening Soviet rule." The defense attorney considered the qualification of V. Moroz's articles as anti-Soviet unjustifiable, and their dissemination by the author himself as unproven. He, allegedly, called the prosecutor's arguments about aggravating circumstances as legally ridiculous. The appearance of the articles abroad, if the accused had nothing to do with their being passed on, should serve neither to aggravate nor to diminish his guilt. Likewise, Section 2 of the Criminal Code of the UkrSSR concerns only those who are being tried for the second time; therefore, the repeated conviction cannot by itself influence the term of the sentence chosen by the court. The defense demanded the acquittal of the defendant or *at least the requalification* of the charge to Article 187-1 of the CC of the UkrSSR, which carries a maximum term of three years.

Valentyn Moroz made a final brief speech, the content of which is not known. It is only known that he did not ask for any leniency and did not dwell on the charges. His last word was a political speech.[7]

[7]*Instead of a Last Word*, p. 1.

In accordance with Article 20 of the CC of the UkrSSR, court verdicts in all cases must be pronounced in an open session. V. Moroz's supporters present near the courthouse demanded, personally and in written applications, to be admitted into the courtroom during the reading of the verdict. The court, however, committed another gross violation of the law. Notwithstanding the great number of troops and KGB personnel, they were afraid to allow anyone from among those present in front of the court into the courtroom. Instead, they summoned by telephone a specially selected audience—deans and lecturers in the social sciences of the medical and teachers' colleges of Ivano-Frankivsk. Some of them were not even told why they were being called to court. Others were warned by the KGB to say, at the entrance of the court, that they were not going to the trial but to the notary's office or to the office of the Lawyer's Guild. This deception soon became apparent, however, and the KGB men and soldiers had to clear the way for the "specially invited" by roughly pushing aside those who had been waiting for two days to gain admittance at least for the reading of the verdict. KGB personnel were also led into the courtroom and stationed in the corridor.

The verdict repeated all the statements of the indictment. Only the authorship of the humorous story *I Saw Mohammed* was dropped from the list of charges as unproven. The fact that all the witnesses in the case refused to testify as a sign of protest against the closed trial was not mentioned in the verdict, and other evidence from the preliminary investigation was distorted. It is probably because of these lies that the witnesses were not permitted in the courtroom at the reading of the verdict. The legally ridiculous assertions of the prosecutor about aggravating circumstances were repeated in the verdict. The court sentenced Moroz to six years of special prison, three years of special-regime camps and five years of exile—a total of fourteen years of punishment.

Valentyn Moroz met the verdict with ironic laughter; the

invited "scholars" listened with confused silence. Then a KGB agent, standing in the aisle, gave the "signal"—he began applauding. Everyone remained silent, so he clapped more vigorously. Here and there, he received some reluctant support. . .

To the judge's question of whether he understood the verdict, Moroz answered—not entirely, because in the verdict it was stated that the trial was held *in camera*, but now he sees many people in the courtroom. The presiding judge explained that, according to the law, the verdict is pronounced in an open session in all cases, and all those who so desire may be present at the reading of the verdict. Moroz, who was obviously waiting for such an explanation, then asked: "Why then, if such is the case, are none of my friends in the courtroom, though they have been standing outside the court for two days, but there are people here whom you have dragged in by the rope?" Instead of giving an answer, the judge ordered the soldiers to take Moroz away and pronounced the trial closed.

During the pronouncement of the verdict, a large crowd of Ivano-Frankivsk residents had gathered near the courthouse; they dared not come near the court for two days. Perhaps fearing a demonstration, the KGB placed several police "Black Ravens," in front of the main entrance as a bluff; V. Moroz was taken away through a back door in an ordinary car.

Attention is also drawn to the cynical behavior of the KGB personnel and the non-Ukrainian soldiers, who had been properly instructed beforehand. People were roughly pushed away from the doors. The soldiers punched S. Hulyk, a pregnant woman from Lviv, in the stomach, when she tried to carry a petition to the Chairman of the Regional Court. The KGB agent contemptuously told those who were near the court: "You are nothing." "Gang." "We will do with you what we like." "We have enough room for all of you." etc.

205

Immediately after the trial, the witnesses composed and sent a letter of protest to the Prosecutor of the UkrSSR and to the Ministry of Justice of the UkrSSR.

25

To the Minister of Justice of the UkrSSR,
Comrade Zaychuk
To the Prosecutor of the Ukrainian SSR,
Comrade Hlukh

ON November 17 and 18, 1970, the Regional Court at Ivano-Frankivsk considered the case of Valentyn Yakovych Moroz, charged under Art. 62-2 of the Criminal Code of the UkrSSR. We have been called as witnesses to this trial. Without any legal grounds and in violation of the Constitution of the USSR, the Constitution of the UkrSSR and the Criminal Procedure Code of the UkrSSR, the trial took place in a closed session. The chairman of the court personally guaranteed us, as also did responsible people from among the security personnel, that we, as witnesses, would be allowed to be present during the pronouncement of the verdict, in which our names could have been mentioned. Anyway, this is our legal right as provided for by Art. 20 of the Criminal Procedure Code of the UkrSSR. In spite of our repeated reminders, we were not admitted to the reading of the verdict, although at the same time many people with special invitations for the reading of the verdict passed by us. Some of them were not even aware of why they were being invited to the Regional Court.

We reserve the right to appeal to the Appellate Court, the Supreme Court of the UkrSSR, to the Ministry of Justice of the UkrSSR and the Prosecutor of the UkrSSR with a justified complaint regarding the illegality of the closed trial of V. Ya. Moroz and its verdict.

November 18, 1970   *B. Antonenko-Davydovych*
                                            I. Dzyuba
                                            V. Chornovil

26

PROTESTS AGAINST TRIAL AND SENTENCE

AT the end of November and the beginning of December, 1970, many people (30 to 40) sent individual telegrams and statements of protest to the Supreme Court of the Ukrainian SSR regarding the cruel treatment of V. Moroz, demanding that the unjust verdict of the Regional Court be annulled and the defendant acquitted.

It is known that petitions to the Supreme Court have been sent by the Kievans—writer B. Antonenko-Davydovych, critic I. Dzyuba, artist Alla Horska, philologists M. Kotsyubynska and Z. Franko, pensioner O. Meshko, medical practitioner M. Plakhotnyuk, teacher O. Serhiyenko, V. Drabata and others; from Lviv—Doctor O. Antoniv, S. Hulyk, a former worker of the Society for the Protection of Historical and Cultural Monuments, teacher O. Horyn, engineer A. Volytska, poet I. Kalynets, artist M. Kachmar-Savka, telephone operator H. Kunytska, trade-union staffer Ya. Kendzyor, poetess and former university student H. Savron, poetess I. Stasiv, journalists P. Chemerys, V. Chornovil, poet H. Chubay, artist S. Shabatura, and others. Appeals were also written by I. Hel[1] (Sambir, Lviv region), N. Karavanska (Odessa), painter P. Zalyvakha, M. Voznyak and L. Lemyk (Ivano-Frankivsk), V. Romanyuk, a priest (Kosmach), and others.

Considered the most legally sound and well-grounded is the extensive petition submitted to the Supreme Court of the Ukrainian SSR, the Prosecutor of the Ukrainian SSR and the Ministry of Justice of the Ukrainian SSR by the witnesses in the case—B. Antonenko-Davydovych, I. Dzyuba and V. Chornovil. The authors refused to allow their statement to

[1]Ivan Hel (b. 1937) : student, locksmith; sentenced in August 1972 to five years of strict-regime labor camp and five years of exile for "anti-Soviet agitation and propaganda"; previously served three years (1966-69) ; married; one child.

be circulated, considering that by this they would demonstrate to the authorities, to whom they were appealing, their sincerity and the lack of any ulterior motives. The contents of the petition is known from a few people who read it at the authors' homes. The petition stresses that in the post-Stalin USSR, no person who had openly—and not covertly—expressed his views in literary and publicist articles has ever been so cruelly punished. The court had incorrectly qualified his articles as anti-Soviet. They authors of the petition think that when in 1969 the KGB men discontinued the investigation in the case of *A Report from the Beria Reservation,* they had no doubts that it had been written by V. Moroz. The fact that the *Report* has again been included in the indictment and the unbelievably cruel sentence are, in the authors' opinion, an indication of the onset of reaction, especially in Ukraine. This is also clear when comparing the sentences in the cases of V. Moroz and the Russian historian Amalrik, who was also tried for the second time for writing considerably sharper articles than had Moroz; he was sentenced to three years of camp imprisonment.

Antonenko-Davydovych, Dzyuba and Chornovil believe that the investigation and the trial did not prove that Moroz personally disseminated his articles. Worthy of note is their opinion that the KGB is capable of artificially creating a criminal situation by circulating someone's works, so that they can later square accounts with their author. They also cited the illegality of a closed trial and expressed indignation that they, as witnesses, were not allowed in the courtroom during the reading of the verdict which distorted their testimony in court and at the preliminary investigation. Finally, citing articles from the Criminal Procedure Code, the authors demanded that the decision of the Ivano-Frankivsk Regional Court be voided.

It is known that the authors of all other statements also cited, first of all, the fact of the closed trial and the unbelievably harsh sentence. We have obtained copies of only a few of these statements to the Supreme Court of the UkrSSR.

27

Phototelegram
To the Supreme Court of the UkrSSR, Kiev

PRECISELY on the eve of Constitution Day of the USSR and the election of judges, the Ivano-Frankivsk people's court allowed itself to ignore Article 91 of the Constitution of the UkrSSR (and Articles 20, 370 and 372 of the Criminal Code of the UkrSSR) about publicity of judicial review, by sentencing historian Valentyn Moroz to fourteen years of imprisonment at a closed trial.

Has the Constitution of the USSR stopped being the fundamental law for all the citizens of the Soviet Union, without exception, or do regional judicial institutions tower above all written laws, inasmuch as by their practice they void Article 92 of the Constitution of the UkrSSR.[1]

If the basis of the Constitution of the UkrSSR is formed by the primary principles and foundations of socialism, then surely this is not the first and not an isolated incident of the destruction of these foundations by the very organs which should sanctimoniously uphold them.

For what then should distinguish the Constitution of the USSR from all others in the world if not the unceasing upholding of democracy and the democratic rights of every citizen?

But does the Constitution sanction a closed trial for Valentyn Moroz, the banning and exclusion by the militia of citizens wishing to be at the trial, more than that, their exclusion from the reading of the verdict?

Will the Constitution of the USSR differ from bourgeois constitutions, if the principle that "not only are the rights of citizens fixed formally, but the primary importance is shifted to the guarantee of these rights, to the means of

---

[1]Article 92 of the Constitution of the UkrSSR states: "The courts are independent and are subservient only to the law."

actual implementation of this guarantee," is violated as easily, cynically and with impunity by regional courts, as it was by the Ivano-Frankivsk Regional Court on November 17th and 18th?

Is this the expression of the substance and the particulars of socialist democracy, of socialist legality and humaneness?

If the Supreme Court confirms the decision of the Ivano-Frankivsk Regional Court, it will force me to refrain from voting for judges who do not want, or are not able, to uphold the letter and the spirit of the law.

Lviv—16, Kirova 33/14 *Olha Horyn*

28

To the Chairman of the Supreme Court of the UkrSSR

ON November 17 and 18, 1970, during the trial of Valentyn Moroz, we were the witnesses of the vicious abuse of power on the part of the members of the Ivano-Frankivsk Regional Court and the Ivano-Frankivsk KGB. In recent history this is unheard of—to sentence a person to fourteen years merely because he thinks.

History knows of many inhuman sentences meted out to the best representatives of its time. But if today we are riled by the ignorance of a world which sentenced Campanella[1] to twenty-five years, which exiled Dante beyond the boundaries of his native land, and which exiled Shevchenko[2] to Siberia, what right have we in our humane 20th century to keep silent and watch indifferently as medieval tortures creep up into broad daylight?

What right have we not to be angry when, under the protection of laws and constitutional rights, a person is imprisoned in the most brutal and cruel manner for four unknown articles which should have been examined not in a courtroom, in a closed session, but in an open auditorium among fellow writers! For what else can we call all that which took place in Ivano-Frankivsk: a closed trial, armed guards at the entrance to the court building, representatives especially invited by telephone for the sentencing, and so on. Are just decisions reached under the cover of secrecy, hidden from the people? Must the words of the prosecutor, if they actually are objective and just, hide behind the unlawful decisions of the court? Why and by what right was there so much contempt for the "mere mortals" who voluntarily arrived for the trial of V.

---

[1]Thomas C. Campanella (1568-1639): Italian Renaissance philosopher and poet; a Dominican.
[2]Taras Shevchenko, greatest Ukrainian poet (see fn. 11, p. 13).

Moroz and whom the representatives of the local KGB called "you are nothing"? Anyway, let us not speak of rights; let us consider some of the representatives of certain agencies.

Various trials are taking place in our time. We are not afraid to try bandits, sadists and murderers in open-door trials. . . . Why, we even let some of them get out on bail. . . . But why, on what basis was Valentyn Moroz tried behind closed doors? Is it not because the wronged truth would suddenly stand beside the defendant?

Soon the works of an outstanding philosopher of the 12th century, R. Bacon, who was also sentenced to fourteen years simply because he did not want to agree with some of the scholastic opinions of his time, will appear in Ukraine. The centuries exonerated and rewarded the prominent scholar. But how many curses, how much contempt has humanity poured today on the heads of those who, donning their black robes, regarded themselves as the guardians of truth on earth. These "guardians of truth," whose bones to this day have no rest, whose descendants have renounced their names and their memory—how many of them there were in each century! And to this day history is subjecting them to its own inexorable trial.

Valentyn Moroz did not break any established laws. But as a person, he has the human right to think. You are not the guardians of all human fate and you wear no black robes. But in your hands you hold today the fate of a human being. And your own as well. For history does not know how to forget. And so that your descendants will not run away from your name, burning with shame, let the biblical wisdom be fulfilled: "Judge not and you shall not be judged."

November 29, 1970   *Iryna Stasiv-Kalynets*

Lviv   *Ihor Kalynets*

29

A Letter to the Supreme Court of the UkrSSR, Kiev,
From Oksana Yakivna Meshko,
born in 1905

ON November 17 and 18, 1970, the trial of Valentyn Moroz
took place.

The man was charged with expressing his thoughts of deep
concern for the preservation of the material, spiritual and
cultural treasures of the nation. When a person with a social
conscience comes into contact with many questions that grieve
him, then, you will agree, if he passes over them, he could not
be regarded as a decent person.

But once this person touches upon them, no matter in what
manner this may have been done, he is repaid with such an
unheard of term of incarceration—nine years of imprisonment and five years of exile.

In essence, there actually was no trial. There was a closed
meeting, after which they did not even allow those wishing
to be present, including witnesses, for the pronouncement of
the sentence.

Such a trial brings about all kinds of rumors and conjec-
tures in which the main thought remains: for openly expressed ideas a man was deprived of his youth and of his
constitutionally guaranteed rights to live freely and work
according to his vocation.

It is difficult to imagine how one can reconcile such a sentence with the concept of socialist legality. But it is not
difficult to imagine that if he had propagated anti-communist
ideas and the most rash of appeals, he would have been tried
by an open court and the press would surely have written
about it as a lesson to the frivolous.

If he had been an indecent person, then he could have been
tried in the press, and this would have found general support.

At my age and with my experience (I was unjustly sentenced during the cult of Stalin to ten years of camp regime, and later rehabilitated), I can say that at such trials a man is blamed for the crimes of others...

Somebody is to blame for the fact that he, a young specialist-historian, who was to defend his dissertation and who, obviously, had lectured well, for no one had any complaints against him, was proclaimed a criminal and given four years of imprisonment.

Naturally, he saw much violence and falsehood there. Then he was set free, but without the possibility of earning enough for bread, for he was not given work; nine months later he was given nine years of imprisonment for highly critical ideas.

This is simply inhuman. Was there not a mistake made here which now has been covered up by cruelty?

I turn to the Supreme Court with my reflections and ask that you consider them and review the case of Valentyn Moroz in the spirit of socialist legality, in which our youth is educated and which it must respect.

Kiev 86, Verbolozna Street 16.   *O. Meshko*

30

To the Chairman of the Supreme Court of the UkrSSR
From Citizen V. P. Drabata,
Kiev 101, Lomonosov 57, Apt. 7.

THE excessively harsh punishment of the young historian, Valentyn Moroz, nine years of severe-regime camps and five years of exile (a total of fourteen years), has come to my attention. I did not know him. I do not know for what he was tried, for the trial was closed. I am not a lawyer and do not understand the articles of the Criminal Code. But I do know that, according to present Soviet laws, the maximum term of imprisonment is fifteen years.

If he committed some terrible crime, wider circles of citizens should have been informed about it. When the reasons for sentencing are concealed, then the impression is formed that we are not dealing with deeds but with opinions and their expression.

In our time, when under the influence of democratic forces humanitarian tendencies are spread throughout the world, the excessively harsh punishment of people whose views, for one reason or another, do not coincide with official ones, can only create a feeling of repression in our own citizens as well as in our foreign friends.

Legal proceedings, particularly in our country, are not always free from error. Facts from our not-too-distant past testify to this.

I regard it my civic duty to bring to your attention the unjustifiably excessive harshness of this sentence, with the aim of seeing it mitigated.

December 11, 1970   *V. Drabata*

216

31

To the Supreme Court of the UkrSSR

ON November 17 and 18, 1970, I, along with a group of people from Lviv, Ivano-Frankivsk, Kiev and Moscow, was a witness to the unprecedented harshness and cynicism of the legal proceedings against the historian and publicist Valentyn Moroz, which were crowned by a fourteen-year term (six years of special prison, three years of labor camps and five years of exile).

Actually, we were not witnesses, in the real sense of the word, for we were not even allowed into the vestibule of the court building. Each of us had at least ten "guards" and "observers," in uniform and in civilian dress, from whom we, though Soviet citizens, heard that we are "nobodies," a "herd," and that they "will do what they please" with us, and so on.

In violation of Soviet laws, which guarantee public trials, they tried Valentyn Moroz within four bare walls, hiding themselves behind armed soldiers. They were even afraid to allow us in for the reading of the verdict. All this provides the basis for regarding the trial as unlawful and amoral. All of us present near the courtroom, therefore, approved the principled behavior of the witnesses who, as a sign of protest against this type of trial, refused to participate in it in any manner.

Moroz was sentenced for trying to form his own convictions, which do not fit into the standard framework. It takes a very evil and tendentious person to see "anti-Soviet propaganda and agitation" in Moroz's essays, especially in those which he wrote after being freed and which became the reason for his arrest.

The judicial qualification of Moroz's essays as anti-Soviet will not stand up under criticism. The inquest and trial also did not uncover any proof that Moroz personally disseminat-

217

ed his works. And that is why this brutal punishment is nothing more than the predaceous revenge of people deprived by nature or by the circumstances of life of those traits which Valentyn Moroz has: compassion, principle, decency, and real, not bought, patriotism.

I beg of you, do not join those who have already dishonored themselves by an act of inhuman retribution and about whom history will have its say, as it did about their spiritual twins of Stalinist times. Upon review of the appeal, annul the ruling of the Ivano-Frankivsk Regional Court as illegal, amoral and harmful to the prestige of our order. Cruelty will not bring you the respect of the people or spiritual contentment. It will always hang as a heavy stone around your necks.

I wish to believe that in examining Moroz's case you will show yourselves to be just and humane.

Lviv,
Partisan Street 12, Apt. 1-a.   *Stefaniya Hulyk*

32

**To the Chief Justice of the
Supreme Court of the UkrSSR**

ON November 17th and 18th of this year, the trial of the writer and publicist Valentyn Moroz was held in Ivano-Frankivsk. The total sentence—fourteen years. I was present at the courtroom doors and am a witness to the violation of the norms of socialist legality. I believe that in our country, which has just celebrated its fifty-third anniversary, closed trials and such brutal sentences given writers are inhumane phenomena and detrimental to the people.

I ask the Court of Appeals to annul the verdict of the Ivano-Frankivsk Regional Court.

November 25, 1970   *Mariya Kachmar-Savka*

33

To the Supreme Court of the UkrSSR

Regarding the sentencing to nine years of imprisonment and five years of exile of the historian Valentyn Moroz

From a priest in the village of Kosmach, Kosiv district, Ivano-Frankivsk region, Vasyl Romanyuk

DECLARATION

WE are living in the time of great acceleration and great contrasts. On the one hand, modern cruelty and new totalitarianism are growing in the world, values are depreciating, traditions are being lost and spiritual devastation is deepening. On the other, there is a painful searching for the roads towards Peace, Goodness and Justice.

And often Evil wins out—the trampling of Christian values which humanity has developed through the ages becomes habitual and even commonplace. . . . Among such depreciated values, we should probably place first and foremost compassion, tolerance, and Christian charity.

These thoughts immediately came to mind when the unbelievably harsh sentence that the Ivano-Frankivsk Regional Court determined for Valentyn Moroz was made known. Fourteen years of imprisonment, of which six years are to be spent in a special prison and three in a special-regime concentration camp—only a murderer or a rapist could have been sentenced thus, and even that would be done with great bitterness, with the understanding of society's debt for the perversion of such an individual. And what did Valentyn Moroz do? He wrote a few essays, openly and on principle, filled with sincere anxiety for the spiritual possesions of his nation, for its fate, for humaneness and justice. A person filled with concern about his nation and its people was tried for "undermining order." It would be worthwhile to consider who actually "undermined" order—Valentyn with his humane articles, or the Ivano-Frankivsk Regional Court with its barbarous, cruel sentence, capable of compromising any kind of order.

I knew Valentyn Moroz personally. I knew him as a fine person, honest, highly moral, and intelligent. And I never heard anything from his lips which could be called criminal.

I am not a lawyer and may not even know on which articles or paragraphs Moroz's sentence was based. But in order to understand that this sentence is not even legal judicially, it was enough for me to learn that Moroz was tried secretly, within four bare walls, under conditions of reinforced security and control.

In turning to you as the court of appeal which will soon examine his case, I ask you to be governed not only by judicial considerations (although there are also enough of them for you to void or lessen the sentence), but more importantly, by the high principles of humaneness and justice.

For even Pontius Pilate, the last resort in the Roman province of Judea, whom it was difficult to suspect of excessive humaneness, did not wish to add his name to the black deeds and slander of the Pharisees towards Jesus Christ and—as the Holy Scriptures say—"washed his hands" of the matter.

November 27, 1970   *Vasyl Romanyuk*

34

To the Chief Justice of the
Supreme Court of the UkrSSR

Regarding the appeal of Valentyn Yakovych Moroz,
sentenced in Ivano-Frankivsk to fourteen years

THE trial of Valentyn Moroz took place in Ivano-Frankivsk
in November. I am deeply disturbed by the term to which
this young writer has been sentenced, because it is difficult
to believe that in our time it is possible to deal so harshly
with human beings. Surely if an individual is being tried
with the possibility of such a term, then the reason for the
trial, the formal charges against Valentyn Moroz, should
have been officially reported to the general public.

As it is now, most of the people know that the trial or
Valentyn Moroz was closed and that none of his friends or
acquaintances were permitted to be present at the reading
of the verdict. It is difficult to believe that such lawlessness
occurred. I believe that the versions which are now beginning to appear in newspapers will be far from reliable, for
it would have been much more reasonable not to have covered up the entire case from the very beginning.

I sincerely hope that the verdict of the Ivano-Frankivsk
Regional Court, which was inspired by some particular extra-
legal motives, will be annulled. This will vindicate Soviet
justice, the authority of which is being undermined by the
provocative actions of the Ivano-Frankivsk officials.

Lviv   *Mariya Voytovych*
December 5, 1970

35

To the Supreme Court of the UkrSSR

RECENTLY Valentyn Moroz was sentenced in Ivano-Frankivsk to nine years of imprisonment and five years of exile. I consider this sentence to be incompatible with the principles of socialist society in its present stage of development.

According to the new program of the CPSU, our country has attained nationwide democracy. There is no socialist basis for socio-political antagonism among us. Therefore, V. Moroz could not have *objectively* done anything that could have presented any actual threat to our society and that would have merited such a brutal sentence. It is, therefore, obvious that the verdict was the product of thoughtless examination of the case or of exalted emotions which are all too common in our courts. For this reason I appeal to the Supreme Court of our Republic to review the case of Valentyn Moroz. In my opinion, it would be unjust merely to reduce the sentence given Valentyn Moroz. He must be *released unconditionally.* Such a decision would indeed be worthy of our State.

In our times, to mete out such unjustifiably brutal sentences to fellow countrymen—allegedly in the interest of Soviet rule—means, in fact, to desecrate and compromise Soviet rule in the eyes of the world and in our own eyes. Spite should not be the judge in a case where objectivity, conscience and a sense of responsibility for one's actions before the people and the Nation should prevail.

Faith in the principle of socialist justice and humanism gives me reason to expect that the Supreme Court of the Ukrainian SSR, in reviewing the case of Valentyn Moroz, will not react contemptuously to these well-meaning reservations.

Respectfully,

Pavlo Chemerys, journalist

Lviv
November 30, 1970

36

Moscow, Kremlin, Council of Ministers
To the Chairman of the Council of Ministers of the USSR
A. N. Kosygin
Moscow, Ministry of Internal Affairs of the USSR
Moscow, Ministry of Health of the USSR
To the Chairman of the Red Cross

I HAVE been delegated by relatives, friends and acquaintances of the historian and writer Valentyn Moroz, arrested on June 1, 1970 and sentenced under Articles 62 of the CC of the UkrSSR to fourteen years of deprivation of freedom, to request that you intervene immediately in the actions of the administration of Vladimir Prison.

It has become well known that Valentyn Moroz is seriously ill in the prison hospital. There is reason to believe that the extreme exhaustion and grave illness of Valentyn Moroz were caused by the inhuman conditions in Vladimir Prison.

I ask that you release Valentyn Moroz, who was wrongfully convicted. (Besides, humane Soviet laws guarantee freedom to seriously ill prisoners.) In the meantime you could at least have him transferred to a camp and allow him to receive a supplementary food parcel.

I request that the Red Cross and the Red Crescent create a commission to investigate the conditions under which political prisoners, among them Valentyn Moroz, are kept, and by their findings bring about a change in these conditions.

Iryna Kalynets

37

APPEAL DENIED

THE Supreme Court of the Ukrainian SSR in Kiev considered the case of Valentyn Moroz on December 24, 1970. It is known that V. Moroz did not submit an appeal to the Supreme Court against the substance of the verdict, but only a protest against the illegal closed trial and a demand to have his case considered once again in an open session. An appeal regarding the substance of the verdict was submitted by Kogan, the defense attorney of the convicted, demanding Moroz's release or at least requalification of the charges to Art. 187-1 of the Criminal Code of the UkrSSR.

Several Kievans who came to the Supreme Court to hear the appeal were not admitted to the courtroom on the grounds that the case was being heard in a closed session. Before the beginning of the trial, the critic Dzyuba, philologist Z. Franko, and medical practitioner M. Plakhtonyuk confronted the Prosecutor of the Ukrainian Republic, Hlukh, in a corridor.

Asked why Moroz was tried in a closed court, he replied that state secrets had been looked into at the trial, namely, "the channels through which Moroz passed his articles abroad, something which apparently could not be discussed in public." This is a conscious lie. Moroz did not pass anything abroad; neither the investigation nor the trial concerned themselves with this, and no "channels" were investigated. When Doctor Plakhtonyuk asked why then was his acquaintance, medical college student Yaroslav Hevrych, tried in a closed court in 1966 (after all, Hevrych did not write anything himself, nor was there any talk about any channels then), the prosecutor could not give an answer. To statements by I. Dzyuba, M. Plakhtonyuk and Z. Franko on the unbelievable cruelty of the sentence, the Prosecutor of the Republic replied (not in Ukrainian but in Russian—transl.

note) : "And if he wants to destroy me, steps on my throat, should I be ceremonious with him? In our country there exists an apparatus of coersion for protection from such people." They retorted that if one was to think like that, then for such innocent articles as *A Chronicle of Resistance,* a better solution than giving fourteen years would be shooting.

The prosecutor also stated that he would demand that the verdict be confirmed because this was necessary as a lesson to others. In answer to Z. Franko's remark that the public would be compelled to send petitions to the United Nations, the Prosecutor ironically waved his hand as if to say: Go on, send your petitions, to your good health. . . .

The Supreme Court left the verdict of the Ivano-Frankivsk Regional Court unchanged. In January 1971, Valentyn Moroz was transported to Vladimir Prison, where he will be kept in conditions of strict isolation during the first six years.

THE reaction of the conscious sector of Ukrainian society to the sentencing of V. Moroz is varied. But everyone agrees that the term of punishment for the open writing of literary and publicist articles was unprecedented in its harshness in post-Stalinist times. Some tend to consider this as an isolated incident brought on by the reaction of the KGB to the sharp criticism of it in his *Report* and to his emphatically highly principled behavior, both in prison and while free. Others regard the Moroz case as a to-be-expected stage in the further advance of reaction and the revival of Stalinist-Beriaist tendencies in the USSR. They think that this trial will be followed by other repressions, perhaps even in mass proportions, certainly no less harsh. Along with this, someone is even spreading provocative rumors about possible candidates for these repressions, naming Ye. Sverstyuk, V. Chornovil and others.

As we have learned, in the United States, Canada and other countries there have been mass demonstrations of Ukrainian youth, particularly students, near Soviet embassies and consulates, as a sign of protest against the anti-democratic, harsh punishment of Valentyn Moroz. However, attention is called to the fact that this is little when compared to the reaction caused by the case of Amalrik, and that the world knows almost nothing about the situation and repressions in Ukraine. In addition, analogy is made with the almost simultaneous widely publicized trials of the Leningrad Jews and the arrest of the American Communist Angela Davis. Moroz's fourteen year sentence does not yield in its severity to the sentences given the Spanish Basques and the Leningrad Jews, but the character of the accusations in his case is altogether different. In all the enumerated cases, the people were tried, or will be formally tried, not for beliefs and their dissemination, but on other (even though perhaps fabricated), purely criminal charges—the killing of a head of the secret police, conspiracy with the aim of hijacking an airplane and the killings of the pilots, the smuggling of weapons to prisoners and aiding in their escape, and so on. Moroz was convicted formally for his beliefs—for the writing and the dissemination, unproven by the court, of a few articles of a critical nature.

The details are also compared. Prior to her trial, Angela Davis enjoys daily contacts with her lawyers, friends and strangers, and with her Party supporters. She writes letters containing criticism of the governmental order of the USA, gives interviews of the same content, and herself guides the campaign for her own defense. If they try her, then undoubtedly it will be done publicly, with correspondents and photographers. As is known from our press, the Americans officially invited Soviet jurists to take part in the inquiry into the case of Angela Davis and in the supervision of adherence to the law. But Valentyn Moroz was kept for almost half a year in conditions of strict isolation, not even allowed to see his wife and eight-year-old son prior to the trial. The trial of the Leningrad Jews was at least formally public, and the renowned defender of democratic rights in the USSR, academician Sakharov, was present at the trial. Even the

Basques in Spain were tried publicly, in the presence of French lawyers and foreign journalists. But Moroz's "trial" took place within four mute walls, under the protection of soldiers who did not understand a single word spoken by the defendant.

It is noted that the central Russian press not only actively came out against lawlessness in Spain and the USA (here are the article titles of only one edition of the newspaper *Pravda* of December 5th: "Stop High-handedness!" "Conscience and Courage in Prison," "The Torture Chamber Will Not Break the Fighters for Freedom," "A Shameful Trial"), but also included, for the first time, articles about the legal meaning of UN documents, not mentioned until now, the Universal Declaration of Human Rights and the International Conventions about Human Rights. Such are, for example, the articles of H. Zadorozhny, Doctor of Law, Professor of International Law and member of the executive of the Soviet Association of Cooperation with the UN (*Pravda* of December 15th), and of V. Romanov, Master of Law (*Pravda* of December 11th). Professor Zadorozhny's idea about the necessity of each nation guaranteeing its citizens the basic minimum of democracy is anemic, because it was precisely for his attempt to take advantage of the most basic minimum of democracy that Valentyn Moroz was so inhumanely punished.

We give, in translation, that portion of the article by Professor of International Law Zadorozhny, where general theoretical principles are stated:

"The right to think freely and express freely one's convictions, the right to assemble, the right to establish associations and trade unions for the protection of one's interests, the right of personal inviolability and other basic human freedoms are transformed by imperialism into crimes against the state that carry the death penalty or the promise of life or lengthy imprisonment. But all nations have under the Charter of the UN taken upon themselves the responsibility to en-

228

courage and develop respect for and observance of human rights and freedoms.

"The Universal Declaration of Human Rights and International Covenants on Human Rights concretely establish human rights and the basic freedoms as forming the minimum of a democracy worthy of contemporary civilization, stressing the obligation that each country has to respect and guarantee these rights and freedoms to all persons who find themselves on its territory and under its jurisdiction.

"The minimum of democracy consists of the condition that no one should suffer arbitrary or illegal interference with his family life, arbitrary or illegal encroachments on the inviolability of his domicile or the secrecy of correspondence, or illegal attempts against his honor and reputation.

"Surveillance, telephone eavesdropping, attempts at total control of thoughts, the arbitrary invasion of personal, occupational and social life, the systematic killing of political and civic activists—these are facts well known to all the world. . . . In truth, it is difficult to find norms of international or constitutional law, statutes of the UN Charter, or covenants on human rights, which have not been fundamentally violated by the forces of international imperialist reaction.

"To stay the hand of executioners, to stop judicial arbitrariness and the mistreatment of the Universal Declaration of Human Rights—the conscience of peoples, the interests of universal peace, democracy, and progress demand this. . . . "

(H. Zadorozhny, "Stop Highhandedness," *Pravda*, Dec. 15, 1970.)

It is believed that the appearance of these articles in the organ of the CC CPSU will possibly lead to the greater popularization in the USSR of UN documents on human rights, which up to now have been hushed-up in the Soviet Union.

During searches, the Universal Declaration of Human Rights was usually removed. Confiscating the Declaration from the political prisoners in Mordovia, the guards declared

"That is for Negroes, what do you need it for?" (Look for this in V. Moroz's article, *A Report from the Beria Reservation* and in the statement of political prisoner I. Kandyba,[1] published in the previous issue.)

At the end of 1970, there appeared in *samvydav* a collection of poems, titled *Prelude*, written by Valentyn Moroz during his first and second terms of imprisonment. The work *First Day*, written in the summer of 1970 after his arrest, has also been widely disseminated. These works testify to the versatility of the author's talent, his uncommon literary skill.

[1]Ivan Kandyba (b. 1930) : lawyer; worked for Lviv—city and regional—judicial agencies; one of the organizers of a political party, Ukrainian Workers' and Peasants' Union, for which he was arrested, tried and sentenced in May 1961 to fifteen years of severe-regime labor camp; has written protests against drugging of camp food.

38

REPRISALS AGAINST MOROZ'S WIFE

RAYISA MOROZ, the wife of the sentenced Valentyn Moroz, has become the object of reprisals. For the past five years she had an unblemished record at the Ivano-Frankivsk Pedagogical Institute, where she teaches German. After her husband's trial, Rayisa Moroz was told, in no uncertain terms, that this would be her last year with the Institute. A job opening for her position will be announced this spring.

The Moroz family had an apartment in a cooperative building. The cooperative had voted earlier to give them a three-room apartment; they paid their fee and moved in. Now, at the direction of the KGB, she is being told to move into a one-room apartment. The chairman of the cooperative does not hide the fact that this is being done because Rayisa Moroz's husband was sentenced for "politics."

39

CONFISCATED BOOKS

IN our previous issues we informed about the search conducted in the home of Rev. Vasyl Romanyuk in the Hutsul village of Kosmach on May 4, 1970, in connection with the Moroz case. After Moroz's trial, the KGB returned to Romanyuk a few religious books. The rest were labeled forbidden and confiscated by the Ivano-Frankivsk KGB. The forbidden books included: a number of religious books published at the end of the 19th and the beginning of the 20th centuries; a play by Lesya Ukrainka *Boyarynya* (a photocopy of a Soviet edition from the 1920's); M. Voznyak, *History of Ukrainian Literature*, vol. 2, 16th-18th centuries, 1921; M. Arkas, *History of Ukraine*, 1909; newspaper clippings from *Nedilya*, 1934-36; a *World History;* as well as almanacs, Christmas carols, poems by Lepky, and the like. They also confiscated letters, notes and abstracts of a religious nature (V. Romanyuk is a student at the Theological Seminary in Moscow). Romanyuk asked: How is it possible to consider anti-Soviet Arkas' *History of Ukraine*, which was published in 1909 and allowed even by the tsarist censors? KGB Captain Pryhornytsky answered: "It may not be anti-Soviet in itself, but it could cause anti-Soviet thoughts."

40

"SCHIZOPHRENICS"

SPEAKING before a meeting of teachers in Kosiv, Ivano-Frankivsk region, a Party lecturer called Ĭ. Dzyuba, I. Svit-lychny, V. Chornovil, and others, "schizophrenics." He added to this group of "psychologically unbalanced" individuals General Hryhorenko (Grigorenko), historian P. Yakir and physicist A. Sakharov.... About V. Moroz it was noted that he managed to do some harm in Kosmach, but he was caught in time.

41

AN "APOSTLE" AND HIS STANDARDS[1]

AGAIN the feverish scratching of pens. Again the full rattle of the bells of the *Radio Liberty*[2] in Munich. Again yellow-and-blue leaflets and magazines, from *Meta* (*The Goal*) and *Ukrainsky Holos* (*Ukrainian Voice*), to the Bandera-ite *Vyzvolny Shlyakh* (*Road to Liberation*) and the Melnykite *Ukrainske Slovo* (*Ukrainian Word*)[3] teem with headlines about "unheard of legal reprisals against an 'innocent'."

What is the cause of all this noise? Who is it that the nationalistic publications so zealously hurry to protect? It is now clear that he is Valentyn Moroz, a former lecturer at the Ivano-Frankivsk Pedagogical Institute convicted of anti-Soviet propaganda. They protect him, first of all, because he has taken the road of actively propogandizing the ideas of bourgeois nationalism and has spread his dirty diatribes with slander of the Leninist nationalities policy of the Communist Party and the Soviet state. Instead of sowing that which is wise, good and eternal, as befits an educator, V. Moroz engaged in criminal activity. And as everyone knows, one must answer for crime and, at that, according to the fullest severity of the law.

Here is what V. Moroz himself disclosed at the inquest the first time (As you see, he is a propagandist with seniority!) he was made to answer for anti-Soviet actions: "When I settled and began to work in Ivano-Frankivsk, taking advantage of my trips on assignment for the management of stu-

[1] "'Apostol' i yoho shtandarty," article in newspaper *Soviet Education* (*Radyanska osvita*), August 14, 1971.

[2] Short-wave radio station, funded by the US Government, but considered private; transmits to Eastern Europe and Soviet Union.

[3] Ukrainian emigre nationalist publications. Bandera-ite and Melnykite refers to factions of the Organization of Ukrainian Nationalists formerly led by Stepan Bandera and Andriy Melnyk, respectively.

234

dent teaching, I also visited the city of Lutsk. I always brought with me anti-Soviet literature, articles with that same content. I disseminated them within the circle of my acquaintances. I spoke to them about the indispensability of the secession of Ukraine from the USSR and its transformation into a bourgeois country. In our aspirations, I told them, we should count on the support, including military support, of Western capitalist countries, in the first place, the USA."

So it is not at all a matter of the "highhandedness" of a Soviet court—this follows from V. Moroz's testimony—but of his anti-Soviet activity, in the course of which he disdained no method, from political double-dealing even to betrayal of the Fatherland. V. Moroz declared, as revealed by a witness, teacher D. P. Ivashchenko, that ". . . the secession of Ukraine is possible with aid of imperialistic nations and that in the event of secession, political power would be bourgeois."

But even these plans, which V. Moroz presented to his friends, far from fully disclosed his real intentions. They are much more fully revealed in certain anti-Soviet writings which came from his pen: *Moses and Dathan, Amid the Snows, A Chronicle of Resistance* and others.

In coming out for a Ukraine torn away from the fraternal family of Soviet people, V. Moroz calls, first of all, for the raising upon a pedestal of the Uniate Church and placing it at the forefront of the spiritual life of the nation. Because, according to V. Moroz's assertion, ". . . the Uniate movement has grown into the living flesh of the Ukrainian spirituality; it has become a national phenomenon." A question arises: Why would V. Moroz want to impose exactly such "spiritual shepherds" on Soviet Ukraine? It is not difficult to understand why: The Uniate Church has always been the source of ideological inspiration of Ukrainian bourgeois nationalism. For it was this Church that sanctified the *Banderivshchyna*,[4]

---

[4]Refers to movement led by Bandera and, often, to Ukrainian Nationalist movement, in general.

that groveled before Hitler; her highest dignitary, Metropolitan Sheptytsky, in his "Epistle to the Clergy Concerning the Organization of the Parish and the Community" wrote: "The pastor must have in readiness a flag of the German army. . . . On it is embroidered a swastika."

The unshakeable loyalty of the people of Soviet Ukraine to V. I. Lenin's ideas, their flaming Soviet patriotism, bring out V. Moroz's fury. He counts himself among the "nation's elite," but he contemptuously calls others "semi-plebeians"; for him, contemporary Ukrainians are "utterly coarsened," "materialized," "immersed in a state of somnambulism."

Disdaining nothing, V. Moroz tries to justify and sow an ideology alien to us, national egotism and enmity among peoples, all of which is nothing but a call for the destruction of all our achievements in the fields of fraternal national interrelations, economics and culture; thus, he engages in undisguised anti-Soviet propaganda.

He calls for an uprising against international feelings, the socialist struggle and the exchange of cadres among Union republics; he speaks about the need for destroying all of this once and for all. In connection with this, he views even the exploratory oil derrick near the village of Kosmach in the Carpathian region as an act . . . hostile to Ukrainian culture; new customs and collective farm songs he calls "bovine folklore"; he terms "piggish" the materialistic philosophy which even our enemies acknowledge, and so on. "De-Christianization, collectivization, industrialization, mass migration from the village to the city," shouts V. Moroz, "all of this was a destruction of traditional structures unprecedented in Ukrainian history, the catastrophic consequences of which have yet to be fully realized."

V. Moroz disseminated by illegal means similar "documents" among certain elements within Ukraine, he passed them on for publication abroad, and always for the sole purpose of defaming the socialist order and its great attainments. He unequivocally writes in his diatribe, *Amid the*

236

Snows: "There is nothing to extinguish in Ukraine as yet, it is still necessary to kindle," because, as is said below in this same diatribe, " . . . there are forty million 'primitives' in our republic! They make up the Ukrainian nation."

And in Munich, they are rubbing their hands with satisfaction. *Radio Liberty* broadcasts these "works"; nationalistic publishing houses abroad unfold noisy campaigns around them. How else? A new "apostle" has appeared in Ukraine.

Where did this hatred of V. Moroz for our order, for socialist reality, come from? Yet for him, as well as for millions of other citizens, the realization of the eternal dream of unification of all Ukrainian lands in one state has opened up the widest paths—to learn, to create, to build a life worthy of a Soviet person. He received a secondary education in his village in Volyn, he entered a university; as all Soviet students he studied free of charge and received a state scholarship, and after finishing the institute, he became a lecturer, first at the Lutsk, then at the Ivano-Frankivsk Pedagogical Institutes.

The fall came not all at once and was not limited to one or a few years. V. Moroz constantly listened to foreign anti-Soviet radio broadcasts, read foreign anti-Soviet literature, and on this basis perfected the forms and methods of the preparation and circulation of anti-Soviet documents. All the while he led a double life; finally, he took the road of betrayal of the interests of the Soviet people.

Above, we cited V. Moroz's confession at the first trial, during which he acknowledged his guilt and seemingly repented. However, he did not learn the necessary lesson.

In September 1969, V. Moroz, having served out his punishment, returned to Ivano-Frankivsk with a firm determination to continue his anti-Soviet activity. He searched for ways of doing battle with our system of government, he wrote *A Chronicle of Resistance* and *Amid the Snows*. Time did not need to be borrowed for these writings. Rather than putting his hands to doing work of social merit, V. Moroz beat a

237

familiar path to the *Radio Liberty* station, to nationalistic journals *Suchasnist* (*Contemporary Times*), *Vyzvolny Shliakh* (*Liberation Path*), and so on.

But when the time came to answer for his crimes, for the preparation and circulation of anti-Soviet documents, he dodged, he tried to cover up his tracks. V. Moroz at first declined the "honor" of being their author, and only when pinned against the wall by the testimony of the witnesses B. D. Antonenko-Davydovych, I. D. Dzyuba and V. M. Chornovil, was he forced to confess.

At the trial, other things were brought out in addition to those presented above. It became cramped for the nationalistic "apostle" within the frames of our republic. He assaults with invectives not only Ukrainian Soviet writers—minstrels of the friendship of nations, internationalists—but also the literati of other republics who came out with criticism of nationalism. And so, having read in the *Literary Gazette* an article in answer to the radio-liars of Munich from the Byelorussian poetess Yevdokiya Los, V. Moroz writes her a letter saturated with nationalistic raving and racism, mixed with the slander of the nationalities policy of the party, threats and insults.

And so, the convicted V. Moroz not only systematically wrote slanderous anti-Soviet "works," but personally disseminated this poison illegally, and conducted anti-Soviet propaganda; for this he stood trial a second time and received his just desserts.

Everything is absolutely clear. What V. Moroz desired, that is what he took a liking to. And whoever, by whatever means, should take it upon himself to defend this "apostle of treason," it is clear to every unbiased person what it is that he wants and what it is that he is demanding. He betrayed our people, he betrayed our multi-national Soviet Fatherland. And traitors—are punished.

Ya. Radchenko

238

42

To the Editors of *Soviet Education*
Esteemed Comrades:

IN the August 14, 1971 issue of your newspaper there appeared an article by Ya. Radchenko entitled "An 'Apostle' and His Standards." It concerns itself with the trial of "the former lecturer at the Ivano-Frankivsk Pedagogical Institute Valentyn Moroz, for anti-Soviet propaganda." But the reader will search in vain in the article for some concrete facts of the substance of the case, for a description of the defendant's crime, for evidence of his guilt, or for the course of the court proceedings. Elementary factual information to which the reader is entitled, as well as ideological and legal argumentation, are substituted for by the use of "strong" words. In his well-practiced art, Ya. Radchenko goes so far as to lightheartedly attribute to V. Moroz nothing more nothing less than "betrayal of the fatherland," although there was no mention of this either during the course of the trial or in Moroz's sentence.

Thus, Ya. Radchenko arbitrarily "reclassified" the official charge, and should bear criminal responsibility for his action.

Moreover, Ya. Radchenko libels not only the defendant but other persons as well. Black on white he writes that Valentyn Moroz denied the authorship of the articles imputed to him, that he "dodged" and "attempted to cover his tracks," etc., and "only when pinned against the wall by the testimony of witnesses B. D. Antonenko-Davydovych, I. M. Dzyuba and V. M. Chornovil was he forced to confess." It appears from the context that the persons referred to were practically Ya. Radchenko's accomplices in baiting Valentyn Moroz.

The fact is that all the witnesses mentioned refused to participate in the legal proceedings against Valentyn Moroz because by conducting the trial in camera the court violated Soviet laws.

At the conclusion of the trial, all three appealed to higher judicial authorities, protesting against the closed trial and the groundless, harsh sentence and requesting a re-examination of the case.

Furthermore, in his rather verbose article, Ya. Radchenko fails to inform his readers about what was most important: the sentence meted out to Valentyn Moroz. How can one account for such absent-mindedness in one who is obviously not just a rank-and-file journalist but who prefers the modest name of "Ya. Radchenko?" He may have simply become confused at this point or perhaps—whoever he may be—he was embarrassed to divulge the fact that for writing several articles (even if they were ideologically erroneous), a young man was immured in prison for nine years, after which five more years of exile await him. This frightening fact does not "harmonize" with an age in which our country, as it is known to the readers of *Soviet Education,* leads the struggle for human rights, for a humane re-ordering of the world, for socialism and democracy.

The appearance of Ya. Radchenko's article redundantly demonstrates to what extent the illegal so-called "closed trials" bring harm to and offend the socialist public.

Besides, had the trial of Valentyn Moroz been open—therefore, legal—the journalist would not have been able to so cynically misinform his readers.

Perhaps it is not within the power of the editors of *Soviet Education* to publish an accurate and objective account of the trial of V. Moroz, as elementary public decency might dictate. But the well-known legal stipulations concerning the responsibility of the press give me the right to demand that they correct to a certain extent the factual error (an error on their part, but a falsification on the part of the author) which concerns me personally and causes me moral harm.

Respectfully,

Kiev   *I. M. Dzyuba*
52 Povitroflotsky Prospect, Apt. 97

43

To the Central Committee of the Communist Party of Ukraine

ON August 14,1971, an article entitled "An 'Apostle' and His Standards," signed by Ya. Radchenko, was published in the newspaper *Soviet Education*. We feel obligated to respond to it, if only because our names were mentioned in it in a false context.

The article by Ya. Radchenko appeared in response to voices in the Western press which were raised as a result of the trial of the historian and publicist Valentyn Moroz, arrested in June and sentenced in November 1970 by the Ivano-Frankivsk Regional Court to nine years in prison and a strict-regime labor camp and five years of exile, a total of fourteen years.

It would have been natural to expect that the author of the article would present the factual side of this—in one way or another—extraordinary trial, that he would give it professional legal interpretation and then, relying on this explanation of the essence of the case, proceed to go into battle against the bourgeois falsifiers.

But such expectations proved naive. In his simplicity (or perhaps as an expert on the rules of the genre) the author of the article probably considers that in an area so sanctified as the fight against "Ukrainian bourgeois nationalism," common sense and elementary logic were not necessarily essential, and that factual accuracy and truth were altogether superfluous luxuries. He assumed that in such a cause all means were justified. For this reason he found it possible to dispense with such "trivialities" as the substance of the case, its factual side, its judicial basis, etc., and by-passing these tedious stages in the development of his theme, he immediately gives free rein to his imagination so that it may paint the most frightening "portrait of the enemy," resembling the devils of Gogol's blacksmith Vakula with which the credulous village mothers used to frighten their children.[1]

Since the level of the named article does not allow us to enter into a serious polemic with its author, we will briefly enumerate only the major deliberate distortions of the facts by Ya. Radchenko.

1. Moroz is referred to as "an apostle of treason" in the article; its author keeps emphasizing that he was sentenced for betraying his fatherland. This assertion is politically and legally groundless. Perhaps it is merely a rhetorical figure of speech. But what right did the author have to resort to "figures of speech" when the fate of human beings and the truthful presentation of the facts to the public are at stake?

Anyway, the country's Constitution and the Criminal Code precisely define the concept of "treason against the fatherland"; there should be no place for fantasy and arbitrariness here.

In fact, Moroz was not tried under Art. 56 of UCC ("treason against the fatherland"), but under Art. 62 ("anti-Soviet propaganda and agitation"). He was not charged with spying, sabotage, acts of terrorism, etc., but merely with the preservation of the culture and the spiritual traditions of his country. The essays of Valentyn Moroz were, according to Art. 62, UCC, interpreted as anti-Soviet; in our opinion, they were qualified as anti-Soviet without sufficient grounds. But how does "treason against the fatherland" figure here?

2. Not finding convincing arguments to justify the case against Moroz in 1970, Ya. Radchenko cites some interrogation records from the first case against Moroz (1965), when the defendant allegedly confessed his intention of establishing an independent bourgeois Ukraine with the aid of the imperialistic countries. Ya. Radchenko's methods are unethical and illegal for two reasons.

[1]An allusion to N. Gogol's (1809-1852) tale *Night Before Christmas* (*Nich pid Rizdvo*).

In the first place, the proof of the present guilt of Moroz must be found in the present case and not in a former case for which he has served his sentence in full.

In the second place, if the testimony cited was in fact recorded in the (interrogation) protocols of 1965, (although we do not exclude the possibility of falsification), their author was certainly not Moroz but the investigator who was conducting the case. After all, an interrogation proceeds according to the scheme of questions of the investigator, who formulates and records the answers. Moreover, it is well known that the majority of those who were sentenced in 1965, including V. Moroz, sent from their places of imprisonment to various legal authorities statements in which they cited the illegal methods used in their interrogations and trials, and denied both their confessions of guilt and the "testimony" attributed to them.

We would like to draw your attention to the fact that this may be the first time in post-Stalinist times that the press quotes from interrogation protocols. Until now, such practices were known mostly from the "experience" of the 1930's.

3. The desire of Valentyn Moroz for the "secession of Ukraine with the aid of imperialistic nations" was allegedly confirmed at the first trial by the witness D. P. Ivashchenko (a teacher).

Again a falsehood. In the V. Moroz case, there was no *witness* Ivashchenko. There was a *prisoner* D. Ivashchenko, who could not have appeared as a witness against V. Moroz because he was a co-defendant with Moroz in the same case. Surely the author had to be aware of such legal axioms.

4. These same "intentions" of V. Moroz are supposedly more fully revealed in some of his anti-Soviet essays: *Moses and Dathan, Amid the Snows, A Chronicle of Resistance,* and others. But the essays of V. Moroz contain nothing even resembling these "intentions." The lie depended on the assumption that not all those who would read Ya. Radchenko would be familiar with the essays of V. Moroz.

5. Plucking phrases out of context from *A Chronicle of Resistance*, Ya. Radchenko writes that V. Moroz advocated "that the Uniate Church be placed at the forefront of the spiritual life of the nation," that it be "imposed" on Soviet Ukraine, etc.

This is a fantasy worthy of a better application. V. Moroz mentioned the Uniate movement only in passing, referring not to Soviet Ukraine, but to Hutsulshchyna of the second half of the eighteenth century, where, after the partition of Poland, this Church ceased to be a means of Polonization and acquired a Ukrainian character. Similar "anti-Soviet" views can be discovered in the research of many contemporary Soviet scholars.

6. Ya. Radchenko performs similar manipulations with the essay *Amid the Snows*, twisting the words of V. Moroz to prove that he allegedly described Ukraine as a nation of "primitives." Actually, Moroz argued against this characterization. Even in the phrase quoted by Ya. Radchenko, the word "primitives" appears in quotation marks.

7. There is absolutely no doubt in Radchenko's mind that V. Moroz "not only systematically wrote slanderous anti-Soviet 'works' but personally disseminated this poison illegally . . . among certain elements within Ukraine (and) passed them on for publication abroad."

That which the investigation was not able to establish during the course of five months, Ya. Radchenko "established" with one stroke of the pen. The investigation did not bring out a single instance of dissemination of his essays by Valentyn Moroz himself (except for one instance of turning for literary advice to Borys Antonenko-Davydovych concerning an unfinished essay) ; no "dissemination" was established at the trial either. Moreover, the question of Valentyn Moroz's passing on anything abroad or instructing anyone else to do so did not even arise.

8. It is asserted that V. Moroz had avoided socially beneficial work. Again a falsehood. V. Moroz was not only not

assigned work in his profession, but was prevented even from finding a position which had nothing to do with ideological questions (as an observer at a meteorological station, an engraver's apprentice, etc.).

9. It is also not true that Valentyn Moroz at first "covered up his tracks" and denied authorship. In fact, he did not give any testimony whatsoever during the investigation, regarding his arrest illegal.

He also boycotted his illegal closed trial, but, as if anticipating the possibility of slander, he announced at the beginning of the trial that he was the author of the four essays *A Report from the Beria Reservation, Moses and Dathan, A Chronicle of Resistance,* and *Amid the Snows.*

10. Finally, Ya. Radchenko arbitrarily enlisted, as his adherents and partners in attacks on Moroz, us—B. D. Antonenko-Davydovych, I. M. Dzyuba and V. M. Chornovil. We supposedly "pinned" V. Moroz "against the wall" and forced him by our testimony to confess to the authorship of the articles. We not only did not "pin" V. Moroz "against the wall," but on the contrary—we announced a protest against the illegal closed trial and refused to give any evidence at all at such a trial.

The question arises: What was the author of "An 'Apostle' and His Standards" counting on when he libeled not only the one who is denied the possibility of refuting him, but us as well? Maybe on the fact that the newspaper would be read by more people than our reply?

We have enumerated above only the instances (not even all of them) where Ya. Radchenko openly distorted concrete facts which do not lend themselves to ambiguous interpretation and subjective appraisals. We leave it on the author's conscience that he saw in the articles of V. Moroz "nationalistic raving and racism," "threats and insults," " a call for the destruction of all our achievements," etc.

It is possible to slander not only by speaking but also by remaining silent. And Ya. Radchenko is silent about too many things: that Moroz was tried illegally in camera; that contrary to the law, no friends of the defendant, not even we, the witnesses, were admitted to the reading of the verdict, which made possible the falsification of our position in the verdict; that V. Moroz was, in fact, not tried for the works mentioned in Radchenko's articles, but primarily for *A Report from the Beria Reservation,* in which he severely criticized the actions of the KGB; that V. Moroz was given an incredibly savage sentence—fourteen years of imprisonment and exile; etc.

It would be possible to interpret Ya. Radchenko's article as a chance excursion into the newspaper technique of the 1930's, if this were an isolated case. But it is enough to mention the article by O. Poltoratsky, "Whom Certain 'Humanitarians' Protect" (*Literary Ukraine,* July 16, 1968) ; the articles by John Weir (*News from Ukraine,* May 1969), Ya. Radchenko and Ya. Klymenko (*Soviet Ukraine,* January 31, 1971), and others, to notice a growing tendency. One thing is characteristic of all these articles: an absence of polemic argumentation, the "convincing" of the reader with the aid of a standard repertoire of vituperative slander. Are not these weapons a bit outdated?

After the Twentieth Congress of the CPSU it was announced that the organs of the KGB will cease to be a state within a state, that effective controls by the Party and government agencies will be established to supervise its actions. Then why should not someone of the highest ranking officials in the Republic undertake to investigate personally any one political case, without relying on the one-sided evidence of the KGB and solely on the secret data of the security agencies, which may be selected tendentiously.

In view of the fact that the case of Moroz has caused an especially strong reaction, within our country as well as abroad, it might be well to make this the test case. Read all of the articles of V. Moroz, the materials of the investigation and the trial, the protests of the Soviet and foreign citizenry,

246

sent through official channels, the press coverage, and the like.

We are certain that after a thorough and unbiased examination of the case you will take steps to either release Valentyn Moroz or reduce his sentence as much as possible, thereby neutralizing the great moral harm done to our society and the Communist ideology by the very fact of such brutal retribution.

September 29, 1971.   *Borys Antonenko-Davydovych*[2]

Ivan Dzyuba

Vyacheslav Chornovil

[2]Although Antonenko-Davydovych was not officially punished for his part in the Moroz case, he did feel repercussions professionally, as a writer. After the trial, he wrote in a letter to a friend: " . . . I wanted to send you a book, but before I got around to it, they had all disappeared in Kiev; the promised second edition (50,000) will not be printed. Why? Apparently, because of the bad civic behavior of its author and the dangerous nature of the book itself, according to Bilodid (director, Language Department, Academy of Sciences of Ukraine—Ed.) and others like him. My improper civic behavior stems from the trial of Moroz, in Ivano-Frankivsk, to which I, along with Dzyuba and Chornovil, was called to be a witness for the prosecution; I declined to testify at the closed trial, basing my refusal on Soviet law, Lenin, the USSR Constitution and my own beliefs. When the judge questioned me on this position, I answered: 'I do not want future generations to judge me—along with you—for having taken part in an illegal act'. Neither will the Minister of Education Udovychenko agree with my behavior; I am enclosing a copy of a letter I have written to him. Officially, I have not been punished for refusing to testify, as could have been expected, but unofficial sanctions have already begun: my story 'Zavyshcheni otsinky', which was cleared for printing, was not published in the *Ukraine* magazine; *Literary Ukraine* no longer publishes my linguistic-notes column 'Vahovyti dribnytsi'; finally, they will not re-publish my book *Yak my hovorymo*. Consequently, I will not be able to 'please my readers with new works' next year, as you suggested. Anyway, the accent in literature today is to write 'industrial' and 'agricultural' novels, at which I am far from being a master. I guess, I'll have to write 'for the future', filing my works under

'When I die, then read!' . . . " (This file heading is a play on words; the poet Shevchenko began his "Testament" with the words "When I die, then bury me . . ."—Ed.) A copy of the above-quoted letter, dated January 6, 1971, was circulated in samvydav, and reached the West.

44

TATYANA KHODOROVYCH[1]

PLEADS FOR MOROZ'S LIFE

"I can endure no more!"

These words belong to Valentyn Moroz, inmate of the penal Vladimir Prison, a human being manly and strong of spirit.

"I can endure no more. . . . "

Valentyn Moroz, a historian by profession and a former lecturer at the Ukrainian Pedagogical Institute in Lutsk, was arrested in July 1970 for the second time and for the second time was sentenced under Article 62 CC UkrSSR ("anti-Soviet agitation and propaganda").

V. Moroz received a most brutal sentence for the books and articles he wrote—fourteen years of deprivation of freedom, six of them in prison. Here is a list of those works which were declared criminal:

1. *A Report from the Beria Reservation.* The work was written in Dubrovlag, where Moroz was serving his sentence —four years of deprivation of freedom—after his first arrest in 1965. In the case of the *Report,* V. Moroz was kept for the entire year 1967 under investigation in solitary confinement in Lefortovo Prison, but, at that time, did not have any more

---

[1]Tatyana Khodorovych, until February 1972 a linguist at the Russian Language Institute of the Academy of Sciences in Moscow, and a member of Dr. Andrei Sakharov's Human Rights Committee, made her statement available to western journalists in Moscow on April 3, 1974 in the hope of reaching Soviet authorities and world opinion. Joining her in the plea for Valentyn Moroz's life was Malva Landa, a geologist and also an active defender of human rights in the Soviet Union.

time added to his sentence for the writing of this work.)

2. *Amid the Snows*—about I. Dzyuba's inconsistency and unprincipled behavior.

3. An article addressed to Byelorussian poetess Yevdokiya Los, whose poems Moroz criticized, in decrying the Russification of Byelorussia, for their lack of the spirit of national self-determination.

Valentyn Moroz was made to serve his sentence in Vladimir Prison. There he was put in a cell with two criminals-sadists. For a long time, they kept V. Moroz from getting any sleep, taking turns at his bed.

All of the appeals of Moroz's wife to have him transferred to another cell were fruitless. "He is in with those just like himself," they told her.

His cellmates once came close to killing Moroz, weakened by the lack of sleep, ripping his stomach open with a knife. The prison authorities were forced to send him to an infirmary. After his release from the infirmary, Moroz was immediately taken to Kiev, as a witness in the case of the so-called Ukrainian nationalists. When they got no testimony of any kind from him, the organs of the KGB sent Moroz back to Vladimir Prison.

After persistent appeals from Moroz's wife, they placed him in a separate cell. He is there now, in a state of complete physical and mental exhaustion. He is on the brink of death.

During a visit on October 9, 1973, Valentyn Moroz asked his wife to try to have him transferred from the prison to a camp. The meeting was very depressing. Usually composed and calm, Moroz was not at all like himself. In a state of complete nervous strain and agitation bordering on hysteria, he accused his wife of not doing enough to ease his fate and begged and at the same time demanded that she do anything to save him, to save his life.

"I can endure no more!"

The philosopher Kant said that two things amazed him

250

most: the stars in the sky and the law of goodness in man.

I write these lines with the hope that this strange law, the law of the goodness that is in man, will win out and that evil will retreat.

But only when the stubborn and calm voice of goodness will resound from the throats of many, only then will it retreat.

Let every person find this goodness within himself and let this voice resound—the voice of good versus evil—and, I believe, evil will retreat.

Valentyn Moroz will not die!

April 3, 1974   *T. Khodorovych*
Moscow

45

NEWS RELEASE—COMMUNIQUE[1]
No. 74 (34) Via Telex, May 8th, 1974.

HOW AND FOR WHAT IS V. MOROZ

SERVING HIS TERM?

"Valentin Moroz is serving his term fully in accordance with the law and in conformity with the sentence passed by a Soviet Court of Justice," said the procurator of the Vladimir region, who in keeping with the law exercises procurator supervision over prison no. 2 in Vladimir, where V. Moroz is inmate.

False Rumours

For more than eighteen months now, since August 1972, the prisoner has been in a cell without any other inmates: His own request was granted by the prison authorities with the consent of the procurator's office. This is an important detail, because it fully refutes all rumours being spread in the West by Moroz's "defenders" about his "conflicts with cell-mates"

---

[1]The News Release—Communiqué, "How and For What Is V. Moroz Serving His Term?" No. 74 (34) appears here in its original, unedited form. It was made available by the Soviet Embassy in Ottawa, Canada, to the general press on May 8, 1974. It was also mailed to some of the 198 signers, mostly professors of Canadian colleges and universities, of the "Appeal on Behalf of Valentyn Moroz to the Authorities of the Soviet Union," which appeared in major Canadian daily newspapers on May 1, 1974.

Editorial comments have been kept to a minimum, although the numerous instances where the release is in conflict with most of the remaining documents in *Boomerang* invite a resolution of discrepancies. The style of the release suggests that the author labored under the assumption that his readers would not have had access to either the works of Moroz or to much of the information in the Moroz case. Compare with Ya. Radchenko, Document 41, p. 234.

As for the prisoner's health, the sanitary department chief of prison no. 2 supplied exhaustive information about it: Moroz is healthy and has no complaints. Between January[2] last year and now he applied to doctors only three times. This is shown by entries in his medical record. Here they are:

"27.4.73—complaints about weakness following an inoculation against gastric and intestinal diseases. Examination revealed no diseases. Calcium chloride, glucose and vitamins were prescribed.

22.9.73—when examined by the chief of the sanitary department he complained of poor sleep and irritability. Was given seduxen. 1.10.73—complained about coughing to the therapeutist. Cough pills were prescribed."

So the information about Moroz's "tragic health condition" is invented. Now to the gist of the matter. What is the guilt of Valentin Moroz?

Recidivist

Prisoner Moroz is qualified as a recidivist. He committed for a second time the crime he had earlier been convicted of. In the early 1960's, V. Moroz, a Ukrainian, born in 1936, was teaching history at Teacher's Training Colleges in the Ukraine, first at Lutsk, then at Ivano-Frankovsk. His criminal activities began at that time. His aim was to abolish Soviet power in the Ukraine and to separate it from the USSR—by any means, including force.[3]

Moroz later described his illegal activities as follows: "I used my business trips to Lutsk from Ivano-Frankovsk to supervise student practice for other purposes. I always brought with me anti-Soviet literature and distributed it

[2]Moroz was reportedly stabbed in the stomach by other inmates in the fall of 1972 and was hospitalized with the injuries until February 1973. See Document 44, p. 249.

[3]This statement is contradicted by the whole of Moroz's writings; nowhere is there reference to the use of force or terrorism in achieving the separation of Ukraine from the USSR.

among students and people I knew. I spoke to them about the need for the Ukraine to secede from the USSR[4] and to become a bourgeois state. In these efforts, I said, we must count on the support of the Western countries and in the first place the USA, including military support".[5]

Such meetings were held regularly at the flat of lecturer D. Ivashchenko. Students—would-be-teachers—to whom society was going to entrust the education of children and teenagers were told there by Moroz to hate the Russians. He stirred up nationalistic strife and justified the terrorism of nationalistic gangs from the smashed OUN underground (OUN is the organisation of Ukrainian Nationalists which collaborated with nazis during the second world war and which aims at abolishing the socialist system in the Ukraine and at wresting it from the USSR).

All that was immoral and, moreover, illegitimate. V. Moroz's actions were fully covered by article 62-1 of the penal code of the Ukrainian Republic, which envisages as punishment the deprivation of freedom for a period of 6 months to 7 years for agitation and propaganda with a view to undermining the Soviet system and for spreading slander vilifying it.

Moroz was exposed by many witnesses and by plenty of evidence. The criminal nature of the meetings at Lutsk was proved. It was found out that through go-betweens Moroz received negative film of an anti-Soviet book published in Munich—"The Deduction of Rights of the Ukraine". It was

---

[4] The Constitution of the USSR guarantees each republic the right to secede from the Union. The Constitution of the Ukrainian SSR likewise reserves for Ukraine the right to secede. See footnote on p. 16.

[5] Both Tkachenko and Ya. Radchenko (see Document 41, p. 234) attribute this quote to Moroz. The style that it is written in is definitely not Moroz's, but it is possible that while he was under investigation following his first arrest, Moroz might have signed such an admission that had been prepared for him by the investigating officer. See Document 15, p. 165, and Document 43, p. 241.

254

issued by the so-called administration of the Chief Ukrainian Liberation Council (Prolog Publishing House) which, together with all the worst enemies of the USSR, dreams of "freeing" the Ukraine from socialism and coducts subsersive work.

Moroz was sentenced to four years imprisonment. In the corrective labour camp he continued his former line. He contacted OUN members who were serving their terms for different crimes, incited them to disobey and violated the regime of the corrective labour institution. At the same time Moroz invented a slanderous "reportage"[6] about the regulations in the colony and sent it to his accomplices abroad.

Court proceedings for slander were instituted against Moroz over his "reportage". He, however, denied any part in that material. The case was closed as there was not evidence enough to prove the accusation. Only later, during the second trial dealing with Moroz's further crimes, that point was proved. . . .

New Crime

On Sept. 1, 1969, Moroz was released and came to Ivano-Frankovsk. He did not try to find a job, however, but lived on the money sent through secret channels by anti-Soviet nationalist organisations from abroad. They believed him to be a "combat unit" operating in the "communist den." Moroz again set about forming and hammering together an anti-Soviet group. He visited Ukrainian cities, carried out agitation against the Soviet system and for secession, prepared and distributed subversive literature.

He was again tried, for a second time, under the same article—62, of the penal code of the Ukrainian Republic. This time however, according to part 2 of the article, Moroz as a recidivist, was to get a more severe punishment—imprisonment between 3 and 10 years. The court found Moroz guilty and sentenced him to 9 years imprisonment.

[6]Reference is to *A Report from the Beria Reservation*, p. 7.

According to reports carried in the Ukrainian press at that time, this decision by the court of justice in Ivano-Frankovsk was met with approval by the public in the Ukraine. Separatist activity and preaching of national discord and chauvinism are deeply resented by Soviet people, who on every occasion show their pride that more than a hundred various nationalities live in accord in their country. The friendship of nations, which was not cultivated in pre-revolutionary Russia, has been gained in the hard and steadfast struggle of several generations of Soviet Society. It is not surprising therefore that encroachments on this gain are regarded here as a blasphemy. In accordance with this view the Soviet law punishes such actions with utmost severity, placing them at the same level as grave crimes against the personality, society and state.

Valery Tkachenko

PART THREE

Dedicated to Valentyn Moroz

IHOR KALYNETS

From the collection *Summing up Silence* (1970) dedicated to Valentyn Moroz

To Valentyn Moroz

I would want that this book
would be for you if but for a moment
the handkerchief of Veronica along the way
of the cross.

I would want that this book
like Veronica's handkerchief would remind
us of the holiness
of your face.

Introduction to the cycle "Stone Windmill"

When I remember
your image

it seems to me
that you emerged
from a dark opening
of flame

and that you will be able always
to return
home

though the patch of Homeland
beneath your feet
is called
a prison cell

and to conquer space
is to gnaw rock

and to conquer time
is to go up against
petrified
windmills

Trenos
at yet another way of the cross

FIRST SORROW

at the golgotha
of a provincial court
they isolated
Your luminous face
by a palisade of rifles

alone
you lug the cross

our back
is still so weak

SECOND SORROW

Ukraine brushed away
from her eye a furtive
tear

Lord
the transparent group
of women-weepers
just shines

but the mother
has nurtured
with her own marrow
a legion of spies

THIRD SORROW

and those two
who were crucified
beside Christ

today
mask
the tall golgotha
with branches of codes

in a prosecutor's toga
they conceal
a cut-throat's knife

FOURTH SORROW

a fresh cross

it's not for nothing
that from it cries
Kosmach resin

oh he
will yet serve
instead of the iconostasis
in our
looted temple

FIFTH SORROW

beggarly little nation
you may safely
bustle
today after all
the earth
did not tremble

and the darkness
which from the sky
like ash
has on your head
settled
prematurely

you don't notice
anyway

SIXTH SORROW

without treachery

sold out
by our feebleness

today still
not just one comrade
will forsake you

even without silver pieces

maybe you will have regret
then
for the biblical judas

SEVENTH SORROW

our father is silent
and mother
throws herself
at the bloody tracks

involve yourself
mother of God
who became
also our mother
on our behalf

let us also
touch
the unextinguished tracks

EIGHTH SORROW

the suffering hands
of the wife
rose
like metal
above the mob

Veronica
you wanted to wipe
the bloodied face

with their feet they shred
the cloth

that will become
a banner

NINTH SORROW

turn your face away
from them

but let it be
that in my soul
always remains

a portrait of your
thorn-crowned
head

TENTH SORROW

out of love for us
you took upon yourself
such dreadful
punishment

to save us
from the greatest
sin

indifference
to *fire*

Hryhir Chubay[1]

From the cycle "Easter," dedicated to V. Moroz, in the collection *Light and Confession* (1970)

Kosmach—1970[2]

all our dwellings and temples are in the valley
and on the hill a dragon
sits and looks into the valley
and then starts painting hutsul
easter eggs so in the valley they'd believe
that this dragon is a local

this time he also took to painting
down the hill rolled easter eggs like soggy
clay

we ran to the gates
to see them more clearly

and on each easter egg
there was a prison painted

[1]See fn. 4, p. 169.
[2]Refers to incident in Kosmach. See Documents 11 (p. 157) and 15 (p. 165).

A CHANCE MEETING

THE Chekists had made a mistake. Chance encounters between prisoners in the corridors of the prison are strictly prohibited. This time something broke down in the finely tuned mechanism. The doors in the lobby of building No. 1 slammed, and I and Valery Ronkin found ourselves face to face with a person in the striped uniform of a prisoner. Momentary bewilderment, pained recognition, and then the two men leaped toward one another.

"Valery!"

"Valentyn!"

Brief half-embraces and already the enraged, winded guards, cursing under their breath (God forbid that their superiors find out that such a meeting occurred), pull the two old friends apart.

When ours and this man's doors clanged shut, Valery asked if I had recognized the man we met. I said I had never before met this person. But I had heard about him, had heard a lot, and I respected and sympathized with him, without having seen him. But even I, who in the past ten years had seen a lot, could hardly imagine that a man could be driven to such a state.

The man was Valentyn Moroz. His name is undoubtedly known to every Ukrainian. Every Ukrainian abroad has probably seen his portrait. Don't believe these portraits now. The Muscovite policemen took pains that this man with a fine, intelligent face and clever eyes will never again resemble his past likeness. Gaunt, sickly, frightening, and dressed as he was in the striped uniform, he brought to mind, in a way that shocked and made the flesh crawl, photographs of the not-yet-dead victims of Auschwitz. The prisoner's robe hung loosely on the body of this grown man as if on a thin wire skeleton. His hair was in sparse tufts of bristles on sallow, dry skin; and the skin itself, horribly greenish

266

like a mummy, was drawn over his high forehead and raw-boned jaws. And the eyes. . . . No, I am not capable of verbalizing that which I saw in those eyes in the few brief moments of that meeting. . . .

Later, we found out that Valentyn had been thrown into the cell next to ours. Osyp Terela, who idolized Moroz, was especially persistent. For a whole month, ignoring danger, we tried to get in touch with Valentyn. We tried knocking on the wall and shouting, but the unfortunate man had been troubled so much by informers and provocateurs in the ward that, until he became convinced that we were the ones in the cell next to his and not some provocateurs who spoke fluent Ukrainian, he neither responded to our knocking nor took our notes from the hiding places. He had become so accustomed (if it is possible at all to get accustomed to this) to daily Chekist provocations, blackmail and the relentless and ruthless inventiveness of the prison inquisitors, that it was only a month later, after seeing us through a crack accidentally left open, that he began to call back and trade magazines and notes with us. And even this he did only when his cellmates had been called away for interrogation, a visit to the doctor, or for a walk.

One time, Valentyn was being taken alone past our cell and, getting ahead of his guard, he succeeded in whispering a prepared phrase, for which we, hiding behind the door, were waiting. It was difficult to believe that this was the same strong-willed, temperamental and wise Moroz, whom we had known from stories about him and from the excerpts of his essays which had reached us. Groans and the sounds of scuffles could often be heard coming from his cell; guards from the "Butzkomand" (an operative pacification squad) would often storm in there with axes—then they would drag someone off, and we would hear hysterical screams. Then everything would quiet down, only to erupt anew a few hours later.

I was to be released in a few months, and so at every oc-

267

casion I would ask Valentyn what message to pass on for him to the outside. He would grimace painfully and repeat with obsessed persistence:

"Pass on just this one thing: they are keeping me with the insane, they create a neverending hell for me! They are trying to turn me into a madman, like those that they throw in here with me. They're murderers and cannibals. I have no air to breathe!"

He repeated this several times in the same memorized words. . . .

And I repeat: one of the most honest and most talented of Ukrainian publicists has been driven to a state of complete exhaustion and to the brink of madness. His mode of existence today is a combination of that a hungry lock-up and of a ward for the insane. He endures the attacks of half-beasts who have completely lost their human likeness, who have lost all national and social traits. His physical and mental tortures do not cease for a single day.

Remember this!

Anatoly Radygin[1]

[1]Soviet Jew who emigrated to Israel; captain of fishing vessel and poet; arrested and tried in 1962 for attempting to flee from USSR; sentenced to ten years of labor camp; served his term in Vladimir Prison and in Mordovian camps.

INDEX

270